Project director	Peter Furtado
Cartographic manager	Richard Watts

Advisory editors

Jeremy Black
Professor of History, University of Exeter, UK

K.M. Chaudhuri
Vasco da Gama Professor of European Exploration, European University Institute, Florence, Italy

Barry Cunliffe
Professor of European Archaeology, University of Oxford, UK

Brian M. Fagan
Professor of Anthropology, University of California, Santa Barbara, USA

J.E. Spence
Associate Fellow, Royal Institute of International Affairs, UK

Academic advisors

J.I. Catto
Oriel College, University of Oxford, UK

Professor Robin Cohen
University of Warwick, UK

Professor J.H. Elliott
Regius Professor of Modern History, University of Oxford, UK

Professor Harold James
Princeton University, New Jersey, USA

Professor Maldwyn A. Jones
University of London, UK

Dr Stewart Lone
Australian Defence Force Academy

Dr Oswyn Murray
Balliol College, University of Oxford, UK

Professor A.J.S. Reid
The Australian National University

Professor Francis Robinson
Royal Holloway, University of London, UK

Dr Kate Spence
Christ's College, University of Cambridge, UK

Professor John K. Thornton
Millersville University, Pennsylvania, USA

This page:
Gold mask from Mycenae, c.1500 BC

Opposite above left:
Saharan rock paintings, c.3500 BC

Opposite centre left:
Bell-breaker drinking cups, c.2000 BC

Opposite centre right:
Assyrian bas-relief of lion hunt, c.650 BC

Opposite below right:
Chavin textile of fanged god, c.400 BC

Following page:
Decorated skull from Jericho, c.8000 BC

Art director	Ayala Kingsley
Art editor	Martin Anderson
Cartographic editor	Tim Williams
Editors	Susan Kennedy
	Peter Lewis
(Encyclopedic dictionary)	BCS Publishing
Cartographer	Nathalie Johns
Picture research	Claire Turner
Production	Clive Sparling
Editorial assistance	Marian Dreier
Typesetter	Brian Blackmore
Illustrations	Charles Raymond
Proof reader	Lynne Elson
Index	Ann Barratt

Metro Books
122 Fifth Avenue
New York, NY 10011

ISBN: 978-1-58663-238-0

7 9 10 8 6 5

Printed and bound in Thailand

Contents

INTRODUCTION

OUTLINE OF WORLD HISTORY

1.01 Human origins • 4,000,000–100,000 years ago

1.02 Peopling the Earth • 100,000–10,000 years ago

1.03 The rise of agriculture • 10,000–500 BC

1.04 The world • 2000 BC

1.05 The world • 1000 BC

1.06 The world • 500 BC

1.07 The spread of writing • 3000 BC–AD 1500

THE MIDDLE EAST

1.08 The first farmers of the Middle East • 10,000–6000 BC

1.09 Advanced farmers of the Middle East • 6500–4300 BC

1.10 The first cities of Mesopotamia • 4300–2334 BC

1.11 The first empires • 2334–1595 BC

1.12 The Hittite and Assyrian empires • 1595–1000 BC

1.13 The Assyrian and Babylonian empires • 1000–539 BC

1.14 The Bible lands • 1000–587 BC

1.15 The Achemenid empires of Persia • 559–480 BC

AFRICA

1.16 Early farming in Africa • 7000–500 BC

1.17 The foundation of Ancient Egypt • 6000–2040 BC

1.18 Middle and New Kingdom Egypt • 2040–332 BC

EUROPE AND THE MEDITERRANEAN

1.19 Upper Paleolithic Europe • 35,000 years ago–5000 BC

1.20 Neolithic Europe • 5000–2000 BC

1.21 Bronze Age Europe • 2000–500 BC

1.22 The first civilizations of the Mediterranean • 2000–1100 BC

1.23 Phoenician and Greek expansion in the Mediterranean • 900–500 BC

1.24 The emergence of the Greek city-states • 1100–500 BC

1.25 Etruscans, Greeks and Carthaginians • 800–4800 BC

ASIA AND THE AMERICAS

1.26 The first civilizations of south Asia • 6000–500 BC

1.27 The first civilizations of east Asia • 6000–500 BC

1.28 The first civilizations of the Americas • 4000–500 BC

1.29 ENCYCLOPEDIC DICTIONARY

ACKNOWLEDGEMENTS

INDEX

INTRODUCTION

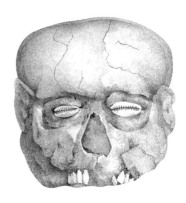

Four million years of biological and cultural evolution are covered in this story of the development of humankind from its origins on the African savanna to the appearance of the literate civilizations and classical empires. The story is the product of research in many disciplines, but the central thread comes from thousands of archeological excavations, of inconspicuous scatters of stone tools and animal bones, hunting camps and farming villages as well as towns and spectacular cities.

Archaeologists study and explain changes in societies, indeed in humanity itself, over immensely long periods of time. Why, for example, did some societies acquire farming skills? And how and why did humans cross from Siberia into Alaska and colonize the Americas? The archaeologist tries to account for such developments in terms of social organization as well as technology and environmental change.

The key intellectual framework for our most distant past derives from the evolutionary theories of Charles Darwin, formulated in 1859. The theory of evolution by natural selection made it possible to imagine a vast antiquity, a blank timescape for human evolution to unfold over hundreds of thousands, if not millions, of years. Darwin and his contemporaries could only guess at the timescales involved. Today, study of the DNA in our body cells tells us that the hominid line – of which *Homo sapiens sapiens* is the culmination – separated from the other apes between four and five million years ago. Today, archaeology tells us that human ancestors appeared in Africa and moved out to populate the rest of the world almost two million years ago, and that modern humanity may also have originated there. With its help, we can not only wonder at the art of 30,000 years ago, but also build up chronologies based on scientific analysis as well as on techniques of stylistic comparison. Archaeology reveals that literate civilizations developed independently in many places around the world. Historians using written sources, and archaeologists using material remains, can then collaborate in piecing together a narrative of these civilizations.

Modern scholars think of evolution like the branches of a tree, with new species emerging as the endlessly proliferating limbs and twigs, which derive from a trunk of remote common ancestors. Human societies have evolved in many ways; but there are similarities, especially in social and political organization and in the ways in which people make their livings. A flexible classification of human societies into "prestate societies" and "state-organized societies" was made by the American anthropologist Elman Service.

The simplest prestate societies were small family bands, egalitarian groups with communal leadership based on experience. Usually hunters and gatherers of plant foods, band societies prevailed for an immensely long time, until the beginnings of farming. Some survived to modern times.

Early farmers lived in permanent villages, and needed new social institutions to settle quarrels and establish land ownership. Many village societies were "tribes", egalitarian groups with kin-based organization to regulate land ownership and undertake communal tasks. "Chiefdoms" were a development of tribes; power lay in the hands of a few people who controlled trade and accumulated wealth. "State-organized societies" or civilizations operated on a larger scale than chiefdoms. They involved cities and saw the development of a writing system. Early civilizations were centralized, with power concentrated in the hands of a supreme ruler at the pinnacle of a socially stratified society.

Four major themes dominate the long early chapter of our history: the origins of humanity, the evolution and spread of humans, the beginnings of agriculture, and the emergence of civilizations. All of these are bound up with the ways in which food has been secured. For 99 percent of all human history, people lived by hunting and gathering. Our earliest ancestors probably used fleetness of foot and opportunism to scavenge their meat from lion and leopard kills. Hunting may have begun at the same time as modern humans appeared. Stone-tipped spears, then barbed antler projectiles and spearthrowers allowed hunters to shoot game from a safe distance. When the bow-and-arrow came into use some 10,000 years ago, humans could hunt animals of every size and birds on the wing. And as the ice sheets retreated, people intensified the quest for food and permanent settlements began to emerge at some favored sites.

Hunting is often seen as the glamorous part of foraging, but edible plant foods formed the essential diet of humanity for four million years. Our ancestors knew which plants to eat as staples, and which to fall back on in lean times. It was only when populations rose at the end of the Ice Age that people began to plant wild grasses and tubers deliberately to extend the range of wild forms that had been gathered for millennia. And, in a remarkably short time – perhaps three thousand years – the growing of crops and the domestication of animals spread very widely.

Farming accelerated the pace of cultural change. At first, civilizations like those of the Egyptians, the S hang and the Sumerians were independent entities. Gradually, though, states became reliant on each other. By 500 BC, empires, much larger entities, played a leading role. But the first four million years had created human biological and cultural diversity and laid the foundations of our own world ■

USING THIS ATLAS

This atlas is part of a six-volume chronological set covering the Ancient (1), Classical (2), Medieval (3), Early Modern (4), 19th Century (5), and Modern (6) worlds. To help the user pinpoint straight away which era any particular map relates to, pages are numbered first by volume, and then by 2-page spread within that volume. Thus, map spread 14 in volume 3 is identified by the page number 3.14.

World map spreads outline global history on the date shown. Different typographical categories (see table opposite) denote different kinds of political or social entity. The text on these spreads includes many cross-references to other relevant spreads. The timelines here are organized by region.

Regional map spreads cover a part of the world over a specific period. Maps for a continent or major region are grouped in a section, named in the heading on the right-hand side of the spread. These sections also appear in the Contents page.

Maps are shown in true cartographic projections. North is generally at the top of the page. Some distortion is evident in those maps that cover huge areas of the world (e.g. Asia). Where necessary location maps have been included.

Each regional map has certain standard features: thick grey lines denote major borders, thin grey lines internal borders. Campaigns or journeys are shown by lines with arrowheads; thicker grey arrows are used for mass movements of people. Trade routes are thinner lines, with arrowheads when the trade is one-way. All map-key items are referred to in text. The main text explains and amplifies the information on the map.

The timelines on regional maps are arranged in geographical or thematic sections. Civilizations, cultures, and dynasties are shown with colored bands; broad historical phases (such as "Bronze Age") are indicated with grey bands. Every regional map also has several numbered "pointers", whose captions offer further historical detail on the places marked. Finally, the panel bottom right cross-refers to other spreads with related information, listing their numbers and themes.

A substantial encyclopedic section at the end of the book contains an A-Z guide to the people, places, and events of the period. It is cross-referenced both within the section and to the information that appears on the map spreads.

The index provides detailed references to the text, timelines, pointer captions and map keys. Space constraints have precluded indexing every location on the maps themselves.

TYPOGRAPHICAL CONVENTIONS	
World maps	
FRANCE	state or empire
Belgian Congo	dependency or territory
Mongols	tribe, chiefdom or people
Anasazi culture	cultural group
Regional maps	
HUNGARY	state or empire
Bohemia	dependency or territory
Slavs	tribe, chiefdom or people
ANATOLIA	geographical region
✳	battle
•	site or town

Human evolution began as the Earth's climate started to cool during the Miocene epoch (25–5 million years ago), and culminated about one million years ago in the Pleistocene Ice Age. During the early Miocene the global climate was warmer than today. Widespread tropical forests in Africa and Eurasia supported diverse populations of early hominoid apes, including a common ancestor of gorillas, chimpanzees and humans.

By the end of the Miocene ice caps had formed at the Poles, and drier conditions in Africa caused tropical forests to shrink. In east Africa, probably the birthplace of the hominids, this was exacerbated by geological movements that led to the uplift of the East African plateau and the formation of the Rift Valley. The ancestral hominids were confined to shrinking "islands" of forest surrounded by open woodland and savanna. As a result they evolved an erect bipedal gait, allowing them to cover long distances on the ground.

The oldest known hominid, 4.4-million-year-old *Ardepithecus ramidus*, was probably bipedal, and the slightly later species *Australopithecus afarensis* certainly was, although (like later australopithecines) it retained a good tree-climbing ability. By 3 million years ago the australopithecines had evolved into two types, known as robusts and graciles. The robusts (named for their massive jaws and teeth) were not human ancestors. The gracile *Australopithecus africanus* had smaller teeth and jaws, and lived on plant foods and meat scavenged from the carcasses of the savanna's herd animals. The first hominid to be considered human, *Homo habilis*, appeared about 2.4 million years ago. This lived in a similar way to the gracile australopithecines, but had a larger brain – almost half the size of a modern human's, compared with a third, for australopithecines and chimpanzees. Whereas the australopithecines used simple tools such as stones and sticks, *Homo habilis* made sharp flakes and chipped pebble tools for butchering large animals. This simple toolmaking culture is known as the Oldowan, for the early hominid fossil site of Olduvai Gorge in the Rift Valley.

About 1.9 million years ago *Homo habilis* was replaced by *Homo erectus*, with a brain size about two-thirds that of modern humans. Over the next million years this proportion grew to three-quarters, the brain evolving rapidly as the climate fluctuated from dry glacial periods to moister, warmer inter-glacial periods. There was little time to adapt physically to new conditions, and intelligent animals that could cope by modifying their

Map labels:
0   600 km
0   400 mi
Hadar Aa
Bodo He
Middle Awash Ar
Melka Kunture
Gadeb
Omo Ra, other
Ra
West Turkana He
Ileret Ra, Hh, He
Koobi Fora Ra, Hh, He
Chesowanja Ra
Olorgasailie
Peninj Ra
Ndutu other
Olduvai Gorge Ra, Hh, He.
Laetoli Aa, other
Kalambo Falls
Kabwe other

Timeline events:
1,600,000 Earliest evidence of the use of fire, at Chesowanja, Kenya and Swartkrans (South Africa)

1,800,000 Populations of *Homo erectus* reach south and southeast Asia

c.3,500,000 "Lucy", the most complete *Australopithecus afarensis* found, lives at Hadar, Ethiopia

c.3,600,000 Hominid bipedal footsteps from this date have been found at Laetoli, Tanzania

c.2,000,000 Stone choppers, from Olduvai Gorge, Tanzania, initiate the Oldowan culture

c.2,400,000 Date of the oldest known stone tools, from Hadar, Ethiopia and the start of the African Lower Paleolithic

1,000,000 Beginning of the modern (Pleistocene) Ice Age

1,000,000 *Homo erectus* reaches Europe and Asia

TIMELINE

4,000,000 years ago (ya)   3,000,000 ya   2,000,000 ya   1,500,000 ya   1,000,00

Ardepithecus ramidus   *Australopithecus afarensis*   *Australopithecus africanus*   *Homo habilis*   *Homo erectus*

Robust Australopithecines

Oldowan culture

LOWER PALEOLITH

PLIOCENE EPOCH

TERTIARY PERIOD

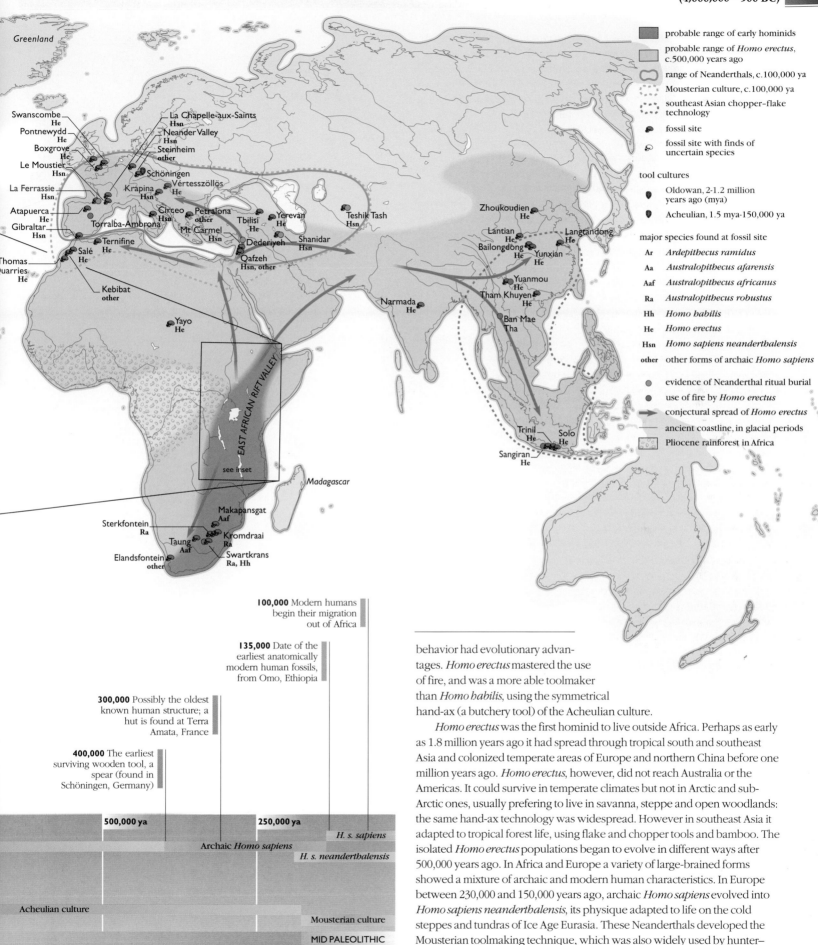

Greenland

Swanscombe
He
Pontnewydd
He
Boxgrove
He
Le Moustier
Hsn
La Ferrassie
Atapuerca
He
Gibraltar
Hsn
Thomas Quarries
He
Salé
He
Kebibat
other
Yayo
He

La Chapelle-aux-Saints
Hsn
Neander Valley
Hsn
Steinheim
other
Schöningen
Krapina
Hsn
Vértesszöllös
He
Circeo
Hsn
Petralona
other
Torralba-Ambrona
Ternifine
He
Mt Carmel
Hsn
Tbilisi
He
Yerevan
He
Dederiyeh
Shanidar
Hsn
Qafzeh
Hsn, other
Teshik Tash
Hsn
Narmada
He

Zhoukoudien
He
Lantian
He
Bailongdong
Langtandong
He
Yunxian
He
Yuanmou
He
Tham Khuyen
He
Ban Mae Tha
Trinil
He
Solo
He
Sangiran
He

EAST AFRICAN RIFT VALLEY
see inset

Madagascar

Makapansgat
Aaf
Sterkfontein
Ra
Taung
Aaf
Kromdraai
Ra
Swartkrans
Ra, Hh
Elandsfontein
other

probable range of early hominids
probable range of *Homo erectus*, c.500,000 years ago
range of Neanderthals, c.100,000 ya
Mousterian culture, c.100,000 ya
southeast Asian chopper–flake technology
fossil site
fossil site with finds of uncertain species

tool cultures
Oldowan, 2-1.2 million years ago (mya)
Acheulian, 1.5 mya-150,000 ya

major species found at fossil site
Ar   *Ardepithecus ramidus*
Aa   *Australopithecus afarensis*
Aaf   *Australopithecus africanus*
Ra   *Australopithecus robustus*
Hh   *Homo habilis*
He   *Homo erectus*
Hsn   *Homo sapiens neanderthalensis*
other other forms of archaic *Homo sapiens*

evidence of Neanderthal ritual burial
use of fire by *Homo erectus*
conjectural spread of *Homo erectus*
ancient coastline, in glacial periods
Pliocene rainforest in Africa

100,000 Modern humans begin their migration out of Africa

135,000 Date of the earliest anatomically modern human fossils, from Omo, Ethiopia

300,000 Possibly the oldest known human structure; a hut is found at Terra Amata, France

400,000 The earliest surviving wooden tool, a spear (found in Schöningen, Germany)

500,000 ya   250,000 ya

H. s. sapiens
Archaic *Homo sapiens*
H. s. neanderthalensis

Acheulian culture

Mousterian culture

MID PALEOLITHIC

PLEISTOCENE EPOCH

QUATERNARY PERIOD

behavior had evolutionary advantages. *Homo erectus* mastered the use of fire, and was a more able toolmaker than *Homo habilis*, using the symmetrical hand-ax (a butchery tool) of the Acheulian culture.

Homo erectus was the first hominid to live outside Africa. Perhaps as early as 1.8 million years ago it had spread through tropical south and southeast Asia and colonized temperate areas of Europe and northern China before one million years ago. *Homo erectus*, however, did not reach Australia or the Americas. It could survive in temperate climates but not in Arctic and sub-Arctic ones, usually prefering to live in savanna, steppe and open woodlands: the same hand-ax technology was widespread. However in southeast Asia it adapted to tropical forest life, using flake and chopper tools and bamboo. The isolated *Homo erectus* populations began to evolve in different ways after 500,000 years ago. In Africa and Europe a variety of large-brained forms showed a mixture of archaic and modern human characteristics. In Europe between 230,000 and 150,000 years ago, archaic *Homo sapiens* evolved into *Homo sapiens neanderthalensis*, its physique adapted to life on the cold steppes and tundras of Ice Age Eurasia. These Neanderthals developed the Mousterian toolmaking technique, which was also widely used by hunter–gatherer groups in North Africa and the Middle East (often called the Near East by archeologists). In Africa archaic humans evolved until anatomically modern humans, *Homo sapiens sapiens*, appeared by 135,000 years ago ■

The earliest known anatomically modern *Homo sapiens sapiens* had appeared in Africa by 135,000 years ago (ya). By 90,000 years ago anatomically modern humans existed in the Middle East; by 75,000 years ago they were in east Asia and by 40,000 in Europe and Australia. By the end of the Ice Age 10,000 years ago, only some oceanic islands, Antarctica and some parts of the high Arctic remained completely uninhabited.

Two rival explanations have been offered for these facts. One argues that the modern human races developed directly from the regional *Homo erectus* populations: modern Africans evolved from *Homo erectus* via African archaic *Homo sapiens*; modern Europeans from *Homo erectus* via European archaic *Homo sapiens* and Neanderthals and so on. Critics point out that parallel evolution of this sort over such a wide area is implausible and that there is no supporting fossil evidence. The second explanation, known as the single-origins or "out of Africa" model, is supported by genetic evidence suggesting that all modern humans derive from African ancestors who lived between about 285,000 and 150,000 years ago, and that all modern non-African humans are descendants of a single group of this ancestral population that migrated out of Africa around 100,000 years ago. According to this model, the descendants of this group spread across Eurasia. The anatomically modern humans had better developed speech abilities than the archaic natives, who could not compete with the newcomers and gradually became extinct.

This model is more compatible with the fossil and archeological evidence than the first. Between 120,000 and 90,000 years ago the African climate was more moist than it is today and bands of hunters and gatherers could have crossed the Sahara. The earliest known fossils of modern humans outside Africa date to about 90,000 years ago and were found in Israel – just the place and date predicted by the single-origins theory. Only in Africa have forms intermediate between archaic and modern humans been found. In Europe, the Neanderthals and early modern humans formed distinct populations that coexisted for over 10,000 years: the Neanderthals did not evolve into modern humans. In east and southeast Asia, the *Homo erectus* populations were replaced by modern humans with no trace of intermediate forms.

When the first modern humans reached the Middle East, the global climate was beginning to enter one of the most severe glacial periods of the Ice Age. Human technology was probably inadequate for survival in the arctic climates of Europe and central Asia, and these areas were left to the hardier Neanderthals. Instead the moderns moved east, reaching China and southeast Asia around 75,000 years ago. Here they developed boat- or raft-building skills and

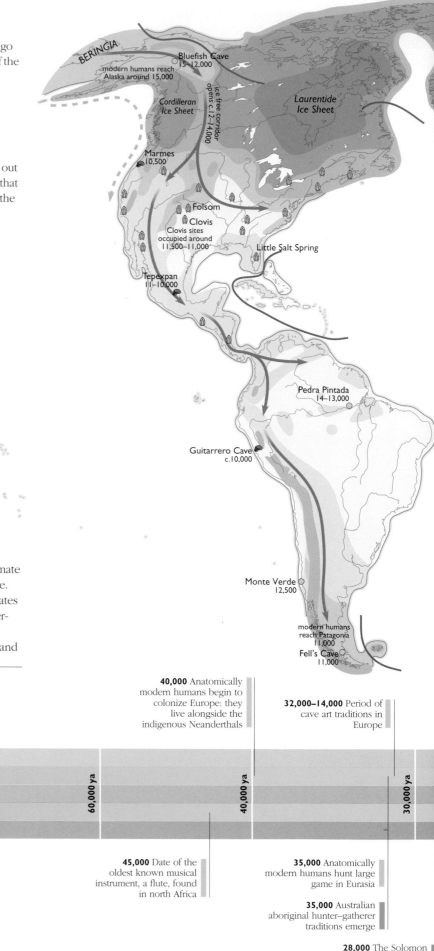

	115,000 Onset of the last glaciation of the (Pleistocene) Ice Age	**90,000** Anatomically modern humans living at Qafzeh, Israel	**40,000** Anatomically modern humans begin to colonize Europe: they live alongside the indigenous Neanderthals	**32,000–14,000** Period of cave art traditions in Europe	

TIMELINE

	100,000 years ago	80,000 ya	60,000 ya	40,000 ya	30,000 ya
The Americas					
Europe					
Middle East					
Africa					
East and South Asia					

c.120,000 Middle Stone Age flake-tool technology is well established in tropical Africa	**c.75,000** Glaciation causes Africa to become arid: the Sahara becomes impassable by humans	**45,000** Date of the oldest known musical instrument, a flute, found in north Africa	**35,000** Anatomically modern humans hunt large game in Eurasia

120,000–90,000 Periods of higher rainfall make the Sahara habitable by humans

75,000 Anatomically modern humans inhabit China and southeast Asia

35,000 Australian aboriginal hunter–gatherer traditions emerge

28,000 The Solomon Islands are settled

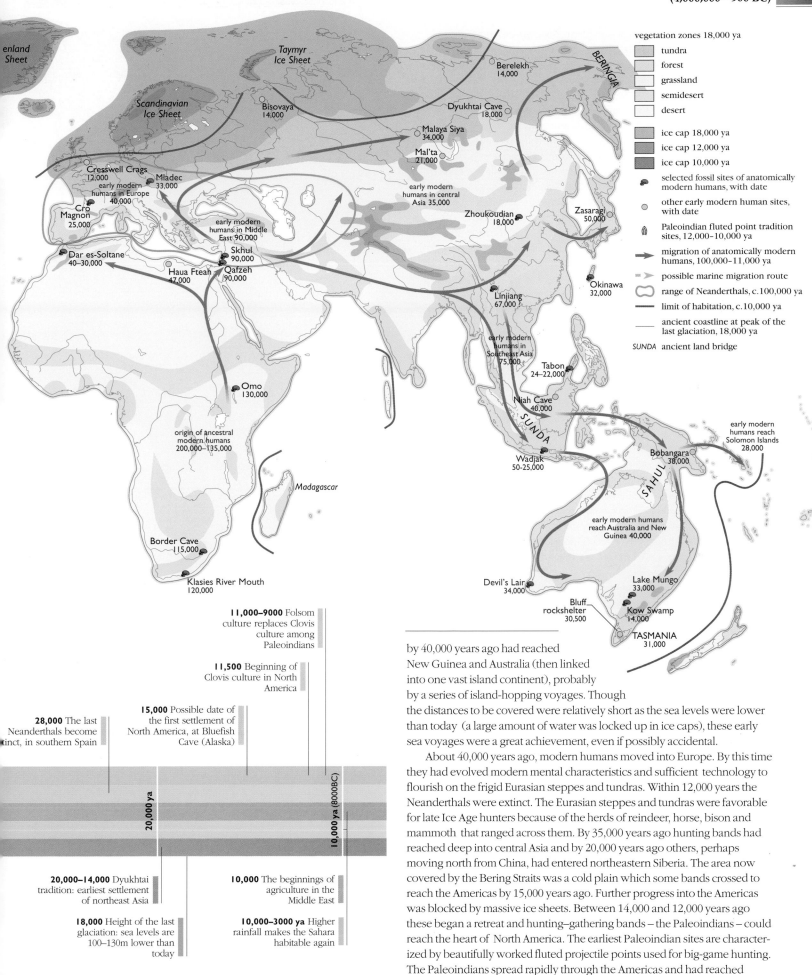

vegetation zones 18,000 ya
- tundra
- forest
- grassland
- semidesert
- desert
- ice cap 18,000 ya
- ice cap 12,000 ya
- ice cap 10,000 ya
- selected fossil sites of anatomically modern humans, with date
- other early modern human sites, with date
- Paleoindian fluted point tradition sites, 12,000–10,000 ya
- migration of anatomically modern humans, 100,000–11,000 ya
- possible marine migration route
- range of Neanderthals, c.100,000 ya
- limit of habitation, c.10,000 ya
- ancient coastline at peak of the last glaciation, 18,000 ya

SUNDA ancient land bridge

Greenland Sheet

Taymyr Ice Sheet

Scandinavian Ice Sheet

Berelekh 14,000

BERINGIA

Bisovaya 14,000

Dyukhtai Cave 18,000

Malaya Siya 34,000

Mal'ta 21,000

Cresswell Crags 12,000
early modern humans in Europe 40,000

Mladec 33,000

Cro Magnon 25,000

early modern humans in central Asia 35,000

Zhoukoudian 18,000

Zasaragi 50,000

early modern humans in Middle East 90,000

Dar es-Soltane 40–30,000

Skhul 90,000

Haua Fteah 47,000

Qafzeh 90,000

Okinawa 32,000

Linjiang 67,000

early modern humans in Southeast Asia 75,000

Tabon 24–22,000

Niah Cave 40,000

SUNDA

Omo 130,000

origin of ancestral modern humans 200,000–135,000

Madagascar

Wadjak 50–25,000

Bobangara 38,000

early modern humans reach Solomon Islands 28,000

SAHUL

early modern humans reach Australia and New Guinea 40,000

Border Cave 115,000

Klasies River Mouth 120,000

Devil's Lair 34,000

Lake Mungo 33,000

Bluff rockshelter 30,500

Kow Swamp 14,000

TASMANIA 31,000

11,000–9000 Folsom culture replaces Clovis culture among Paleoindians

11,500 Beginning of Clovis culture in North America

15,000 Possible date of the first settlement of North America, at Bluefish Cave (Alaska)

28,000 The last Neanderthals become extinct, in southern Spain

20,000 ya

10,000 ya (8000BC)

20,000–14,000 Dyukhtai tradition: earliest settlement of northeast Asia

18,000 Height of the last glaciation: sea levels are 100–130m lower than today

10,000 The beginnings of agriculture in the Middle East

10,000–3000 ya Higher rainfall makes the Sahara habitable again

by 40,000 years ago had reached New Guinea and Australia (then linked into one vast island continent), probably by a series of island-hopping voyages. Though the distances to be covered were relatively short as the sea levels were lower than today (a large amount of water was locked up in ice caps), these early sea voyages were a great achievement, even if possibly accidental.

About 40,000 years ago, modern humans moved into Europe. By this time they had evolved modern mental characteristics and sufficient technology to flourish on the frigid Eurasian steppes and tundras. Within 12,000 years the Neanderthals were extinct. The Eurasian steppes and tundras were favorable for late Ice Age hunters because of the herds of reindeer, horse, bison and mammoth that ranged across them. By 35,000 years ago hunting bands had reached deep into central Asia and by 20,000 years ago others, perhaps moving north from China, had entered northeastern Siberia. The area now covered by the Bering Straits was a cold plain which some bands crossed to reach the Americas by 15,000 years ago. Further progress into the Americas was blocked by massive ice sheets. Between 14,000 and 12,000 years ago these began a retreat and hunting–gathering bands – the Paleoindians – could reach the heart of North America. The earliest Paleoindian sites are characterized by beautifully worked fluted projectile points used for big-game hunting. The Paleoindians spread rapidly through the Americas and had reached Patagonia in South America by 11,000 years ago ■

F arming communities arose independently in many parts of the world between 10,000 and 5000 BC as a response to the environmental changes that followed the end of the Ice Age. The warmer climate was not an unmixed blessing: sea levels rose as the ice sheets melted, flooding huge areas of lowland hunting grounds. The savannas, steppes and tundras, all abundant in big game, shrank as the forests advanced.

In many areas, hunter–gatherers began to exploit small game birds, fish and plants to a greater extent than before. It was among these communities that agriculture first arose. Probably the first stage was planting the seeds of favored wild plant foods to guarantee their continuing availability. Next was the domestication of food plants by breeding strains with desirable characteristics. Because their seeds had a high carbohydrate content and were easy to store, the most important domesticated plant foods were strains of the cereals – wheat, barley, oats, rice, millet and maize – that still form the staple food crops today. Relatively few animal species have been domesticated; most of those have been herd animals, whose tendency to "follow the leader" makes them easier to manage. Animal domestication began with the management and selective culling of wild herds. Penning the animals followed, then selective breeding for desirable qualities. Most early centers of agriculture were rich in wild plants and animals suitable for domestication. Elsewhere agriculture relied on the introduction of crops and livestock from established farming areas.

Some communities of hunter–gatherers moved from casual cultivation of wild plants (incipient agriculture) to a full farming economy far more quickly than others. Farmers have to work harder than hunter–gatherers, and few made the transition willingly. Rising populations probably forced many to adopt cultivation to supplement wild food supplies. In the Fertile Crescent of the Middle East, where farming first developed, (▷ 1.08) the transition from incipient agriculture to dependence on domesticated cereals took only three centuries, 8000–7700 BC, and domesticated animals replaced hunted wild animals a millennium later. In Mesoamerica a full farming way of life developed within a few centuries of the domestication of maize (▷ 1.28). In eastern North America hunting and gathering remained the main source of food for some three millennia after the first cultivation of domesticated food around 2500 BC. Even farmers who grew most of their food still exploited wild food sources.

Agriculture led to far-reaching technological developments. Most hunter–gatherers had to carry everything from camp to camp: farmers were sedentary, so weight became less critical. New tools, such as polished stone

EASTERN N AMERICA
goosefoot
gourds
marsh elder
sumpweed
sunflowers
c.1000

Hawaiian Islands

c.2300

Bahamas

Cuba
Jamaica
Hispaniola
Puerto Rico

c.1000

MESOAMERICA
avocados
beans
cotton
gourds
maize
peppers
pumpkins
squashes
tomatoes
turkeys

c.3500

c.4000

LOWLAND S AMERICA
manioc
peanuts
pineapples

c.3000

c.2000

ANDES
alpacas
beans
chili peppers
gourds
guinea pigs
llamas
potatoes

c.1000
c.500

5400–4500 Bandkeramick culture: first farmers of central Europe

6000 Farming spreads across southern Europe

c.6000 The first cattle are domesticated in the Middle East

9000 Wild sheep flocks are managed in the Zagros mountains, Iraq

6200 Copper smelting and textile manufacture in Chatal Huyuk (Turkey)

9000–8000 Incipient agriculture (cultivation of wild cereals) in the Fertile Crescent

10,000 BC Natufian hunter–gatherers harvest wild cereals in Syria

8000-7700 Wheat and barley are domesticated in the Fertile Crescent

5000 Irrigation agriculture begins on the Mesopotamian plains

TIMELINE	10,000 BC		8000		6000		4000
The Americas							
Europe							
Middle East							
Africa							
East and South Asia							

c.12,000 BC Jomon hunter–gatherers make the first pottery in Japan

8000 End of the last glaciation, worldwide

6500 Rice cultivation in the Yangtze valley

4500 Farming is adopted in the Ganges plain

6000 Wheat, barley and sheep farming begins in Egypt

3800 The earliest bronze working is carried out in the Middle East

6000 Earliest evidence for farming in the Indian subcontinent

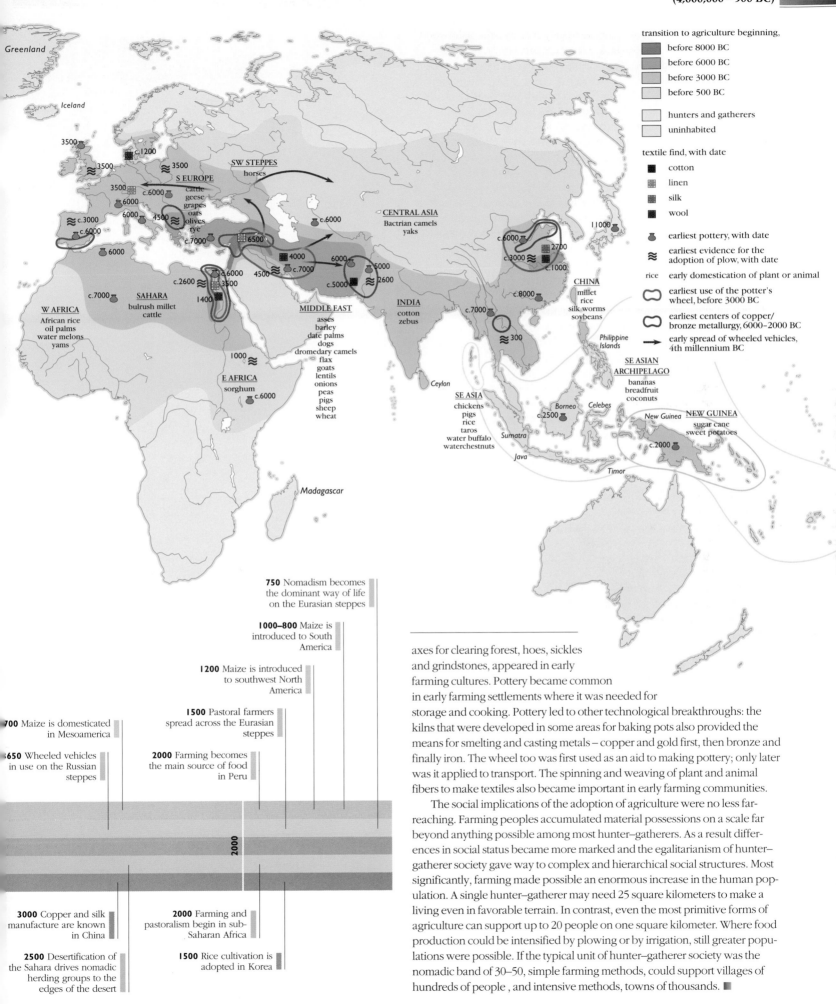

Legend:

transition to agriculture beginning,

- before 8000 BC
- before 6000 BC
- before 3000 BC
- before 500 BC
- hunters and gatherers
- uninhabited

textile find, with date

- cotton
- linen
- silk
- wool

earliest pottery, with date

earliest evidence for the adoption of plow, with date

rice — early domestication of plant or animal

earliest use of the potter's wheel, before 3000 BC

earliest centers of copper/bronze metallurgy, 6000–2000 BC

early spread of wheeled vehicles, 4th millennium BC

Map labels:

Greenland

Iceland

SW STEPPES
horses

S EUROPE
cattle
geese
grapes
oats
olives
rye

CENTRAL ASIA
Bactrian camels
yaks

CHINA
millet
rice
silk worms
soybeans

W AFRICA
African rice
oil palms
water melons
yams

SAHARA
bulrush millet
cattle

MIDDLE EAST
asses
barley
date palms
dogs
dromedary camels
flax
goats
lentils
onions
peas
pigs
sheep
wheat

INDIA
cotton
zebus

E AFRICA
sorghum

Ceylon

Madagascar

Philippine Islands

SE ASIA
chickens
pigs
rice
taros
water buffalo
waterchestnuts

SE ASIAN ARCHIPELAGO
bananas
breadfruit
coconuts

NEW GUINEA
sugar cane
sweet potatoes

Borneo

Celebes

New Guinea

Sumatra

Java

Timor

Timeline:

750 Nomadism becomes the dominant way of life on the Eurasian steppes

1000–800 Maize is introduced to South America

1200 Maize is introduced to southwest North America

1500 Pastoral farmers spread across the Eurasian steppes

700 Maize is domesticated in Mesoamerica

3650 Wheeled vehicles in use on the Russian steppes

2000 Farming becomes the main source of food in Peru

2000

3000 Copper and silk manufacture are known in China

2000 Farming and pastoralism begin in sub-Saharan Africa

2500 Desertification of the Sahara drives nomadic herding groups to the edges of the desert

1500 Rice cultivation is adopted in Korea

Body text:

axes for clearing forest, hoes, sickles and grindstones, appeared in early farming cultures. Pottery became common in early farming settlements where it was needed for storage and cooking. Pottery led to other technological breakthroughs: the kilns that were developed in some areas for baking pots also provided the means for smelting and casting metals – copper and gold first, then bronze and finally iron. The wheel too was first used as an aid to making pottery; only later was it applied to transport. The spinning and weaving of plant and animal fibers to make textiles also became important in early farming communities.

The social implications of the adoption of agriculture were no less far-reaching. Farming peoples accumulated material possessions on a scale far beyond anything possible among most hunter–gatherers. As a result differences in social status became more marked and the egalitarianism of hunter–gatherer society gave way to complex and hierarchical social structures. Most significantly, farming made possible an enormous increase in the human population. A single hunter–gatherer may need 25 square kilometers to make a living even in favorable terrain. In contrast, even the most primitive forms of agriculture can support up to 20 people on one square kilometer. Where food production could be intensified by plowing or by irrigation, still greater populations were possible. If the typical unit of hunter–gatherer society was the nomadic band of 30–50, simple farming methods, could support villages of hundreds of people , and intensive methods, towns of thousands. ■

By 2000 BC the revolutionary impact of agriculture had become clear. Farming was practiced on every continent and would overtake hunting and gathering as the way of life of most people well before the Christian era.

Not all early farming societies developed the same level of complexity. Poor soil, climate, endemic diseases of humans or livestock or a lack of suitable crops limited development in many areas. The greater the resources possessed by a society, the more complex it could become; in a few favorable environments (such as the northwest of North America), hunter-gatherer societies too achieved greater levels of social complexity.

Most early farming societies were kinship-based tribes of hundreds or a few thousand people living in villages or dispersed homesteads. Although they recognized ties of kinship, religion or language with others, each tribe was essentially independent. Differences of rank and status existed but leaders could rarely exercise coercive power over other tribes' people. Archeologically, such societies (known to anthropologists as "segmentary societies") can be recognized by communal burial practices, the remains of permanent homesteads and villages and communal works such as the megalithic tombs of prehistoric western Europe. In 2000 BC segmentary farming societies were dominant in south and southeast Asia, New Guinea, north Africa, northern Europe and parts of Mesoamerica and South America.

Where intensive agricultural techniques could be used, largescale hierarchical communities of up to 20,000 people, known as "chiefdoms", could develop. Rank and status were linked to lineage: the senior person of the senior lineage was the chief, who was thereby the ruler of the whole community. Chieftains could exercise coercive power, often through a warrior class, and support specialist craftsmen. Archeologically, chiefdoms show major construction projects requiring large resources of labor and wealth, such as Stonehenge in southern Britain (▷ 1.20). In chiefdoms the quantity and quality of grave goods placed with burials indicate the rank and status of the individual and a few burials are lavishly furnished. Chiefdoms commonly had a dominant central site such as a stronghold or ceremonial center, and smaller satellite settlements. In 2000 BC chiefdoms were established in the Middle East and southwest central Europe, in China and the Andes. In western Europe segmentary farming societies were giving way to chiefdoms at this time.

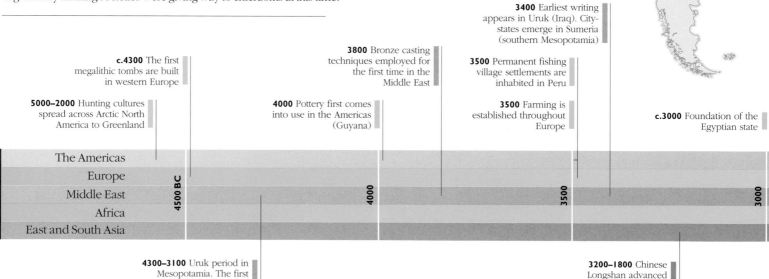

3400 Earliest writing appears in Uruk (Iraq). City-states emerge in Sumeria (southern Mesopotamia)

c.4300 The first megalithic tombs are built in western Europe

3800 Bronze casting techniques employed for the first time in the Middle East

3500 Permanent fishing village settlements are inhabited in Peru

5000–2000 Hunting cultures spread across Arctic North America to Greenland

4000 Pottery first comes into use in the Americas (Guyana)

3500 Farming is established throughout Europe

c.3000 Foundation of the Egyptian state

TIMELINE

The Americas				
Europe	**4500 BC**	**4000**	**3500**	**3000**
Middle East				
Africa				
East and South Asia				

4300–3100 Uruk period in Mesopotamia. The first cities are built.

3200–1800 Chinese Longshan advanced farming cultures; first towns are built in China

3000 Ancestral Austronesians migrate from Taiwan to the Philippines

3000–1700 Pastoral farming is established on the central Asian steppes (Afanasevo culture)

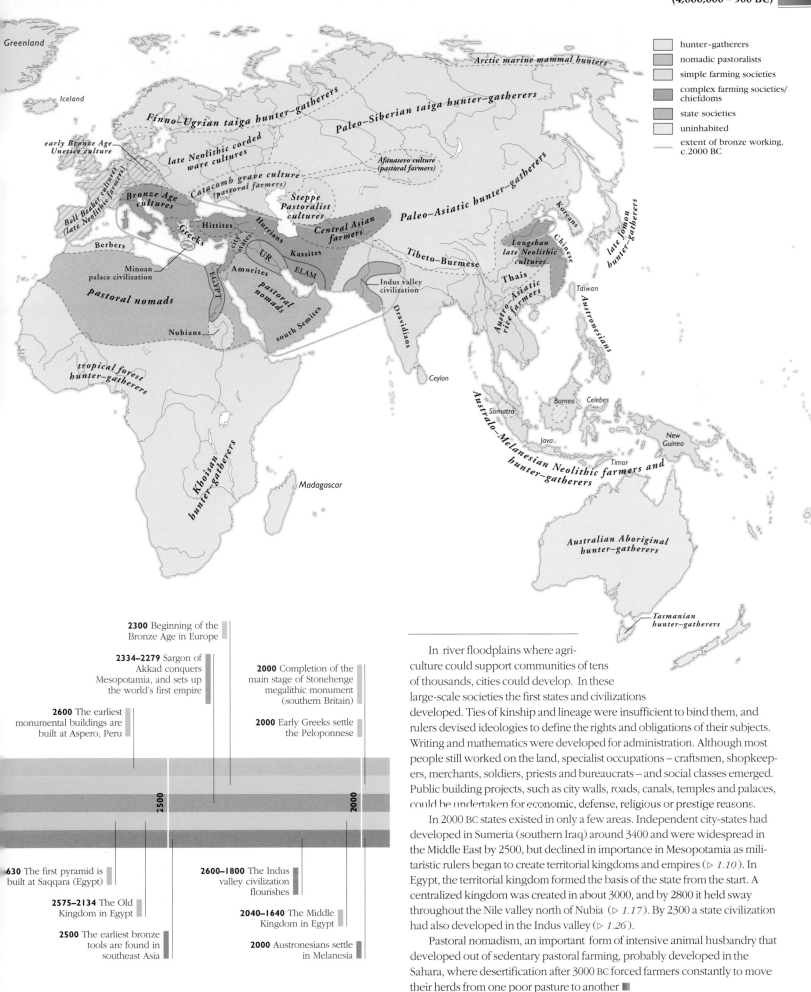

Legend:
- hunter-gatherers
- nomadic pastoralists
- simple farming societies
- complex farming societies/chiefdoms
- state societies
- uninhabited
- extent of bronze working, c.2000 BC

Greenland

Iceland

Arctic marine mammal hunters

Finno–Ugrian taiga hunter–gatherers

Paleo–Siberian taiga hunter–gatherers

early Bronze Age Unetice culture

late Neolithic corded ware cultures

Afanasevo culture (pastoral farmers)

Bell Beaker cultures (late Neolithic farmers)

Catacomb grave culture (pastoral farmers)

Bronze Age cultures

Steppe Pastoralist cultures

Central Asian farmers

Paleo–Asiatic hunter–gatherers

Koreans

Greeks

Hittites

Hurrians

late Jomon hunter–gatherers

Berbers

city states

Kassites

Tibeto–Burmese

Chinese

Longshan late Neolithic cultures

Minoan palace civilization

UR

ELAM

Amorites

Thais

Austro–Asiatic rice farmers

Taiwan

EGYPT

pastoral nomads

Indus valley civilization

Austronesians

Pastoral nomads

Nubians

south Semites

Dravidians

Ceylon

tropical forest hunter–gatherers

Borneo

Celebes

Sumatra

Java

New Guinea

Timor

Australo–Melanesian Neolithic farmers and hunter–gatherers

Khoisan hunter–gatherers

Madagascar

Australian Aboriginal hunter–gatherers

Tasmanian hunter–gatherers

Timeline:

2300 Beginning of the Bronze Age in Europe

2334–2279 Sargon of Akkad conquers Mesopotamia, and sets up the world's first empire

2000 Completion of the main stage of Stonehenge megalithic monument (southern Britain)

2600 The earliest monumental buildings are built at Aspero, Peru

2000 Early Greeks settle the Peloponnese

2500

2000

630 The first pyramid is built at Saqqara (Egypt)

2600–1800 The Indus valley civilization flourishes

2575–2134 The Old Kingdom in Egypt

2040–1640 The Middle Kingdom in Egypt

2500 The earliest bronze tools are found in southeast Asia

2000 Austronesians settle in Melanesia

In river floodplains where agriculture could support communities of tens of thousands, cities could develop. In these large-scale societies the first states and civilizations developed. Ties of kinship and lineage were insufficient to bind them, and rulers devised ideologies to define the rights and obligations of their subjects. Writing and mathematics were developed for administration. Although most people still worked on the land, specialist occupations – craftsmen, shopkeepers, merchants, soldiers, priests and bureaucrats – and social classes emerged. Public building projects, such as city walls, roads, canals, temples and palaces, could be undertaken for economic, defense, religious or prestige reasons.

In 2000 BC states existed in only a few areas. Independent city-states had developed in Sumeria (southern Iraq) around 3400 and were widespread in the Middle East by 2500, but declined in importance in Mesopotamia as militaristic rulers began to create territorial kingdoms and empires (▷ 1.10). In Egypt, the territorial kingdom formed the basis of the state from the start. A centralized kingdom was created in about 3000, and by 2800 it held sway throughout the Nile valley north of Nubia (▷ 1.17). By 2300 a state civilization had also developed in the Indus valley (▷ 1.26).

Pastoral nomadism, an important form of intensive animal husbandry that developed out of sedentary pastoral farming, probably developed in the Sahara, where desertification after 3000 BC forced farmers constantly to move their herds from one poor pasture to another ∎

The fragility of the first civilizations was evident during the second millennium BC. Sumeria had vanished as a political entity shortly before 2000 BC though its achievements were built upon by the Babylonian and Assyrian states which arose in the early second millennium (▷ 1.11). The rivalry between these two states was to endure until the middle of the first millennium. The other major power of the Middle East was the Hittite kingdom of Anatolia. One of the secrets of Hittite success is thought to have been their early mastery of iron working, in about 1500 BC. Meanwhile, Egypt expanded far south into Nubia and north into the Levant (▷ 1.18). In the eastern Mediterranean, the Minoans of Crete were replaced by the Mycenaean civilization that emerged on the Greek mainland around 1600. Around 1400 the Mycenaeans conquered Crete and introduced the Greek language; they also settled on Cyprus and in Anatolia (▷ 1.22).

This civilized world was thrown into chaos about 1200 by a wave of invasions. Mycenae was destroyed by invaders from the north, plunging Greece into a 400-year-long "dark age". Thracians, Phrygians and Anatolian Luvians overthrew the Hittite empire and nomadic Aramaeans occupied much of Mesopotamia. Egypt was invaded by mysterious Sea Peoples. Their fleets were driven from the Nile, but they settled in the Levant where they were known as the Philistines.

By 1000 stability was returning. The Hittites survived though as a shadow of their former selves. The Aramaeans had settled and were assimilating with the urbanized peoples of the conquered territories: their language became the common tongue of the Middle East for the next millennium. Assyria and Babylon were beginning to recover (▷ 1.12). The Levant was a mosaic of tiny states: of these, the Phoenician city-states and Israel acquired a historical importance out of all proportion to their size (▷ 1.14). Egyptian power was in decline and the Nubians, after a millennium of Egyptian domination, set up the kingdom of Kush. In sub-Saharan Africa, the transition to a farming way of life was beginning.

In Asia, the Indus valley civilization had collapsed around 1700; about 200 years later the Aryans, an Indo-European pastoralist people, migrated into India. In northern China the Neolithic Longshan cultures developed into the urbanized Shang state around 1766, marking the start of Chinese civilization. Around 1122 the Shang dynasty was ousted by the ruler of the Zhou sub-kingdom (▷ 1.27).

The Austronesian farming peoples continued to colonize the southeast Asian archipelagoes; by 2000 they had bypassed New Guinea and settled the western Pacific Bismarck archipelago around 1500 BC. The Lapita culture,

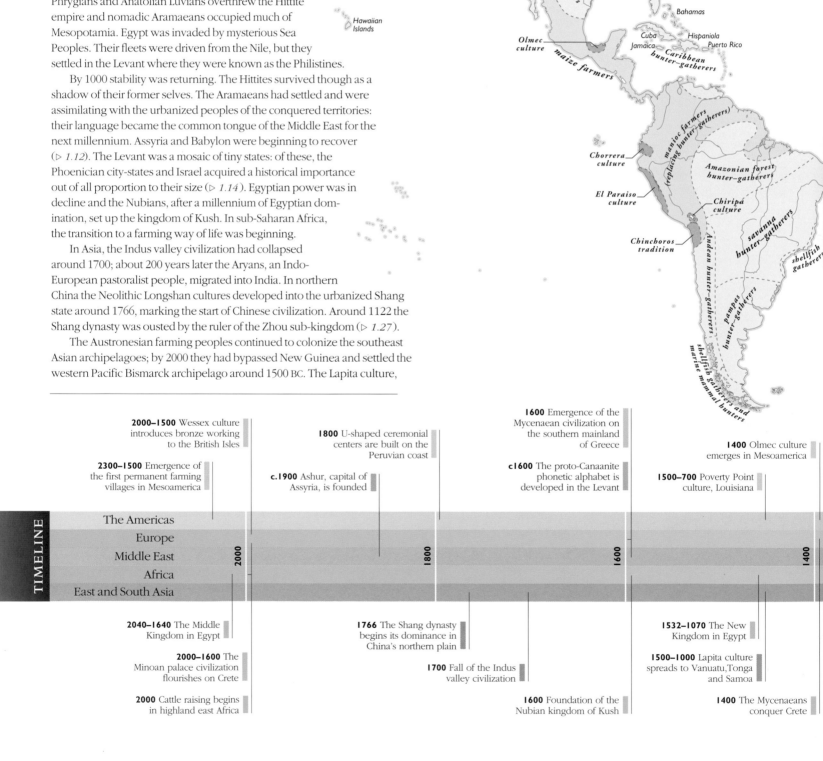

TIMELINE

2000–1500 Wessex culture introduces bronze working to the British Isles

2300–1500 Emergence of the first permanent farming villages in Mesoamerica

1800 U-shaped ceremonial centers are built on the Peruvian coast

c.1900 Ashur, capital of Assyria, is founded

1600 Emergence of the Mycenaean civilization on the southern mainland of Greece

c1600 The proto-Canaanite phonetic alphabet is developed in the Levant

1400 Olmec culture emerges in Mesoamerica

1500–700 Poverty Point culture, Louisiana

	2000	1800	1600	1400
The Americas				
Europe				
Middle East				
Africa				
East and South Asia				

2040–1640 The Middle Kingdom in Egypt

2000–1600 The Minoan palace civilization flourishes on Crete

2000 Cattle raising begins in highland east Africa

1766 The Shang dynasty begins its dominance in China's northern plain

1700 Fall of the Indus valley civilization

1600 Foundation of the Nubian kingdom of Kush

1532–1070 The New Kingdom in Egypt

1500–1000 Lapita culture spreads to Vanuatu, Tonga and Samoa

1400 The Mycenaeans conquer Crete

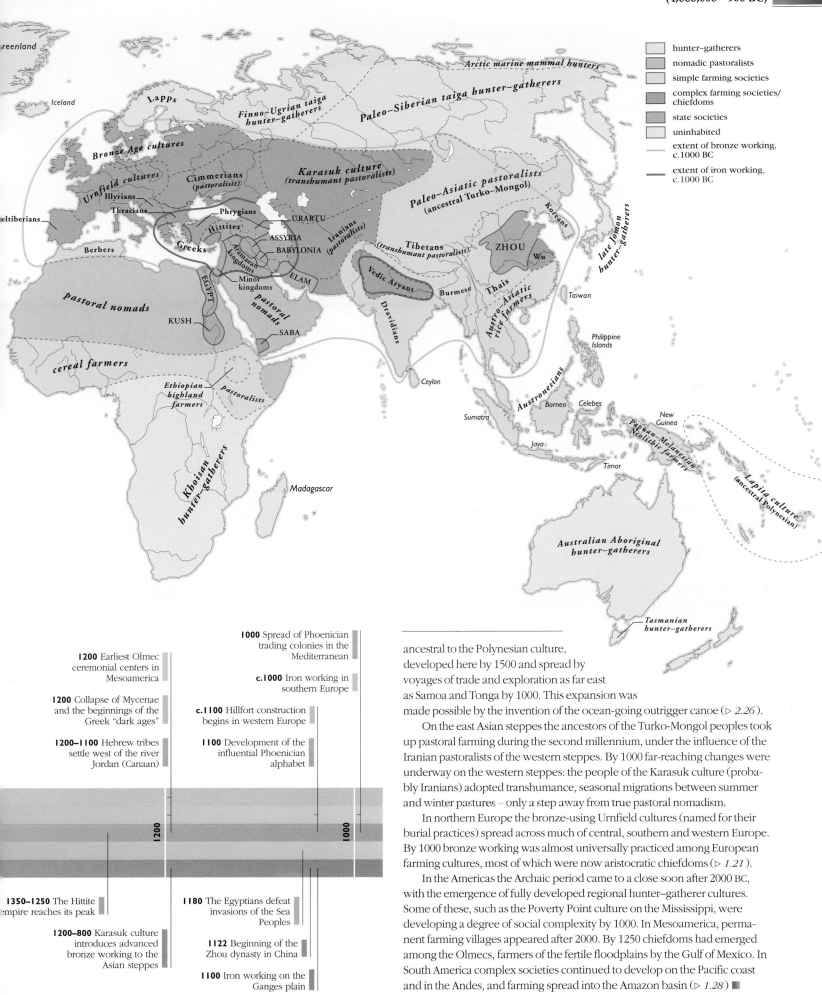

hunter-gatherers
nomadic pastoralists
simple farming societies
complex farming societies/chiefdoms
state societies
uninhabited
extent of bronze working, c.1000 BC
extent of iron working, c.1000 BC

1200 Earliest Olmec ceremonial centers in Mesoamerica

1200 Collapse of Mycenae and the beginnings of the Greek "dark ages"

1200–1100 Hebrew tribes settle west of the river Jordan (Canaan)

1000 Spread of Phoenician trading colonies in the Mediterranean

c.1000 Iron working in southern Europe

c.1100 Hillfort construction begins in western Europe

1100 Development of the influential Phoenician alphabet

1350–1250 The Hittite empire reaches its peak

1200–800 Karasuk culture introduces advanced bronze working to the Asian steppes

1180 The Egyptians defeat invasions of the Sea Peoples

1122 Beginning of the Zhou dynasty in China

1100 Iron working on the Ganges plain

ancestral to the Polynesian culture, developed here by 1500 and spread by voyages of trade and exploration as far east as Samoa and Tonga by 1000. This expansion was made possible by the invention of the ocean-going outrigger canoe (▷ 2.26).

On the east Asian steppes the ancestors of the Turko-Mongol peoples took up pastoral farming during the second millennium, under the influence of the Iranian pastoralists of the western steppes. By 1000 far-reaching changes were underway on the western steppes: the people of the Karasuk culture (probably Iranians) adopted transhumance, seasonal migrations between summer and winter pastures – only a step away from true pastoral nomadism.

In northern Europe the bronze-using Urnfield cultures (named for their burial practices) spread across much of central, southern and western Europe. By 1000 bronze working was almost universally practiced among European farming cultures, most of which were now aristocratic chiefdoms (▷ 1.21).

In the Americas the Archaic period came to a close soon after 2000 BC, with the emergence of fully developed regional hunter–gatherer cultures. Some of these, such as the Poverty Point culture on the Mississippi, were developing a degree of social complexity by 1000. In Mesoamerica, permanent farming villages appeared after 2000. By 1250 chiefdoms had emerged among the Olmecs, farmers of the fertile floodplains by the Gulf of Mexico. In South America complex societies continued to develop on the Pacific coast and in the Andes, and farming spread into the Amazon basin (▷ 1.28) ∎

The number and size of organized states in the Middle East, India and the Mediterranean rose sharply between 1000 and 500 BC. A succession of empires dominated the Middle East. The first was the Assyrian empire which stretched from the Zagros mountains to Egypt by the 7th century. Assyrian rule was harsh and in 625 the Babylonians rebelled and seized most of the empire for themselves (▷ 1.13). Then the Iranian Medes pushed west, conquering the Caucasus and eastern Anatolia. In 550 Cyrus II "the Great", an Iranian king, seized the Median kingdom and founded the Persian empire. He then took western Anatolia and the Babylonian empire. By 500 the Persian empire extended from Egypt to the Indus (▷ 1.15).

State-organized societies had also spread throughout the Mediterranean world. By 700 Greece was a patchwork of independent city-states: by 500 these cities, and Athens in particular, entered a period of intellectual creativity unparalleled in world history (▷ 1.24). The Greeks and Phoenicians also founded trading colonies throughout the Mediterranean. Although the Phoenicians lost their independence by 500, Carthage, their colony in north Africa, was the leading power of the western Mediterranean. The Greek cities of Sicily and southern Italy had a powerful influence, notably on the Etruscans who dominated northern Italy by 500. North of the Alps the Urnfield cultures of central Europe were replaced by the aristocratic iron-using Celtic Hallstatt culture c.600 (▷ 1.25).

States reappeared in the Indian subcontinent in the 9th century. The focus this time was the Ganges plain where Vedic Aryan chiefdoms began to coalesce into kingdoms and republics. By 500 the largest was the kingdom of Magadha. At the same time the Aryans extended southward, conquering the Dravidians and imposing Hindu religion on them (▷ 1.26). The Chinese Zhou kingdom expanded to the southeast after 1000, but what it gained in area it lost in internal cohesion. The Zhou kingdom was a decentralized feudal state and by the 8th century the powerful warlords had so undermined the power of the monarchy that it was power-less to prevent the kingdom from breaking up (▷ 1.27). Meanwhile the first chiefdoms emerged around 500 in Korea and in Van Lang in southeast Asia.

One far-reaching development of the early first millennium was the change in lifestyle of the Iranian peoples (Scythians, Sarmatians, Sakas and Yue Qi) of the Eurasian steppes from transhumant pastoralism to nomadic pastoralism. The steppe peoples had been pioneers in the use of horses: they had domesticated them for their meat around 4000 BC, they had harnessed them to wagons (4th millennium) and war chariots (2nd millennium) and by 1000 BC they had mastered riding on horse-

---

700–100 Adena culture burial mound builders in the eastern woodlands of North America

800 Zapotecs develop hieroglyphic script in Mesoamerica

700 City-states flourish in Greece and the Aegean

800–500 Greek coloniza-tion of the Mediterranean and Black Sea

c.750 Emergence of the Celtic Hallstatt Iron Age culture north of the Alps

900–700 Nomadism becomes the dominant way of life on the Eurasian steppes

800 Emergence of the Etruscan civilization in Italy

1000 Emergence of the kingdom of Israel

750–705 Assyrian power reaches its peak

612 The collapse of the Assyrian empire

TIMELINE		1000		900		800		700		600
The Americas										
Europe										
Middle East										
Africa										
East and South Asia										

1000–500 Formative period of Hinduism

900 The first states emerge on the Ganges plain

814 Foundation of the Phoenician colony of Carthage

712–671 Egypt is ruled by a Kushite dynasty from Nubia

600 Iron and bronze working develop in west Africa

800 The Aryans expand into southern India

600 Introduction of iron working into China

770–481 The "Springs and Autumns" period in China: the Zhou kingdom breaks up into minor states

c.590 The Nubian capital established at Meroë

Arctic marine mammal hunters

Aleuts

sub-Arctic forest hunter-gatherers

west coast foraging hunting and fishing peoples

plateau fishers and hunter-gatherers

desert hunter-gatherers

plains bison hunters

east woodlands hunter-gatherers

Adena complex

maize farmers

Hawaiian Islands

Bahamas

Cuba
Jamaica

Hispaniola
Puerto Rico

Caribbean hunter-gatherers

Zapotec culture

Maya

Olmec culture

maize farmers

manioc farmers

Chorrera culture

Chavin culture

Yaya–Mama religious tradition

savanna hunter-gatherers

Paracas culture

Chinchoros tradition

Andean hunter-gatherers

pampas hunter-gatherers

shellfish gatherers

shellfish gatherers and marine mammal hunters

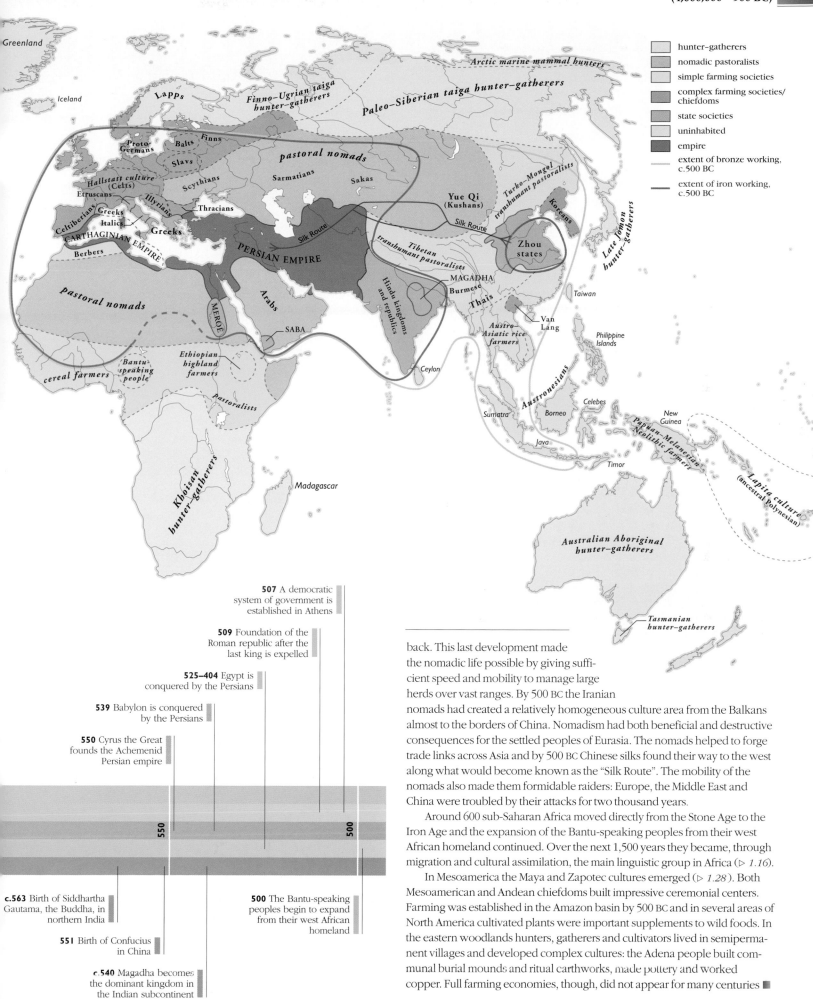

Legend:

- hunter-gatherers
- nomadic pastoralists
- simple farming societies
- complex farming societies/chiefdoms
- state societies
- uninhabited
- empire
- ——— extent of bronze working, c.500 BC
- ——— extent of iron working, c.500 BC

Map labels:

Greenland · Iceland · Lapps · Finno–Ugrian taiga hunter-gatherers · Arctic marine mammal hunters · Paleo-Siberian taiga hunter-gatherers · Proto-Germans · Balts · Finns · Slavs · pastoral nomads · Turko–Mongol transhumant pastoralists · Koreans · Late Jomon hunter-gatherers · Hallstatt culture (Celts) · Etruscans · Illyrians · Scythians · Sarmatians · Sakas · Yue Qi (Kushans) · Zhou states · Celtiberians · Greeks · Italics · Greeks · Thracians · Silk Route · Silk Route · Tibetan transhumant pastoralists · MAGADHA · CARTHAGINIAN EMPIRE · Berbers · PERSIAN EMPIRE · Burmese · Thais · Taiwan · pastoral nomads · Arabs · Hindu kingdoms and republics · Van Lang · MEROË · Austro-Asiatic rice farmers · Philippine Islands · SABA · Ceylon · Austronesians · cereal farmers · Bantu-speaking people · Ethiopian highland farmers · Celebes · New Guinea · Pastoralists · Sumatra · Borneo · Papuan–Melanesian Neolithic farmers · Java · Timor · Lapita culture (ancestral Polynesian) · Khoisan hunter-gatherers · Madagascar · Australian Aboriginal hunter-gatherers · Tasmanian hunter-gatherers

Timeline:

507 A democratic system of government is established in Athens

509 Foundation of the Roman republic after the last king is expelled

525–404 Egypt is conquered by the Persians

539 Babylon is conquered by the Persians

550 Cyrus the Great founds the Achemenid Persian empire

550

500

c.563 Birth of Siddhartha Gautama, the Buddha, in northern India

500 The Bantu-speaking peoples begin to expand from their west African homeland

551 Birth of Confucius in China

c.540 Magadha becomes the dominant kingdom in the Indian subcontinent

back. This last development made the nomadic life possible by giving sufficient speed and mobility to manage large herds over vast ranges. By 500 BC the Iranian nomads had created a relatively homogeneous culture area from the Balkans almost to the borders of China. Nomadism had both beneficial and destructive consequences for the settled peoples of Eurasia. The nomads helped to forge trade links across Asia and by 500 BC Chinese silks found their way to the west along what would become known as the "Silk Route". The mobility of the nomads also made them formidable raiders: Europe, the Middle East and China were troubled by their attacks for two thousand years.

Around 600 sub-Saharan Africa moved directly from the Stone Age to the Iron Age and the expansion of the Bantu-speaking peoples from their west African homeland continued. Over the next 1,500 years they became, through migration and cultural assimilation, the main linguistic group in Africa (▷ 1.16).

In Mesoamerica the Maya and Zapotec cultures emerged (▷ 1.28). Both Mesoamerican and Andean chiefdoms built impressive ceremonial centers. Farming was established in the Amazon basin by 500 BC and in several areas of North America cultivated plants were important supplements to wild foods. In the eastern woodlands hunters, gatherers and cultivators lived in semipermanent villages and developed complex cultures: the Adena people built communal burial mounds and ritual earthworks, made pottery and worked copper. Full farming economies, though, did not appear for many centuries ■

Writing was invented as an aid to administration in communities that had grown so complex that human memory could no longer store all the information needed for efficient government. The earliest known writing has been found on clay tablets from the Sumerian city of Uruk (in modern Iraq), from about 3400 BC but, as this was already a complete system with over seven hundred signs, development must have begun much earlier.

The earliest Sumerian signs are pictographs – for example the sign for barley is a simplified picture of an ear of barley. More complex ideas were expressed by combining signs: thus a head and a bowl together meant "to eat". The signs were inscribed on wet clay tablets which were then dried. This proved to be a very durable medium and many thousands of clay tablets have survived (▷ 1.10). After about 2900 BC the signs were gradually simplified and inscribed with a rectangular-ended reed stylus. This left wedge-shaped strokes from which this script derives its name (cuneiform, from the Latin *cuneus*, "wedge").

Cuneiform was gradually refined so that a sign could also stand for the phonetic value of the word: if this system were used for modern English, the sign for "man" could also be used in combination with another sign, such as that for "age", to make another word, "manage". Syllable signs were also introduced, enabling cuneiform to record accurately all elements of human speech. Most early Sumerian documents were accounts and records of transactions. It was not until about 2400 that writing was used to record law codes, letters, chronicles, religious beliefs or for literature.

The Sumerian writing systems were widely adapted to other languages. Elamite and Indus valley pictographic derive from Sumerian pictographic (▷ 1.26) and although Egyptian hieroglyphic writing (a system that is almost as old as the Sumerian) was unique, the idea was probably based on Sumerian pictographs (▷ 1.17). Cuneiform was adapted successfully to the Akkadian, Assyrian, Babylonian, Elamite, Hittite, Hurrian and Urartian languages among others. Nevertheless, hundreds of different signs had to be learned, and scribes needed several years to master cuneiform and hieroglyphic scripts; as a result literacy remained the preserve of a tiny minority of specialists, and the cultural impact of its introduction was limited.

In the early 16th century BC the much simpler proto-Canaanite phonetic alphabet, with only 28 letters, was developed in the Levant or eastern Mediterranean coastal region (▷ 1.12). The letters were based on Egyptian hieroglyphs, but they stood for syllables that could be combined to spell out the sound of a word. By 1000 BC many variants of the proto-Canaanite script had developed, most important among them the Phoenician, Aramaic and the Arabian Sabean and Nabatean alphabets. The Aramaic alphabet was adopted by the Assyrians by the 8th century and replaced cuneiform as the main script of the Middle East. Adaptations of Aramaic were introduced into India in the 7th century and became the basis of modern Indian scripts and, ultimately, of the Indian-derived scripts of southeast and central Asia. Nabatean developed into the Arabic script in the 7th century AD while Sabean crossed the Red Sea to form the basis of Ethiopic, which was the only independent script to emerge in sub-Saharan Africa.

The Phoenician alphabet was the basis of the Old Hebrew and Greek alphabets. The Greeks adapted the Phoenician alphabet in the 8th century by introducing separate letters for consonant and vowel sounds (▷ 1.23). This was more precise than any syllabic alphabet. The Greek alphabet was in turn adapted to form new scripts by the peoples of Anatolia, the Balkans and Italy, including the Etruscans whose script was developed by the Romans into the Latin alphabet. Alphabetic scripts were easier to learn and use and they permitted literacy to become a widespread accomplishment, rather than just the preserve of professional scribes and administrators.

China, Mesoamerica and Polynesia each saw the independent development of writing. In Shang Dynasty China, a script with both pictographic and phonetic elements appeared around 1600 BC. Most early examples record the results of divinations on animal bones, but the script was also used for record-keeping (▷ 1.27). This script was constantly refined and standardized over the centuries, and the modern Chinese writing system is still based on its principles. The Chinese script became the basis of Japanese and Korean scripts (though the Koreans later adopted an alphabetic script).

In Mesoamerica the Zapotecs began to develop a hieroglyphic script about 800 BC, from which the later Mesoamerican scripts derive (▷ 1.28). Of these, only the Mayan was a fully developed literary language capable of expressing all aspects of spoken language. Writing did not develop in the Andean civilizations although the Inca *quipu*, a mnemonic device made of knotted strings, fulfilled some of the functions of a simple script. Colored strings symbolized different commodities or services while the number of knots represented quantities held or required.

Another script to arise independently of any other was the hieroglyphic script developed in the Polynesian chiefdoms of Easter Island about AD 1500. Known as Rongorongo, it fell out of use before Europeans reached Easter Island and has not been deciphered ∎

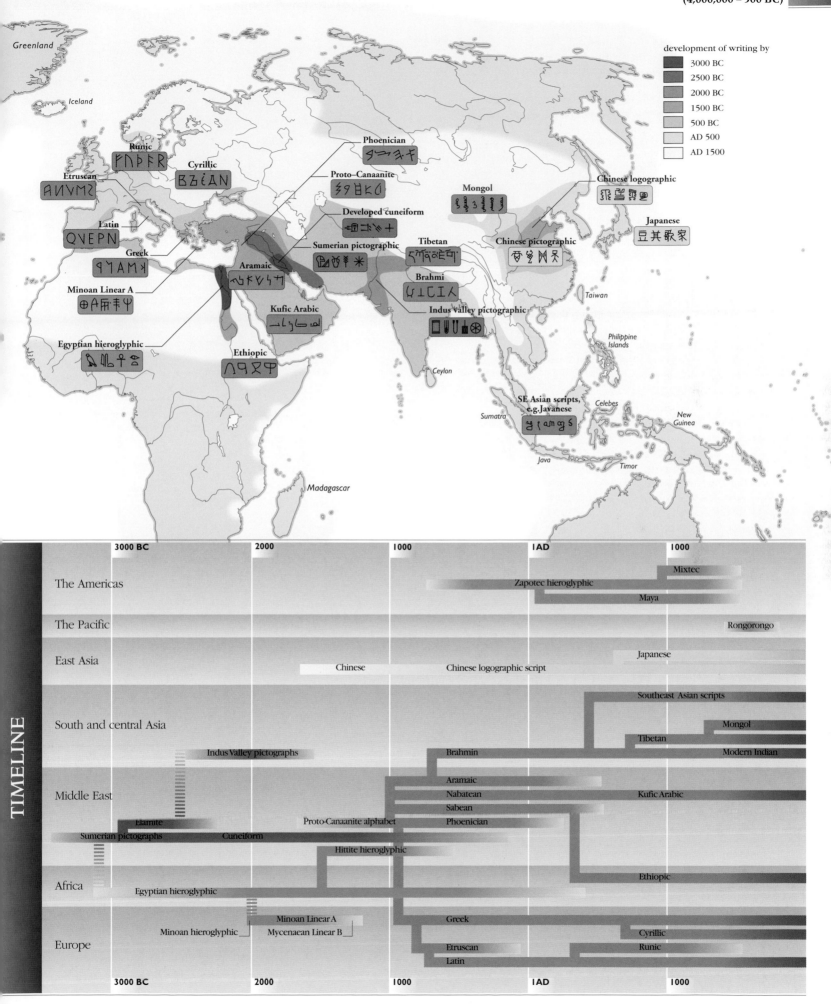

development of writing by

- 3000 BC
- 2500 BC
- 2000 BC
- 1500 BC
- 500 BC
- AD 500
- AD 1500

Greenland

Iceland

Runic

Cyrillic

Etruscan

Latin

Greek

Minoan Linear A

Egyptian hieroglyphic

Phoenician

Proto–Canaanite

Developed cuneiform

Sumerian pictographic

Aramaic

Kufic Arabic

Ethiopic

Mongol

Chinese logographic

Japanese

Chinese pictographic

Tibetan

Brahmi

Indus valley pictographic

Taiwan

SE Asian scripts, e.g.Javanese

Philippine Islands

Ceylon

Sumatra

Celebes

New Guinea

Java

Timor

Madagascar

TIMELINE

	3000 BC	2000	1000	IAD	1000
The Americas				Zapotec hieroglyphic	Mixtec / Maya
The Pacific					Rongorongo
East Asia		Chinese	Chinese logographic script		Japanese
South and central Asia		Indus Valley pictographs	Brahmin	Tibetan	Southeast Asian scripts / Mongol / Modern Indian
Middle East	Sumerian pictographs	Elamite / Cuneiform	Proto-Canaanite alphabet	Aramaic / Nabatean / Sabean / Phoenician	Kufic Arabic
		Hittite hieroglyphic			
Africa	Egyptian hieroglyphic				Ethiopic
Europe		Minoan hieroglyphic / Minoan Linear A / Mycenaean Linear B	Greek	Etruscan	Cyrillic / Runic
			Latin		

| 3000 BC | 2000 | 1000 | IAD | 1000 |

The earliest communities to rely on farming for most of their food grew up in the area known as the Fertile Crescent. This region of good soils and light but reliable rainfall extends in an arc from the foothills of Iraq's Zagros mountains, through south Turkey to western Syria, the Lebanon and Israel. Toward the end of the Ice Age it was colonized by plants such as wild emmer and einkorn wheat, wild barley, wild pulses, and almond, oak and pistachio trees. The supply of cereals and nuts was so rich that in some areas the hunter–gatherer population could settle in semi-permanent villages.

Among these sedentary hunter–gatherers were the Natufians of the Levant, whose way of life developed about 10,500 BC. Except for short stays at seasonal camps, the Natufians lived in villages of substantial wooden huts with stone foundations. They hunted gazelle intensively but their staple food was wild cereals, which they harvested with bone-handled reaping knives, stored in stone jars and processed with querns, grindstones, and mortars and pestles. Settled living and abundant food led them to abandon the egalitarianism of the nomadic hunter–gatherer band. A wide variation in the range and quality of goods found in individual burials points to the existence of social ranking.

During the 9th millennium they began to cultivate wild cereals close to their settlements. In some places, such as at Tell Mureybet in Syria, wild cereals may even have been introduced to areas where they did not naturally occur. The climate was changing and the natural range of wild cereals was shrinking, so these developments were probably an attempt to secure the food supply. Around 8000 BC these early farmers learned to breed wild cereals selectively for characteristics that increased the yield and made them easier to harvest. Within a few centuries domesticated strains of barley, emmer and einkorn wheat had appeared. Although cultivated plants were important to the economies of these transitional, or "proto-Neolithic", farmers, hunting and gathering continued to be crucial sources of food. As the population began to outstrip the environment's

capacity to support the old lifestyle, the dependence on farming increased. By about 7500 BC communities with a full farming economy had developed, marking the proper beginning of the Neolithic or "New Stone Age" (the period between the adoption of agriculture and that of metal working).

One of the most impressive proto-Neolithic sites is at Jericho, where a walled settlement of 1,500 people had grown up near a permanent spring by about 8000 BC. Domesticated barley and emmer wheat, pulses and figs were cultivated, but wild animals – gazelle and wild sheep and goats – were also important food sources. The people lived in huts built of sun-dried mud bricks, the earliest known use of what became the most important building material of the Middle East. Mud brick was easy to produce; when a house fell into disrepair it was simply knocked down and replaced by a new one. Over the centuries, successive rebuildings on the same site produced a high mound of debris,

Map labels:

7

spread of domesticated emmer wheat and barley to southeast Europe, 7th millennium

Aegean Sea

Lake Tuz

Ashikli Huyuk

Hacilar

Suberde
Can Has

TAURUS

Cyprus

Khirokitia

Mediterranean Sea

Legend:

	wild strains of einkorn wheat only
	wild strains of emmer and einkorn wheat, and barley
	distribution of wild sheep and goats
....	southeastern limit of range of aurochs
....	southern limit of dry farming
⬛	area of Epipaleolithic Natufian sites, 10,500–8500
▲	proto-Neolithic settlement, 8500–7500
⬢	aceramic Neolithic farming village, 7500–6500
⬢	aceramic site with population of over 1000
✦	obsidian source
➤	distribution of Armenian obsidian
➤	distribution of Anatolian obsidian
—	modern coastline and drainage where altered

0 _____ 300 km
0 _____ 200 mi

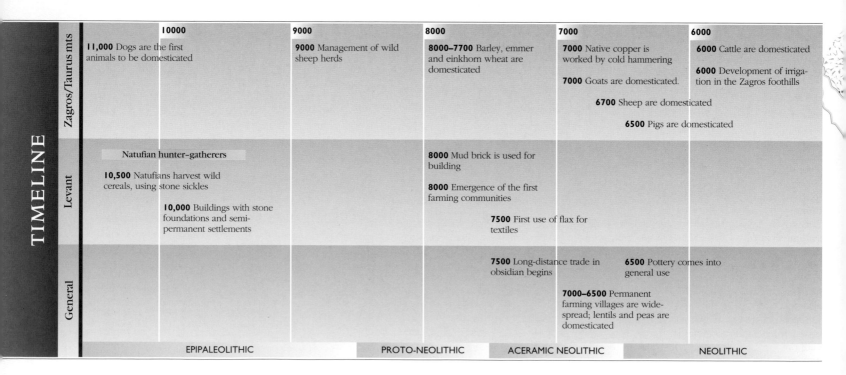

TIMELINE

		10000	9000	8000	7000	6000
Zagros/Taurus mts		**11,000** Dogs are the first animals to be domesticated	**9000** Management of wild sheep herds	**8000–7700** Barley, emmer and einkorn wheat are domesticated	**7000** Native copper is worked by cold hammering **7000** Goats are domesticated. **6700** Sheep are domesticated **6500** Pigs are domesticated	**6000** Cattle are domesticated **6000** Development of irrigation in the Zagros foothills
Levant		Natufian hunter-gatherers **10,500** Natufians harvest wild cereals, using stone sickles **10,000** Buildings with stone foundations and semi-permanent settlements		**8000** Mud brick is used for building **8000** Emergence of the first farming communities	**7500** First use of flax for textiles	
General					**7500** Long-distance trade in obsidian **7000–6500** Permanent farming villages are widespread; lentils and peas are domesticated	**6500** Pottery comes into general use

EPIPALEOLITHIC	PROTO-NEOLITHIC	ACERAMIC NEOLITHIC	NEOLITHIC

Black Sea

CAUCASUS MOUNTAINS

Kura

Caspian Sea

hunter–
gatherers

Araks

ANATOLIA

Kizil Irmak

Acigol

Chiftlik

Bingol

5

Chayonu

Cafer Huyuk

Nemrut Dag

Lake
Van

Lake
Urmia

Murat

ZAGROS MOUNTAINS

Coban

Gritille

2

Zawi Chemi Shanidar

Tigris

Great Zab

Qermez Dere

Tell Aswad

MESOPOTAMIA

Karim Shahir

Jarmo

Orontes

Tell Mureybet

Abu Hureyra

6

Diyala

Euphrates

Ganj Dareh

Ugarit

1

Bouqras

Tepe Abdul
Hosein

Syrian Desert

Tepe Guran

Tamarkhan

Karkheh

Labwe

LEVANT

Tell Ramad

Beisamoun

Ali Kosh

Nahal
Oren

8

Choga Bonut

Munhatta

Hatula

Ain Ghazal

Abu Gosh

Jericho

El Khiam

3

Nahal
Hemar

Persian Gulf

4

Beidha

Basta

HUMAN skulls, like this one
found at Jericho, were often
buried separately.
Sometimes they were deco-
rated with paint, shells and
modeled clay features.

called a *tell* in Arabic, *huyuk* in Turkish and *tepe* in Persian. These settlement mounds are the most characteristic archeological sites of the region.

Farming also began to develop in southern Anatolia and the Zagros mountains. In the mountains hunter–gatherers intensified their management of flocks of wild sheep and goats. Animal bones from a settlement at Zawi Chemi Shanidar (9000 BC) show that the inhabitants killed mainly immature sheep. Since hunting would have resulted in a more random distribution of ages, the sheep had probably been penned and selectively culled. Pollen samples also suggest that wild cereals were cultivated at Zawi Chemi Shanidar. By the 7th millennium, domesticated sheep and goats were an important part of the economy of villages such as Chayonu (now in eastern Turkey).

Farming had not yet begun on the greater part of the fertile but almost rainless Mesopotamian plain. Only along the eastern edges, which caught some of the rainfall of the Zagros mountains, was farming possible before the development of irrigation and heat-resistant cereal strains in the 6th millennium.

The early farming communities had no pottery; this period of the Neolithic is known as the aceramic or prepottery Neolithic. The first pottery appeared by 7000 BC, but such was its usefulness for cooking and storage that its use had become widespread within five centuries. By this time bread wheat had also been developed, flax – the raw material of linen cloth – had been domesticated, as had the pig, and cattle were introduced from southeastern Europe where farming was just beginning.

The sedentary way of life meant that communities became less self-sufficient and long-distance trade, particularly in salt and toolmaking stone, became more important. The finest toolmaking stone, obsidian (volcanic glass), was traded over long distances. Obsidian from Anatolia has been found in early Neolithic sites almost as far south as the Red Sea, while obsidian from the region by Lake Van reached the Mediterranean and the Persian Gulf.

1 Abu Hureyra was a village of 300-400 people, living by hunting gazelles and harvesting wild cereals, c.9500.

2 Zawi Chemi Shanidar, a summer settlement c.9000, shows evidence for intensive management of wild sheep herds.

3 Jericho was a permanent settlement by 8500 BC, and was walled by 8000.

4 Nahal Hemar, an aceramic Neolithic site, has the earliest evidence for textile manufacture (flax).

5 At Chayonu, native copper was used 7300–6500 to make tools and ornaments.

6 Before 6000 BC Mesopotamia was only sparsely populated with hunter–gatherers.

7 Cultivation of emmer wheat and barley began in southeast Europe c.6000 BC, probably as a result of trade contacts with the Middle East.

8 Ali Kosh was one of the earliest farming communities on the Mesopotamian plain, founded 8000 BC.

See also 1.03 (rise of agriculture),
1.09 (MiddleEast), 1.16 (Africa)

By the time that pottery came into widespread use in the Fertile Crescent, around 6500 BC, the densest concentration of farming settlements was still to be found in the uplands of the Levant, southern Anatolia and the Zagros mountains, where there was reliable rainfall. Most villages had no more than a few hundred inhabitants and had relatively egalitarian social structures; the simple subsistence economies were based on cereals and herds of sheep, goats or cattle.

An important exception was the town-sized settlement which grew up around 6700 BC at Chatal Huyuk in Turkey. This settlement of densely packed mud-brick houses is the largest Neolithic settlement yet found. Long-distance trade in obsidian from nearby volcanoes, and improved agricultural yields resulting from the adoption of simple irrigation techniques, may have played a role in the town's growth. Chatal Huyuk had rich artistic traditions of wall-painting and sculpture, and a great many elaborately decorated shrines have been found. Many other crafts were practiced, including weaving, basketry, copper working (the earliest known evidence of copper smelting has been found here), fine stone toolmaking and pottery. Chatal Huyuk, however, was a precocious development. The local environment could not sustain longterm urban growth: the site was abandoned after about a thousand years and the pattern of dispersed settlements, typical of the rest of Neolithic Anatolia, was resumed.

The conditions for sustainable urban growth were first achieved in Mesopotamia. Farming was still confined to the fringes of the Mesopotamian plain in 6500 BC but it had spread throughout the region by 5500. The expansion of farming settlement across the plain is reflected by a series of cultures, each of which can be identified by a distinctive pottery style. The first of these was the Hassuna culture (6500–6000), centered on northern Mesopotamia and mostly within the dry farming zone. The Hassuna people grew emmer, einkorn and barley, bred sheep, goats, pigs and cattle and hunted a little. There is evidence for copper and lead

smelting and the Hassuna culture was the earliest to produce painted pottery and fire it in purpose-built kilns. Stamp seals, later used widely in Mesopotamia to indicate ownership, were also first used in the Hassuna culture.

The Hassuna culture was replaced around 6000 by the Halafian culture. A storehouse excavated at Arpachiyeh, containing a concentration of fine pottery, jewelry, sculpture and flint and obsidian tools, suggests that the Halafians were ruled by chiefs who amassed considerable personal wealth and controlled the community's trade contacts. The influence of the Halafian culture was confined almost entirely to the dry farming zone but the same was not true of the contemporary, and overlapping,

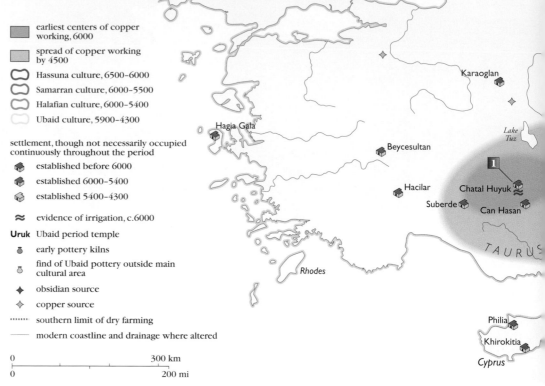

Mediterranean Sea

1 Chatal Huyuk had a population of about 6000 people, mainly farmers, between 6700-5700 BC.

2 Tell Umm Dabaghiyeh was a permanent hunter settlement c.6000, trading hides for grain with the northern farmers.

3 Choga Mami is the site of the earliest known irrigation canals; 5500 BC.

4 The fertile but rainless south Mesopotamia plain was colonized by farmers after the development of irrigation c.5500 BC.

5 Kilns were first used for firing pottery in Hassuna c.6000 BC.

6 The Ubaid settlement of Tell Awayli had a grain storehouse with a total area of 200 m².

7 Eridu was the oldest town in southern Mesopotamia. It had a large temple and a population of five thousand by the end of the Ubaid period.

8 Ubaid pottery from Ur found here indicates trade links between Mesopotamia and Arabia.

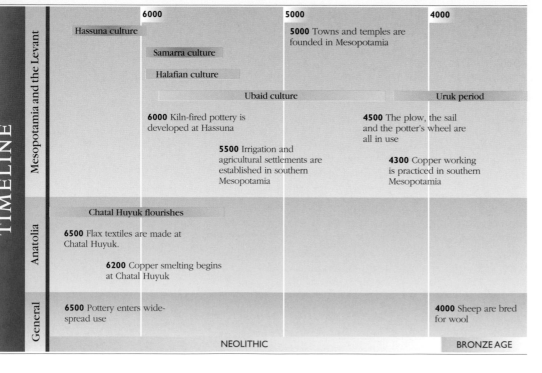

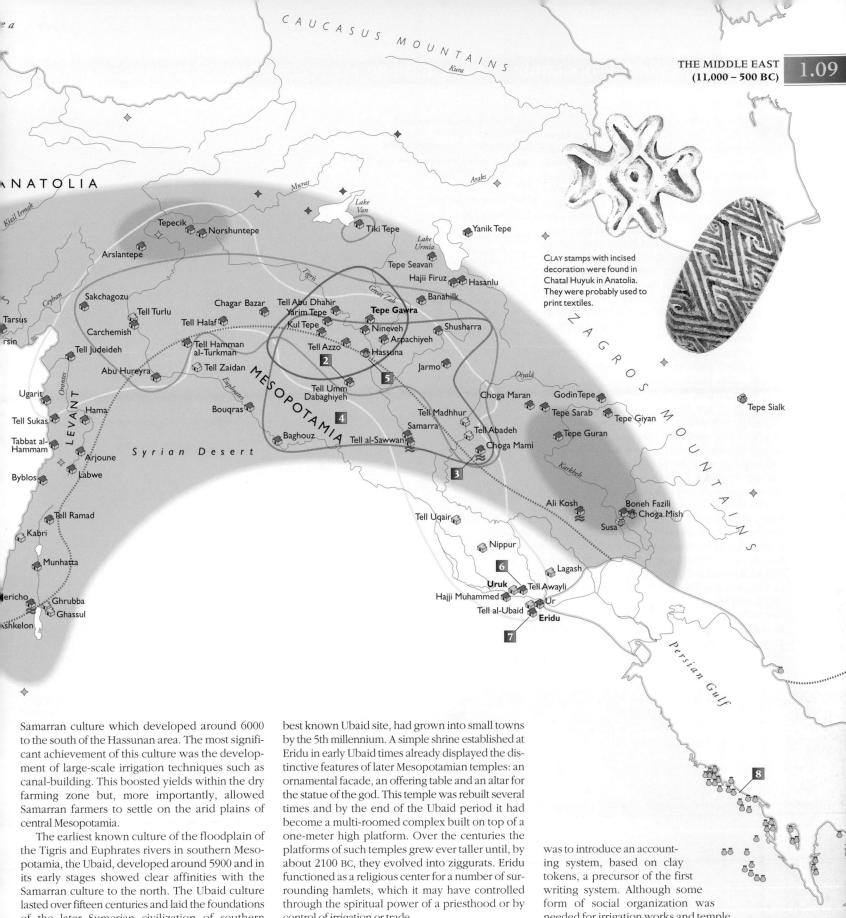

CLAY stamps with incised
decoration were found in
Chatal Huyuk in Anatolia.
They were probably used to
print textiles.

Samarran culture which developed around 6000 to the south of the Hassunan area. The most significant achievement of this culture was the development of large-scale irrigation techniques such as canal-building. This boosted yields within the dry farming zone but, more importantly, allowed Samarran farmers to settle on the arid plains of central Mesopotamia.

The earliest known culture of the floodplain of the Tigris and Euphrates rivers in southern Mesopotamia, the Ubaid, developed around 5900 and in its early stages showed clear affinities with the Samarran culture to the north. The Ubaid culture lasted over fifteen centuries and laid the foundations of the later Sumerian civilization of southern Mesopotamia. The first inhabitants of this almost rainless region depended mainly on fishing, hunting and herding but the introduction of irrigation techniques from the north transformed the settlement pattern. Irrigation allowed the enormously productive potential of southern Mesopotamia's fertile alluvial soils to be realized. Productivity received another boost in the 5th millennium with the invention of the plow. Intensive agriculture meant that the population rose rapidly and many new farming villages were founded. Some of these, like Eridu, the

best known Ubaid site, had grown into small towns by the 5th millennium. A simple shrine established at Eridu in early Ubaid times already displayed the distinctive features of later Mesopotamian temples: an ornamental facade, an offering table and an altar for the statue of the god. This temple was rebuilt several times and by the end of the Ubaid period it had become a multi-roomed complex built on top of a one-meter high platform. Over the centuries the platforms of such temples grew ever taller until, by about 2100 BC, they evolved into ziggurats. Eridu functioned as a religious center for a number of surrounding hamlets, which it may have controlled through the spiritual power of a priesthood or by control of irrigation or trade.

Southern Mesopotamia lacks many essential raw materials, including building timber, metals and stone for toolmaking (and, later for building and sculpture) and semi-precious stone: as a result trade links were of vital importance to – and helped to spread the influence of – the Ubaid culture. By 5400 the Ubaid culture had replaced the Halafian culture in northern Mesopotamia while Ubaid pottery manufactured around Ur has been found throughout the Persian Gulf region.

An important innovation of the Ubaid culture

was to introduce an accounting system, based on clay tokens, a precursor of the first writing system. Although some form of social organization was needed for irrigation works and temple building, burial practices of the Ubaid period suggest that society was still basically egalitarian. When the Ubaid period came to a close in about 4300 BC, the population of southern Mesopotamia was still on the increase and the succeeding Uruk period saw the development of a far more complex and hierarchical society.

See also 1.03 (the rise of agriculture),
1.10 (earliest cities), 1.20 (southeast Europe)

By the end of the Early Dynastic period Sumeria, though still wealthy and populous, was being overtaken by Akkad as the leading center of Mesopotamian civilization. The rise of Akkad is reflected in the career of the first great conqueror known to history, Sargon "the Great" of Agade (r.2334–2279). Sargon's origins are obscure. He claimed that his father had been a date-grower and that he himself had been an official to the king of the Akkadian city of Kish. How he came to power is unknown but he may have staged a coup against his employer to become king of Kish. Sargon's first task was to eliminate the most powerful ruler in Mesopotamia, Lugalzagesi of Umma and Uruk, which he did in three hard-fought battles. He went on to conquer the rest of Sumeria, Akkad and Elam before pushing west to the Mediterranean and Anatolia. The island of Dilmun (Bahrain) and parts of Iran may also have been conquered. Sargon united peoples of many different ethnic and cultural identities to create an entirely new kind of state, an empire. To celebrate his conquests he founded the city of Agade, which has yet to be located. His empire reached its peak of power under his grandson Naram-Sin (r.2254–2218) but thereafter declined and collapsed about 2193, probably as a result of invasions by the Gutians and Amorites. For eighty years the old pattern of competing city-states returned until a Sumerian revival occurred.

Using diplomacy as much as force, Ur-Nammu (r.2112–2095), the first king of the Third Dynasty of Ur, built a new empire stretching as far north as Assyria. Ur-Nammu's reign saw the construction of the first ziggurats, the high temple platforms that are Mesopotamia's most distinctive monuments. About 2034 the empire of the Third Dynasty came under pressure from the nomadic Amorites of the Syrian desert but it was a knockout blow from the Elamites, who sacked Ur in 2004, that led to the fall of the empire. Sumeria never regained its preeminence.

The two centuries following the fall of the Third Dynasty are a confusion of minor states and of inroads by the Amorites. The Amorites were a strong influence in the rise of the two states that were to dominate the next one and a half millennia of Mesopotamian history: Assyria and Babylon. Assyria emerged as an important trading power in the 19th century BC but it was only after the Amorite Shamshi-Adad tookthe capital Ashur, along with most of northern Mesopotamia, in about 1813 that it became a major territorial power. An Amorite dynasty had also set up at Babylon around 1894 and when Hammurabi came to the throne in 1792 Babylon controlled most of Akkad (subsequently known as Babylonia). Five years later Hammurabi marched south and conquered Sumeria. In 1781 Shamshi-Adad died and, weakened by attacks from Eshnunna and the Elamites, most of his kingdom was under Hammurabi's control by 1757. Two years later Hammurabi conquered the last Mesopotamian power, Eshnunna. Babylon now became the religious and cultural center of Mesopotamia.

In the 17th century BC new and threatening powers began to gather on the borders of Mesopotamia. The most important of these were the Hurrians and the Hittites. The Hurrians were a tribal people from Armenia who overran Assyria around 1680. The Hittites were an Indo-European people who had invaded Anatolia from Thrace about 1800 and had emergedas a powerful kingdom by 1650.

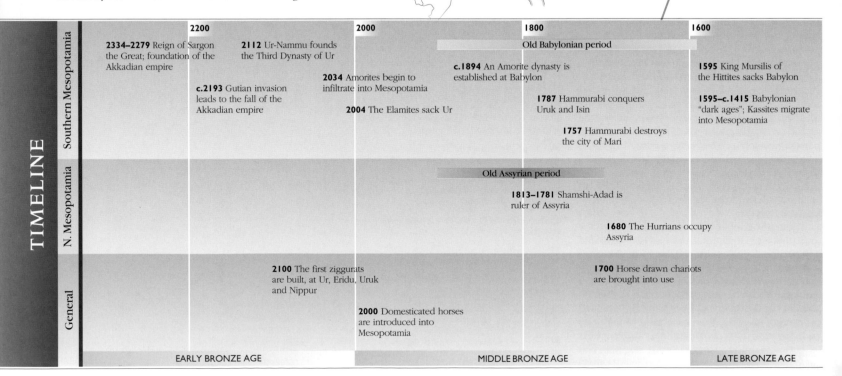

		2200		**2000**		**1800**		**1600**	
TIMELINE	**Southern Mesopotamia**	**2334–2279** Reign of Sargon the Great; foundation of the Akkadian empire	**2112** Ur-Nammu founds the Third Dynasty of Ur			Old Babylonian period		**1595** King Mursilis of the Hittites sacks Babylon	
			c.2193 Gutian invasion leads to the fall of the Akkadian empire	**2034** Amorites begin to infiltrate into Mesopotamia	**2004** The Elamites sack Ur	**c.1894** An Amorite dynasty is established at Babylon	**1787** Hammurabi conquers Uruk and Isin	**1595–c.1415** Babylonian "dark ages"; Kassites migrate into Mesopotamia	
							1757 Hammurabi destroys the city of Mari		
	N. Mesopotamia					Old Assyrian period			
							1813–1781 Shamshi-Adad is ruler of Assyria		
								1680 The Hurrians occupy Assyria	
	General			**2100** The first ziggurats are built, at Ur, Eridu, Uruk and Nippur	**2000** Domesticated horses are introduced into Mesopotamia			**1700** Horse drawn chariots are brought into use	
		EARLY BRONZE AGE				MIDDLE BRONZE AGE		LATE BRONZE AGE	

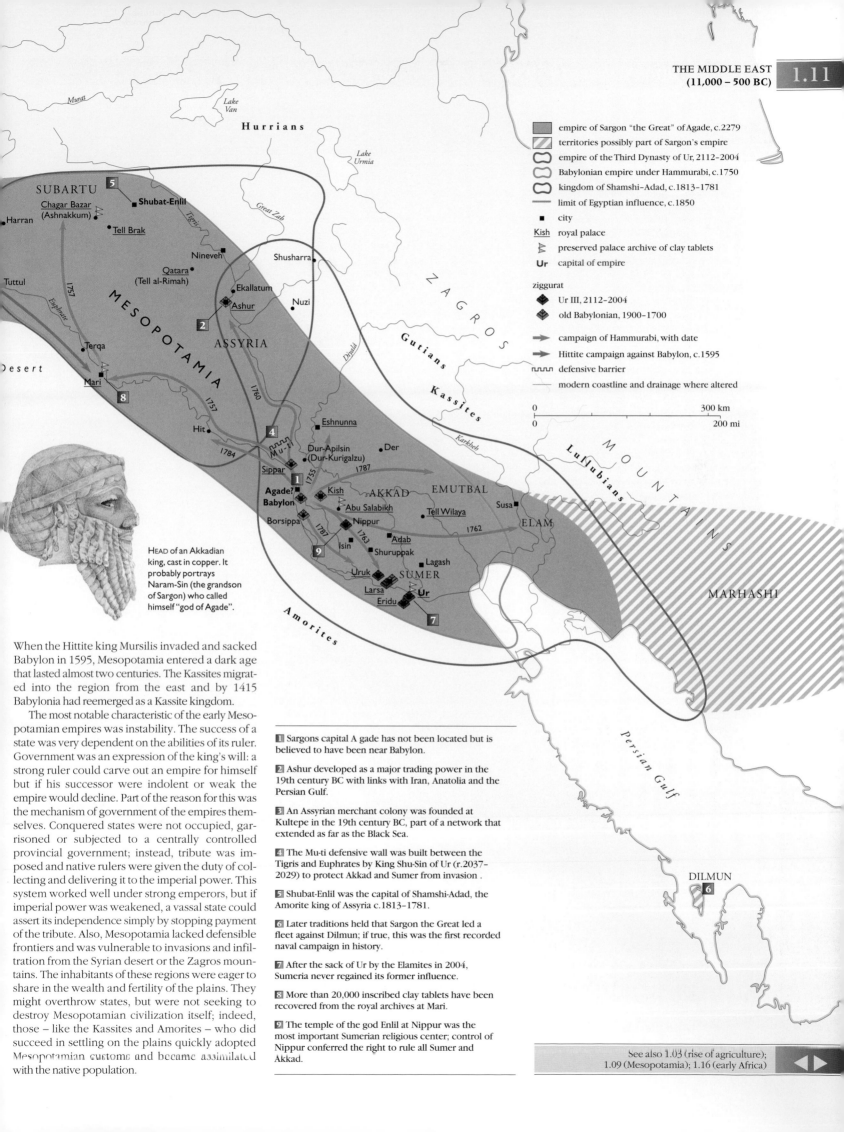

Legend:

- empire of Sargon "the Great" of Agade, c.2279
- territories possibly part of Sargon's empire
- empire of the Third Dynasty of Ur, 2112–2004
- Babylonian empire under Hammurabi, c.1750
- kingdom of Shamshi-Adad, c.1813–1781
- limit of Egyptian influence, c.1850
- ■ city
- Kish royal palace
- ⚐ preserved palace archive of clay tablets
- Ur capital of empire

ziggurat
- ◆ Ur III, 2112–2004
- ◆ old Babylonian, 1900–1700
- → campaign of Hammurabi, with date
- → Hittite campaign against Babylon, c.1595
- ⌁ defensive barrier
- — modern coastline and drainage where altered

0 — 300 km
0 — 200 mi

HEAD of an Akkadian king, cast in copper. It probably portrays Naram-Sin (the grandson of Sargon) who called himself "god of Agade".

When the Hittite king Mursilis invaded and sacked Babylon in 1595, Mesopotamia entered a dark age that lasted almost two centuries. The Kassites migrated into the region from the east and by 1415 Babylonia had reemerged as a Kassite kingdom.

The most notable characteristic of the early Mesopotamian empires was instability. The success of a state was very dependent on the abilities of its ruler. Government was an expression of the king's will: a strong ruler could carve out an empire for himself but if his successor were indolent or weak the empire would decline. Part of the reason for this was the mechanism of government of the empires themselves. Conquered states were not occupied, garrisoned or subjected to a centrally controlled provincial government; instead, tribute was imposed and native rulers were given the duty of collecting and delivering it to the imperial power. This system worked well under strong emperors, but if imperial power was weakened, a vassal state could assert its independence simply by stopping payment of the tribute. Also, Mesopotamia lacked defensible frontiers and was vulnerable to invasions and infiltration from the Syrian desert or the Zagros mountains. The inhabitants of these regions were eager to share in the wealth and fertility of the plains. They might overthrow states, but were not seeking to destroy Mesopotamian civilization itself; indeed, those – like the Kassites and Amorites – who did succeed in settling on the plains quickly adopted Mesopotamian customs and became assimilated with the native population.

1 Sargons capital A gade has not been located but is believed to have been near Babylon.

2 Ashur developed as a major trading power in the 19th century BC with links with Iran, Anatolia and the Persian Gulf.

3 An Assyrian merchant colony was founded at Kultepe in the 19th century BC, part of a network that extended as far as the Black Sea.

4 The Mu-ti defensive wall was built between the Tigris and Euphrates by King Shu-Sin of Ur (r.2037–2029) to protect Akkad and Sumer from invasion.

5 Shubat-Enlil was the capital of Shamshi-Adad, the Amorite king of Assyria c.1813–1781.

6 Later traditions held that Sargon the Great led a fleet against Dilmun; if true, this was the first recorded naval campaign in history.

7 After the sack of Ur by the Elamites in 2004, Sumeria never regained its former influence.

8 More than 20,000 inscribed clay tablets have been recovered from the royal archives at Mari.

9 The temple of the god Enlil at Nippur was the most important Sumerian religious center; control of Nippur conferred the right to rule all Sumer and Akkad.

See also 1.03 (rise of agriculture); 1.09 (Mesopotamia); 1.16 (early Africa)

In the two centuries following the Hittite sack of Babylon in 1595, the kingdom of Mittani controlled most of northern Mesopotamia and, at its peak, southern Anatolia. Mittani was founded about 1550 by the Hurrians, who had begun to encroach on northern Mesopotamia early in the previous century. As its power spread west into the Levant (the part of the Fertile Crescent bordering the Mediterranean), Mittani came into conflict with the Egyptians. Under Tuthmosis I (r.1504–1492), Egypt controlled all of the Levant and established a frontier on the Euphrates.

The Egyptians were unable to maintain this frontier and over the next century Mittani regained control over the northern Levant and pushed the Egyptians south of the Orontes river. Then, during the reign of Tuthmosis IV (r.1401–1391) Egypt and Mittani formed an alliance. The peace initiative probably came from Mittani which was faced with a revival of Hittite power in the north, while in the east the Assyrians had won back their independence. When Egypt became preoccupied with internal affairs during the reign of Akhenaten (r.1353–1335), Mittani was left exposed.

The Hittite king Suppiluliumas (r.1344–1322) spent the early part of his reign establishing Hittite dominance in Anatolia, and then in about 1340 sacked Washukanni, Mittani's capital, before sweeping on into the Levant. Mittani began to crumble and when he launched a second campaign around 1328 (or 1323) the western half of the kingdom fell. Suppiluliumas established a puppet ruler at Washukanni, intending western Mittani to become a buffer state against Assyria. As such it was a failure, and fell to the Assyrians by 1300.

The Hittites, who now held the same commanding position in the Levant that Mittani had held in the 15th century, incurred the enmity of Egypt, where a new dynasty had come to power in 1307, eager to reestablish Egypt's position in the Levant. By 1290 the Egyptians had recovered Canaan, which had become independent under Akhenaten, and in 1285 pharaoh Ramesses II (r.1290–1224) launched a major invasion of Hittite territory. The Hittite king

Muwatallis II (r.1295–1271) was prepared and, in a battle between two fleets of chariots at Qadesh, Ramesses was defeated (though he claimed a great victory). The Egyptians withdrew and Hittite control was extended as far south as Damascus. Relations between the two empires remained difficult until 1258 when they agreed an alliance, as the Hittites were alarmed at the growth of Assyrian power.

Assyrian expansion had begun under Ashur-uballit I (r.1363–1328), who seized Nineveh from the crumbling Mittanian kingdom in about 1330, and was continued in the 13th century. Tukulti-Ninurta I (r.1243–1207) waged campaigns against the Hittites and the Kassite kingdom of Babylonia and built an empire that stretched from the upper Euphrates to the Persian Gulf. However, the empire fell apart after he was murdered by discontented nobles.

TIMELINE		1400		1200		1000
Mesopotamia	**1595** Babylon is sacked by the Hittites and enters a "dark age"		Middle Assyrian empire		**1076** Fall of the Middle Assyrian empire	
		c.1415 The first recorded Kassite king of Babylon		**c.1220** Babylon is under Assyrian control		**1000** Chaldeans occupy Ur
	c.1550 Foundation of the kingdom of Mittani		**1400** Assyria regains independence		**1160–1130** Babylon is occupied by the Elamites	**950** Assyria and Babylon begin to recover from the Aramaean invasions
		c.1472 Mittani annexes Assyria	**c.1328** Western Mittani is conquered by the Hittites		**1115** The Assyrians repel a Mushki invasion	
			c.1300 Eastern Mittani is conquered by the Assyrians		**c.1080** The Aramaeans invade Mesopotamia	
Levant and Anatolia	**1600** The Canaanites invent the first alphabetic script			**1285** Peak of Hittite power: battle of Qadesh between Hittites and the Egyptians	**1180** The "Sea Peoples" are driven from Egypt and settle in Canaan five years later	
		c.1500 The Egyptian empire is extended as far as the Euphrates		**1220–1100** The Hebrews settle Canaan		
		1500 Ironworking emerges in the Hittite empire		**c.1200** The Phrygians invade Anatolia; fall of the Hittite empire		
		LATE BRONZE AGE			IRON AGE	

Black Sea

CAUCASUS MOUNTAINS

Caspian Sea

Kaskas

Mushki
(Mysians)

1

ttusas
oghazkoy)

HATTI

Kizil Irmak

• Kanesh

c.1340

Malatya •

Hurrians

Urartians

Lake
Van

Lake
Urmia

Murat

c.1328

Carchemish

Washukanni
(Tell al-Fakhariyeh)

2

MITTANI

5

1115×

Tigris

Great Zab

KIZZUWATNA

Ceyhan

• Tarsus

Aleppo •

Nineveh •
Kalhu •

• Arbil

Kar-Tukulti-Ninurta

ASSYRIA

Ugarit •

LEVANT

Orontes

Ashur •

• Nuzi

Diyala

Gutians

Arvad •

Syrian Desert

Euphrates

MESOPOTAMIA

6

Qadesh
1285

×

4

Byblos •

Tadmor
(Palmyra) •

• Hit

Damascus •

Aramaeans

Sippar •

Dur-Kurigalzu • • Der

• Babylon

BABYLONIA

• Susa

ELAM

Al-Untash-Napirisha ■

• Tyre

3

• Nippur

ZAGROS MTS

CANAAN

• Jerusalem

• Isin

• Uruk

•Ur

Chaldeans

Persian Gulf

Hebrews

HITTITE metalworkers of
around 1200 BC
demonstrate their skill with
this silver ceremonial
drinking cup in the shape
of a stag.

Legend

	major kingdom, c.1400
	Hittite
	Hurrian kingdom of Mittani
	Assyria
	Kassite kingdom of Babylon
	New Kingdom of Egypt

maximum extent of Hittite empire, c.1322

Mycenaean civilization, c.1300

maximum extent of the Middle
Assyrian empire , 1243-1207

maximum northern expansion of Egyptian
kingdom of Tuthmosis I, 1504-1492

■ capital city

➜ campaign of Suppiluliumas, 1344-1323

campaign of Assyrian king

➜ Adad-nirari, 1305-1274

➜ Shalmaneser I, 1273-1244

➜ Tukulti-Ninurta I, 1243-1207

➜ Tiglath-pileser I, 1115-1076

➜ migration, 12th and 11th centuries

— modern coastline and drainage where altered

0	300 km
0	200 mi

Around 1200 new waves of migrations brought chaos to the region. Shortly after 1205 the Hittite kingdom collapsed, destroyed by the Phrygians, who had entered Anatolia from Thrace. At the same time Egypt came under attack from a group known to the Egyptians as the Sea Peoples. Their origin is uncertain. Some may have come from the Aegean islands and Anatolian coast but they were joined by others already settled in the Levant and Libya. The Sea Peoples were driven from Egypt in 1180 but settled in Canaan where they became known as the Philistines. Nomadic Hebrew tribes, related to the Aramaeans, were also moving into Canaan.

At the end of the 12th century Assyria was attacked by a confederation of Mushki (probably Mysians – relatives of the Phrygians) and native Anatolian peoples including the Kaskas and Hurrians. The new Assyrian king Tiglath-pileser I (r.1115–1076), forced the invaders to retreat into Anatolia, but he had less success against the nomadic Aramaeans who, despite 28 campaigns against them, had made considerable settlements in Assyria before his death. Tiglath-pileser's successors failed

to contain the Aramaeans and by 1000 Assyria was reduced to its heartland around Ashur and Nineveh.

Babylonia's main problem from the 14th to 12th centuries was the kingdom of Elam. Devastating Elamite invasions of Babylon in the mid 12th century led to the fall of the Kassite dynasty. Babylon recovered under a native dynasty around 1130 and defeated the Elamites so thoroughly that they disappeared from history for 300 years. Then, in the 11th century Babylonia, like Assyria, had problems with migrating nomads – Aramaeans in the north, Chaldeans in the south – and, also like Assyria, was unable to do much about them. The nomads' tribal structures provided no central authority to destroy or negotiate with, and they had no cities that could be taken nor crops to be burned. The powerful Assyrian and Babylonian armies had no target to attack.

The period saw key technological advances, glass, glazed pottery and bricks and iron-smelting all appearing for the first time. Iron did not supplant bronze as the main metal for tools and weapons until around 900, but its use was widespread by 1200, the date accepted as the start of the Iron Age.

1 Hattusas became the Hittite capital in about 1650, and was destroyed about 1200, probably by Phrygian invaders.

2 Tell al-Fakhariyeh is the likely site of Washukanni, capital of Mittani, sacked by the Hittites in 1340 and the Assyrians c.1304-1274.

3 Babylon was sacked by the Hittites in 1595, and was under Kassite rule by 1415, held by the Assyrians 1220-1213 and the Elamites 1160-1130.

4 The Egyptians and Hittites clashed at Qadesh over control of Syria; this is the first battle in history well enough recorded for historians to reconstruct its course.

5 Tiglath-pileser I defeated an invading army of 20,000 Mushki in the upper Tigris valley.

6 On reaching the Mediterranean, Tiglath-pileser I went sailing and claimed to have harpooned a whale.

See also 1.13 (later Assyria), 1.14 (Bible lands),
1.18 (Egypt)

The Hebrew kingdoms of the Bible lands were dwarfed in scale and longevity by the great empires of the Middle East, yet their significance in world history is at least as great. The period of the independent monarchy, from the time of David to the Babylonian conquest in 587, was a formative time for Judaism and gave Jews a sense of historical destiny, driving them to preserve their religion and identity through centuries of foreign rule, exile and worldwide dispersal. Christianity and Islam both owe so much to Judaism that neither religion would have its present form had Judaism not survived.

The Hebrews migrated into Canaan in the early 12th century, a time when the great powers of the region were neutralized by troubles of various kinds. In their initial attacks under Joshua, the Hebrews occupied most of Canaan, which they settled in tribal units under chieftains (the "judges" of the biblical Book of Judges). However, many Canaanite enclaves remained and Hebrew expansion to the southwest was blocked by the Philistines who had settled in the area after being repulsed from Egypt in 1180. Most of the Canaanite enclaves were mopped up in the 11th century but the Hebrews began to lose ground in the southwest to the Philistines.

The need for effective defense against the Philistines led the Hebrew tribes to unite under a monarchy. According to the Bible, the first king of the Hebrews was Saul (r.c.1020–c.1006) but it was his successor David who was responsible for consolidating the monarchy and creating the first Hebrew state. David conquered the Philistines, Ammonites, Moabites and Edomites and forced several of the Aramaean tribes of the Levant to accept his overlordship. These were great achievements, but he was aided by the temporary impotence of the powers who might otherwise have intervened. It was also to his advantage that the Aramaeans of the Levant (who had moved into the area after the fall of the Hittite empire) had settled in urban communities by 1000, and so were more vulnerable to attack than the still-nomadic Mesopotamian Aramaeans. Perhaps the most important event of David's reign was his capture of Jerusalem from the Canaanite Jebusites. By making Jerusalem his capital David ensured its lasting importance as a religious center.

David was succeeded by his son Solomon. Solomon's reign was largely peaceful, but maintaining his splendid court life and ambitious building projects, including the temple at Jerusalem, proved burdensome to his people. Some Hebrews were used as forced labor and territory was ceded to Tyre in return for supplying craftsmen and materials. He was criticized for tolerating the pagan religious practices of the many non-Hebrew wives he had acquired from diplomatic marriages. When his successor Rehoboam (r.928–911) dealt tactlessly with the economic complaints of the northern tribes, the kingdom split in two halves, Israel and Judah, and most of the non-Hebrew provinces fell away.

probable border of the kingdom of Saul, c.1006

kingdom of David and Solomon
— border, 1006–928
under direct rule
vassal states and tributaries
campaigns of David, c.1006–965
Canaanite enclaves conquered by David
area ceded to Tyre by Solomon
fortress built by Solomon
other major building project by Solomon

0   200 km
0   150 mi

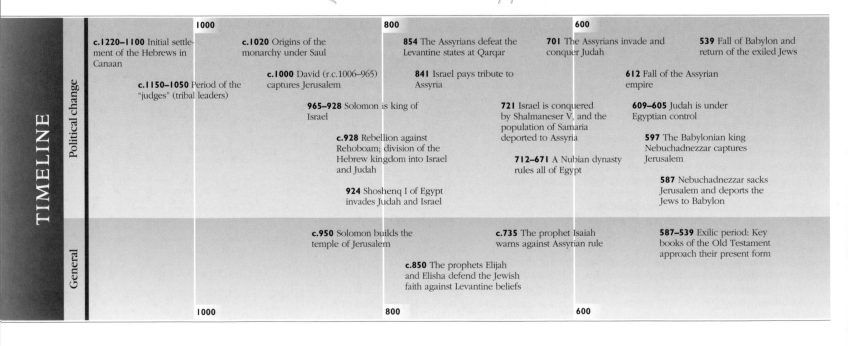

Political change

c.1220–1100 Initial settlement of the Hebrews in Canaan

c.1150–1050 Period of the "judges" (tribal leaders)

c.1020 Origins of the monarchy under Saul

c.1000 David (r.c.1006–965) captures Jerusalem

965–928 Solomon is king of Israel

c.928 Rebellion against Rehoboam; division of the Hebrew kingdom into Israel and Judah

924 Shoshenq I of Egypt invades Judah and Israel

854 The Assyrians defeat the Levantine states at Qarqar

841 Israel pays tribute to Assyria

721 Israel is conquered by Shalmaneser V, and the population of Samaria deported to Assyria

712–671 A Nubian dynasty rules all of Egypt

701 The Assyrians invade and conquer Judah

612 Fall of the Assyrian empire

609–605 Judah is under Egyptian control

597 The Babylonian king Nebuchadnezzar captures Jerusalem

587 Nebuchadnezzar sacks Jerusalem and deports the Jews to Babylon

539 Fall of Babylon and return of the exiled Jews

General

c.950 Solomon builds the temple of Jerusalem

c.850 The prophets Elijah and Elisha defend the Jewish faith against Levantine beliefs

c.735 The prophet Isaiah warns against Assyrian rule

587–539 Exilic period: Key books of the Old Testament approach their present form

1000   800   600

Map Legend

- border of former kingdom of Solomon
- greatest extent of kingdom of Israel
- greatest extent of kingdom of Judah
- border of state gaining independence from kingdoms of Israel or Judah
- kingdom of Egypt, 924
- Assyrian empire, 722
- Babylonian empire, 597

campaigns in Israel and Judah
- pharaoh Shoshenq I, 924
- Sennacherib, 701

0 ——— 150 km
0 ——— 100 mi

Map labels

Aleppo · Euphrates · Qarqar 854 · Hamath · Syrian Desert · ARAM · Tadmor · Ugarit · Arvad · LEVANT · Riblah · ARAM-ZOBAH · Byblos · Cyprus · Sidon · Damascus · PHOENICIA · Tyre · Dan · ARAM-DAMASCUS · Acco · Hazor · Mediterranean Sea · Megiddo · Sea of Chinnereth (Sea of Galilee) · Beth-shean · Samaria · Shechem · Joppa · AMMON · Rabbah · KINGDOM OF ISRAEL · Eltekeh 701 · Gezer · Ashkelon · Jerusalem · Bethlehem · Gaza · Lachish · MOAB independent of Israel, 843 BC · Arad · Salt Sea (Dead Sea) · PHILISTIA · KINGDOM OF JUDAH · EGYPT · EDOM independent of Judah, 843 BC · Ezion-geber · Orontes

Disunity was a luxury the Hebrews could ill afford, as the power of both Egypt and Assyria was reviving. In 924 the pharaoh Shoshenq I (r.945–924) led a campaign through Philistia, Judah and Israel, sacking many cities and imposing tribute, although both kingdoms survived. In the 9th century relations between Israel and Judah was usually hostile and Israel often suffered attacks from Aram–Damascus which was frequently allied to Judah. Under Omri and Ahab Israel became the most powerful kingdom in the region and played a leading role in attempts by the Levantine states to check the growing power of Assyria under Shalmaneser III. However, under Ahab's successor Jehu, Israel was forced to pay tribute to Assyria. In the early 8th century the kingdoms enjoyed relative peace and prosperity with Assyria in a period of decline, until Tiglath-pileser III (r.744–727) overran the Levant and forced vassal status on Israel and Judah. When Hoshea, king of Israel, rebelled against Assyria in 724 his capital Samaria was taken after a three-year siege and its population deported to Assyria. Despite receiving Egyptian support, a rebellion by Hezekiah, the king of Judah, was also put down by the Assyrians. As Assyrian power entered terminal decline in the 630s, Judah briefly regained independence under Josiah (r.640–609) who extended his authority over the old kingdom of Israel until he was killed in battle with the Egyptians at Megiddo. The Egyptians occupied the Levant but were defeated by the Babylonians at Carchemish in 605, after which Judah became a vassal state of Babylon.

In 597 Judah rebelled against Babylonian rule and was crushed by Nebuchadnezzar. Jerusalem was captured, the temple plundered and many of its citizens were deported to Babylonia. Ten years later Judah rebelled again but Jerusalem was taken after an eighteen-month siege. This was the end for independent Judah. Its last king Zedekiah was blinded and imprisoned with most of his nobles and more Hebrews were deported. Many others fled into exile in Egypt. Though a disaster in political terms, the Babylonian captivity was a creative period in Jewish history. Exile caused a great deal of religious reflection and it was the period when much of the Old Testament was written up in something close to its present form. Nor perhaps were the conditions of the exile too harsh. When Cyrus the Great of Persia destroyed the Babylonian empire in 539 and gave the Jews leave to return home, thousands chose to remain where they were. Many others remained in Egypt. It was the beginning of the Diaspora.

HEBREW captives march into exile after the fall of Lachish in 701. Sennacherib commissioned this relief to record his triumph.

1 Saul was killed in battle against the Philistines at Gilboa c.1006.

2 Hebron was David's capital before his capture of Jerusalem from the Jebusite Canaanites c.1000.

3 The Aramaeans of Hamath submitted after David defeated the Aramaeans of Zobah and Damascus.

4 Solomon built a fleet at Ezion-geber to trade on the Red Sea with east Africa and Arabia.

5 Northern tribes rebelled against Rehoboam and formed the breakaway kingdom of Israel.

6 A coalition of Levantine states including Israel briefly checked Assyrian expansion at Qarqar, 854 BC.

7 Aram–Damascus emerged as a major rival to Israel in the 850s, but was conquered by Assyria in 732.

8 Samaria, the capital of Israel, was taken by the Assyrians in 721 after a three-year siege.

9 Jerusalem, capital of Judah, was sacked after the rebellion of 587, and its population deported to Babylon; they stayed until 539 when the victorious Achemenid Persians allowed them to return.

See also 1.07 (writing), 1.13 (Assyrians and Babylonians), 1.23 (eastern Mediterranean)

The Persians who took Babylon in 539 were comparative newcomers to the region. An Indo-Iranian people, the Persians had followed their close relations the Medes from central Asia to Iran in the 8th century. The founder of the Persian monarchy was Achemenes, who gave his name to the dynasty, but it is uncertain when he ruled. In 648, when Ashurbanipal destroyed the Elamite kingdom and occupied western Elam, the Persians seized the opportunity to take its eastern territories. Despite this Persia was overshadowed by, and often subject to, the powerful Median kingdom. It was in the reign of Cyrus the Great that Persia rose to empire.

Cyrus' career as a great conqueror started when his nominal overlord, the Median king Astyages, invaded Persia around 550 following a rebellion. Astyages was deserted by his army and captured when he met Cyrus in battle at Pasargadae. Cyrus followed up this easy victory by taking the Median capital at Hamadan (Ecbatana). Cyrus was now the most powerful ruler in the region. In 547 he repulsed an invasion of Media by King Croesus of Lydia, who withdrew to his capital Sardis and disbanded his army for the winter. Cyrus, however, had nothing against winter campaigns and, when he arrived unexpectedly, Sardis fell after a siege of only fourteen days. Leaving his generals to complete the conquest of Lydia and the Ionian Greeks, Cyrus marched east to push deep into central Asia. In 539 he crowned his career by conquering Babylonia. Discontent over the religious unorthodoxy of its king Nabonidus was rife and, by posing as a servant of the god Marduk and restorer of orthodoxy, he was even welcomed in Babylon.

In little more than a decade Cyrus had built the largest empire the world had yet seen, with remarkably little hard campaigning. Clearly the close relationship between the Medes and Persians aided in what was more of a dynastic takeover than a conquest, and in Mesopotamia the experience of incorporation in the Assyrian and Babylonian empires had long-since mixed cultures, weakened local identities and accustomed people to imperial rule. As a result there was little spirit of resistance to what amounted, in practice, to no more than the advent of a new imperial dynasty. Cyrus was diplomat as well as soldier and the consolidation of his empire owed much to his moderation. Demands for tribute were modest, he did not interfere with local customs, upheld the rights of the local priesthood and left local institutions of government intact.

Cyrus was killed in 530 on campaign against the Sakas in central Asia and was succeeded by his son Cambyses. Cambyses added Egypt and Libya to the empire before dying in mysterious circumstances,

Map legend

- Persia at the accession of Cyrus, 559
- conquered by Cyrus, 559–550
- conquered by Cyrus, 550–530
- conquered by Cambyses, 530–522
- conquered by Darius, 521–486
- tributary region or vassal state
- border of pre-Achemenid state
- uncertain border of pre-Achemenid state
- border of Persian empire, 496
- royal road
- ■ capital of Persian empire
- Susa   major royal palace
- LYDIA   conquered state
- Caria   region paying tribute to Persia in 500
- modern coastline and drainage where altered

major Persian campaign
- → Cyrus
- -▶ Cyrus, conjectural
- ➡ Cambyses
- ➡ Darius
- -▶ Darius, conjectural
- ➡ Xerxes

Map labels

Scythia
Scythians
THRACE
Black Sea
Skudra — horses, weapons
Bosporus
Sinope
MACEDON
Cappadocia — 300 talents of silver, clothing, horses
GREEK CITY STATES
Hellespont
LYDIA
Pteria — 547
Plataea 479 — Marathon 490
Salamis 480 — Athens
Sardis 547–546
Lydia — 500 talents of silver, vessels
Lake Tuz
Kizil Irmak
Sparta
Ionia — clothing, vessels
Cilician Gates
TAURUS MTS
Xanthus
Crete
Rhodes
Cilicia — 360 white horses
Aleppo
Caria — 400 talents of silver with Ionia, chariots, weapons
Cyprus — 350 talents of silver with Palestine and Phoenicia
Sidon
Tyre
Phoenicia
Syria
Mediterranean Sea
Barca
Cyrene
Libya — chariots, goats
525
Jerusalem
Palestine
Pelusium — 525
Siwa Oasis
Memphis
KINGDOM OF EGYPT
Arabia — camels, cloth, frankincense
Egypt — 700 talents of silver, bulls, cloth
El Kharga Oasis
Thebes
526
523
Red Sea
Nile
Kingdom of Meroë (Nubia) — elephant tusks, giraffe, vessels
513

TIMELINE

Persian empire

600	550	500
c.850 The Medes migrate into Iran from central Asia.	559 Accession of Cyrus, who seizes the Median throne in 550	513 Darius invades southeast Europe
c.750 The Persians migrate into southern Iran from central Asia	547–546 Cyrus captures Lydia	499 The Ionian Greeks rebel against Persian rule
c.640 Persia becomes a vassal state of Media	539 Cyrus takes Babylon	490 The Greeks defeat the Persians at Marathon
c.630–553 Life of Zoroaster, the prophet of Iran and founder of the Parsee religion	525–523 Cambyses (r.530–522) conquers Egypt	480 The Greeks halt Xerxes (r.486–465) at Salamis
	520 Darius (r.521–486) campaigns against the pointed-hat Scythians	
	518 Conquest of the Indus valley by the Persians	

General

600	550	500
612 Fall of Nineveh and collapse of Assyria's empire	520 Darius links the Nile and Red Sea by a canal	
	562 Decline of Babylon after the death of Nebuchadnezzar	507 Kleisthenes lays the basis for democracy in Athens

0 _____ 600 km
0 _____ 400 mi

GOLD bracelets like this were shown as part of the Lydians' tribute, depicted on reliefs at Persepolis

Sakas

Aral Sea

Pointed-hat Scythians
250 talents of silver, clothing, jewelry, horses

Pointed-hat Scythians

Caspian Sea

Syr Dar'ya

Sogdiana
horses, jewelry, weapons

3
Kyreskhata

Marakanda (Samarkand)

Bactria
360 talents of silver, camels, vessels

Amu Dar'ya

HINDU KUSH

Indus

Bactra

Capisa

Peshawar (Caspatyrus?)

Kabul

Taxila

Chenub

CAUCASUS MTS
Colchis
25 boys, 25 girls

Armenia
400 talents of silver, clothing, horses, vessels

Murat

Lake Van
Van

Lake Urmia

Araks

MEDIAN

Media
450 talents of silver, animal hides, clothing, jewelry, vessels, weapons

Turan Lowland

Chorasmia
300 talents of silver with Parthia and Aria, horses, jewelry, weapons

546–539

Aria
camels, lionskin cloaks, vessels

Herat

Gandhara
170 talents of silver, bulls, weapons

Jhelum

Sutlej

520

Parthia
camels, vessels

EMPIRE

Hamadan

ZAGROS MOUNTAINS

Tigris

547

Assyria
animal hides, cloth, eunuchs, metals, rams, vessels

Nineveh
Arbil

Diyala

BABYLONIAN EMPIRE

539

Dasht-e Lut

Kandahar

c.518

HINDU KINGDOMS

Desert

Euphrates

539✕

Sippar

Opis

Elam
300 talents of silver, lioness & cubs, weapons

550

Drangiana
camels, lionskin cloaks, vessels

Sind
360 talents of gold dust, axes, weapons

Babylon
Nippur

Susa

1

Sagartia
600 talents of silver, cloth, horses

Arachosia
animal hides, camels, vessels

Indus

Babylonia
1000 talents of silver with Assyria, bulls, cloth, eunuchs, vessels

550✕ Pasargadae
Persepolis

PERSIA

Maka

Persian Gulf

Gulf of Oman

Arabian Sea

possibly murdered by his brother Smerdis. Smerdis was quickly overthrown and killed by Darius (r.521–486), a member of a junior Achemenid house. Darius faced rebellions from one end of the empire to the other but suppressed them all within a year and by 520 he was secure enough to campaign against the Caspian Scythians. In 518 he extended Persian control as far as, and possibly a little beyond, the Indus and in 513 he crossed into Europe; though he conquered Thrace, the expedition failed in its main objective of subduing the Black Sea Scythians. This failure encouraged a rebellion by the Ionian Greeks in 499. This was put down in 494 and Darius dispatched an expedition to punish the mainland Greeks for supporting the rebels. When this force was defeated by the Athenians at Marathon in 490, Darius began to plan for the conquest of Greece. The expedition was finally launched by his son Xerxes but the decisive defeat of his fleet at Salamis in 480 and of his army at Plataea the following year brought the expansion of the empire to a halt.

Darius reorganized the empire into about twenty provinces under governors or satraps, often relatives or close friends of the king. The system of taxation was regularized and fixed tributes, based on the wealth of each province, were introduced. Only Persia, which was not a conquered province, was exempt. The Assyrian imperial post system was expanded and the roads improved. Local garrison commanders remained directly responsible to the king. The official capital of the empire under Cyrus had been Pasargadae, but Hamadan was effectively the administrative capital. Darius moved the administrative capital to Susa and founded a new official capital at Persepolis. Under Darius the imperial administration used various local languages transcribed into cuneiform and written on clay tablets for documents, but his successors abandoned this system in favor of writing on parchment using the widespread Aramaic language and alphabet.

The Persian empire was a thoroughly cosmopolitan state which united elements of all the major civilizations of its time except the Chinese. By throwing together peoples from so many backgrounds the empire promoted the diffusion and mixing of cultures and ended the isolation of the old civilizations.

1 Astyages, king of Media, was defeated by Cyrus at Pasargadae; Cyrus then took Hamadan and seized the Median throne.

2 Cyrus repulsed a Lydian invasion at Pteria, then captured the Lydian capital Sardis and King Croesus.

3 Kyreskhata was the strongest of a chain of forts built by Cyrus to protect the northern frontier.

4 After a hard-fought battle at Pelusium Cambyses captured Memphis (525) and took pharaoh Psammeticus III to Susa in chains.

5 A Persian force sent by Cambyses to capture Siwa vanished in the desert.

6 Darius built a bridge of boats over the Bosporus (513) to invade Europe; Xerxes did the same over the Hellespont in 480.

7 Persian expansion to the west was decisively halted by the Greeks at the naval battle of Salamis.

See also 1.14 (Babylon); 1.24 (Greece)

The end of the Ice Age, about 10,000 years ago, brought major climatic changes. Africa had been an arid continent during the last glaciation: rainforests were small and the Sahara desert formed a virtually impenetrable barrier between central and northern Africa. When the last glaciation ended rainfall increased over the whole continent, with most of the Sahara now able to support semi-arid grassland, diverse wildlife and large permanent lakes. Some 9,000 years ago hunter–gatherer bands lived in most of the area, exploiting game, lake-fish and wild plants of all kinds. Most groups became sedentary around favored watercourses or lakes and produced pottery decorated with a wavy-line motif while they exploited wild plants and hunted over the semi-arid neighborhood. They have yielded bone fishing harpoons, small stone tools and a pottery style decorated with wavy line patterns.

Some of Africa's earliest farming communities developed among these Saharan groups, perhaps as early as 6000 BC. Even though wetter than today, the Sahara suffered long drought cycles that affected the availability of both game and wild plant foods. One survival strategy was to supplement cereal grass yields by planting small gardens in areas where these wild grasses flourished. Over many centuries this resulted in a permanent dependence on crops such as bulrush millet, sorghum and African rice.

In the eastern Sahara, farming based on barley and wheat and domesticated indigenous wild cattle was established by 6500 BC. Farming probably began in the Nile valley soon after. A period of low Nile floods around this time probably reduced supplies of fish and other aquatic animals on which the local hunter–gatherers depended, and forced them to adopt farming. The fertile soils and reliable water supply of the Nile valley made it the richest and most densely populated farming area in Africa by the 4th millennium BC. Wheat and barley spread from Egypt throughout north Africa and to the Ethiopian highlands by about 500 BC, but they were unsuited to the climate of tropical Africa.

Another early center of agriculture in Africa was the Ethiopian highlands, where farming may have begun by 5000 BC based on teff, an indigenous Ethiopian cereal, and finger millet, a cereal of unknown origin. Other Ethiopian domesticates included noog, an oil plant, and ensete, a relative of the banana grown for its starchy root. Of these, only finger millet became important outside Ethiopia. Ethiopia's relative isolation meant that many food plants, including barley, flax, emmer wheat, peas and lentils, developed strains unique to the area.

Farming along the margins of the west African forest zone had begun by the 2nd millennium with indigenous plants such as yams, cowpeas and the oil palm. African rice, adapted to grow in flooded savanna waterholes, became a staple west of the Bandama river. Farmers spread using a technique of shifting agriculture in clearings cut or burned out of the forest.

The introduction of cattle, sheep and goats about 5000 BC revolutionized farming in the central Sahara. By the 4th millennium cattle- and sheep-herding and limited cultivation of cereals were widespread. The herders were seminomadic, and drove their animals between seasonal pastures. The Saharan herders left a vivid record of their way of life in thousands of naturalistic rock paintings found widely across the central Sahara. By about 3000 BC desertification intensified, perhaps in part because of overgrazing. The herders' response was to move out to the Sahel region of semi-arid savanna at its southern margins. South of the Sahara, cattle-herding was restricted by areas of dense rainforest and by the widespread tsetse fly. However, herder groups spread onto the east African highlands by 2000 BC and moved south.

Copper was worked in the southern Sahara in the 2nd millennium, but sub-Saharan Africa moved straight from the Stone Age to the Iron Age. Knowledge of iron working may have developed indigenously in the southern Sahara; alternatively it may have been introduced either down the Nile valley or from the Phonecian colonies in north Africa. Iron was being worked in the Nubian kingdom of Kush by about 600 BC, while it is attested in northern Nigeria at about the same time, where the Nok culture developed by the late 6th century.

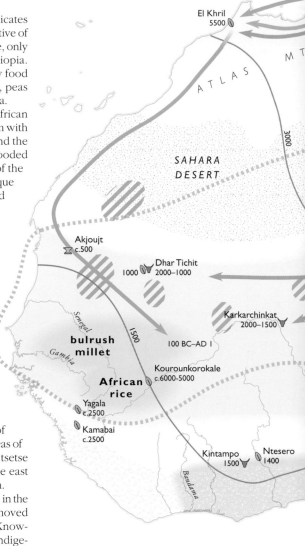

ATLANTIC OCEAN

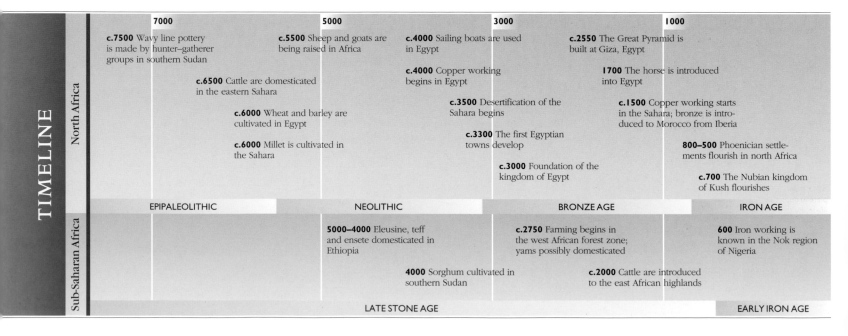

TIMELINE

	7000	5000	3000	1000
North Africa	**c.7500** Wavy line pottery is made by hunter–gatherer groups in southern Sudan	**c.5500** Sheep and goats are being raised in Africa	**c.4000** Sailing boats are used in Egypt	**c.2550** The Great Pyramid is built at Giza, Egypt
			c.4000 Copper working begins in Egypt	**1700** The horse is introduced into Egypt
	c.6500 Cattle are domesticated in the eastern Sahara		**c.3500** Desertification of the Sahara begins	**c.1500** Copper working starts in the Sahara; bronze is introduced to Morocco from Iberia
	c.6000 Wheat and barley are cultivated in Egypt		**c.3300** The first Egyptian towns develop	
	c.6000 Millet is cultivated in the Sahara		**c.3000** Foundation of the kingdom of Egypt	**800–500** Phoenician settlements flourish in north Africa
				c.700 The Nubian kingdom of Kush flourishes

EPIPALEOLITHIC	NEOLITHIC	BRONZE AGE	IRON AGE

Sub-Saharan Africa		**5000–4000** Eleusine, teff and ensete domesticated in Ethiopia	**c.2750** Farming begins in the west African forest zone; yams possibly domesticated	**600** Iron working is known in the Nok region of Nigeria
		4000 Sorghum cultivated in southern Sudan	**c.2000** Cattle are introduced to the east African highlands	

LATE STONE AGE			EARLY IRON AGE

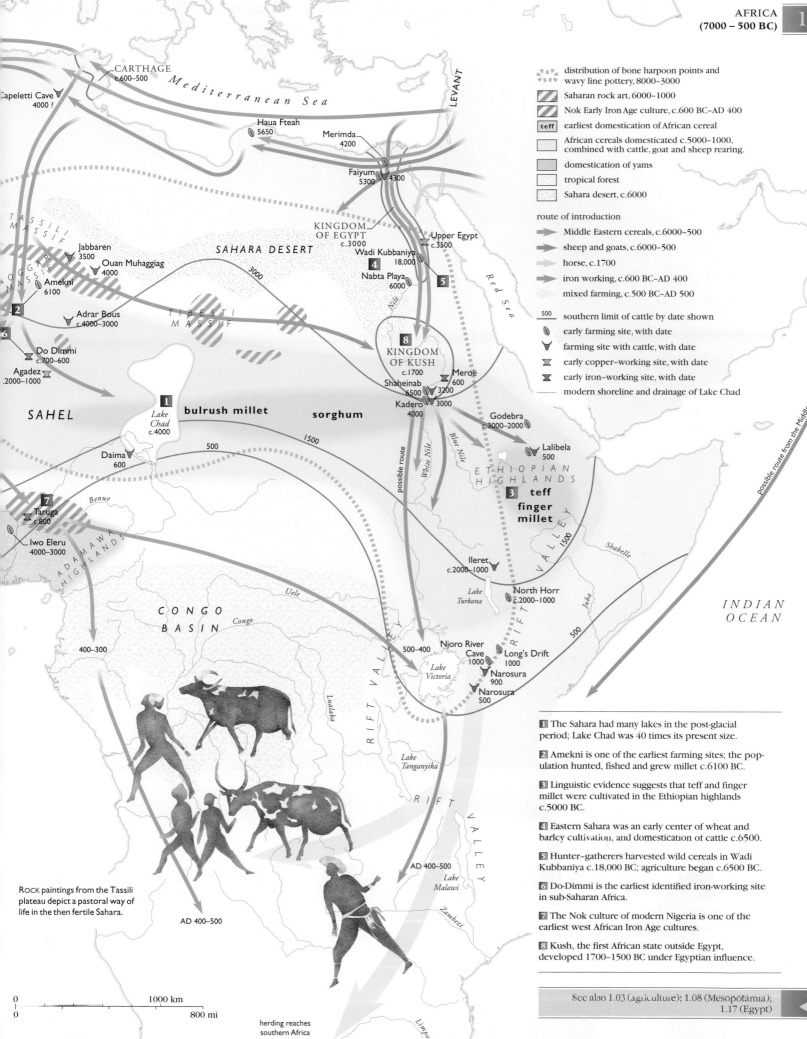

Legend

- distribution of bone harpoon points and wavy line pottery, 8000–3000
- Saharan rock art, 6000–1000
- Nok Early Iron Age culture, c.600 BC–AD 400
- **teff** earliest domestication of African cereal
- African cereals domesticated c.5000–1000, combined with cattle, goat and sheep rearing.
- domestication of yams
- tropical forest
- Sahara desert, c.6000

route of introduction
- Middle Eastern cereals, c.6000–500
- sheep and goats, c.6000–500
- horse, c.1700
- iron working, c.600 BC–AD 400
- mixed farming, c.500 BC–AD 500

- 500 southern limit of cattle by date shown
- early farming site, with date
- farming site with cattle, with date
- early copper-working site, with date
- early iron-working site, with date
- modern shoreline and drainage of Lake Chad

Map labels

CARTHAGE c.600–500
Mediterranean Sea
LEVANT
Capeletti Cave 4000 ?
Haua Fteah 5650
Merimda 4200
Faiyum 5300 4300
TASSILI MASSIF
HOGGAR MASSIF
Jabbaren 3500
Ouan Muhaggiag 4000
Amekni 6100
Adrar Bous c.4000–3000
Do Dimmi c.700–600
Agadez c.2000–1000
SAHARA DESERT
KINGDOM OF EGYPT c.3000
Upper Egypt c.3500
Wadi Kubbaniya 18,000
Nabta Playa 6000
TIBESTI MASSIF
3000
Red Sea
SAHEL
Lake Chad c.4000
bulrush millet
sorghum
Nile
KINGDOM OF KUSH c.1700
Meroë 600
Shaheinab 6500
Kadero 4000 3000 3200
Godebra c.3000–2000
Lalibela 500
ETHIOPIAN HIGHLANDS
teff finger millet
Daima 600
500
1500
White Nile
Blue Nile
possible route
Benue
Taruga c.800
Iwo Eleru 4000–3000
ADAMAWA HIGHLANDS
Ileret c.2000–1000
North Horr c.2000–1000
Lake Turkana
Shabelle
Juba
RIFT VALLEY
1500
500
INDIAN OCEAN
CONGO BASIN
Uele
Congo
400–300
Lualaba
Njoro River Cave 1000
Long's Drift 1000
Narosura 900
Narosura 500
500–400
Lake Victoria
RIFT VALLEY
Lake Tanganyika
RIFT VALLEY
AD 400–500
Lake Malawi
AD 400–500
Zambezi
Limpopo
possible route from the Middle East or India

Notes

1 The Sahara had many lakes in the post-glacial period; Lake Chad was 40 times its present size.

2 Amekni is one of the earliest farming sites; the population hunted, fished and grew millet c.6100 BC.

3 Linguistic evidence suggests that teff and finger millet were cultivated in the Ethiopian highlands c.5000 BC.

4 Eastern Sahara was an early center of wheat and barley cultivation, and domestication of cattle c.6500.

5 Hunter-gatherers harvested wild cereals in Wadi Kubbaniya c.18,000 BC; agriculture began c.6500 BC.

6 Do-Dimmi is the earliest identified iron-working site in sub-Saharan Africa.

7 The Nok culture of modern Nigeria is one of the earliest west African Iron Age cultures.

8 Kush, the first African state outside Egypt, developed 1700–1500 BC under Egyptian influence.

ROCK paintings from the Tassili plateau depict a pastoral way of life in the then fertile Sahara.

herding reaches southern Africa around AD 1

0 1000 km
0 800 mi

See also 1.03 (agriculture); 1.08 (Mesopotamia); 1.17 (Egypt)

Ancient Egypt was totally dependent on the Nile. Below the First Cataract, the Nile flows through a narrow valley and, except where it broadens out into the Delta, its flood plain is nowhere more than a few kilometers wide, often less. The flood plain was probably the most favorable area for agriculture anywhere in the ancient world. The Nile flooded annually in the late summer, falling in the autumn and leaving the fields moist and fertilized with fresh silt ready for sowing. The crops grew through the warm Egyptian winter and were harvested in the spring before the next cycle of flooding. Egypt had little need of the complex irrigation systems and flood defenses of Mesopotamia, where the rivers flooded in spring, after the start of the growing season. Canals, however, were used to spread the floodwaters and increase the cultivable area. High yields were possible year after year: the farmers' surpluses were taken to state storehouses for distribution to administrators, craftsmen and priests, for trade or to build up reserves against the famine that would follow if the Nile flood failed. The Nile was also Egypt's main highway. The prevailing winds in Egypt blow north to south, enabling boats to travel upstream under sail and return downstream with the flow. Few settlements were far from the river, making it relatively easy to transport heavy loads of grain or stone over long distances. On either side of the narrow 800-kilometer fertile strip was the desert which isolated Egypt from the influence of other civilizations and protected it from invaders: Egyptian civilization was over 1,300 years old before it suffered its first major invasion.

Farming began in the Nile valley before 6000 BC and by 4000 BC it was densely populated by subsistence farmers. Chiefdoms and towns appeared by 3300. In the narrow confines of the valley competition was probably intense. Eventually, the chiefdoms amalgamated into two coalitions or kingdoms, centered respectively in Upper and Lower Egypt, which fought each other for supremacy. The first king known to have ruled all Egypt was Narmer, king of Upper Egypt who conquered Lower Egypt about 3000. This unification was consolidated by the foundation of Memphis as a new capital.

By the same date the hieroglyphic system of writing had appeared. The system worked on similar principles to the Sumerian pictographic script, but hieroglyphs were developed from symbolic motifs used to decorate pottery in Egypt's Predynastic period. Early hieroglyphs appear on slate palettes which Narmer had carved to commemorate his victories. These palettes show that the principle of theocratic kingship that would be the basis of the ancient Egyptian state was already well established. During the ensuing Early Dynastic period (2920–2575) the kings developed an efficient administration which made possible a dramatic increase in royal power at the beginning of the Old Kingdom (2575–2134): named for the kingdom ruled from Memphis by a succession of four dynasties.

The annual Nile flood was seen as a gift from the gods. The king claimed to be able to control the flood, but if the flood failed, his authority could be called into question. He was believed to be of divine descent and was held to be immortal. At his death immense effort was put into preserving his body and to providing it with a suitably regal tomb furnished with the luxuries of everyday life. Early royal tombs were built on platforms known as *mastabas*, but these were superseded by pyramids in the reign of King Djoser (r.2630–2611). Pyramid building climaxed in about 2550 with the 146-meter-high Great Pyramid, built for Khufu, and the slightly smaller pyramid of his son Khephren. These enormous buildings are impressive evidence of the power the kings exercised over their subjects. However the large pyramids strained the resources of the kingdom: later ones were more modest and none were built after the 17th century BC, by which time ideas of the afterlife had changed.

Egypt was governed by an efficient central and local bureaucracy. The kingdom was treated as the personal property of the king and the central bureaucracy was an extension of the royal household. The highest official was the vizier who supervised the administration of justice and taxation. Below the vizier were chancellors, controllers of stores and other officials, supported by a staff of scribes trained in mathematics and writing. For the purposes of local government, Egypt was divided into provinces, or *nomes*, under governors selected from the royal or noble families.

During the 5th Dynasty (2465–2323) the monarchy was weakened by granting out lands as rewards and favors to the nobility. The provincial governorships became hereditary and drifted out of the control of the king. A period of low Nile floods then began around 2150, bringing famine and starvation, and the remaining royal authority crumbled. The Old Kingdom state collapsed and Egypt was divided between rival dynasties in Upper and Lower Egypt in what is known as the First Intermediate period.

THIS pottery lion, with a stylized mane resembling a headcloth, was found in the temple at Hierakonpolis. It dates from about the 3rd Dynasty.

Mediterranean Sea

to Libya

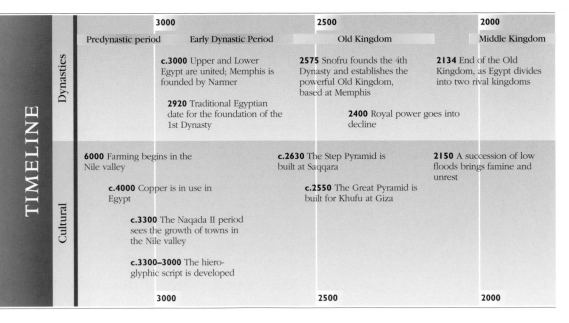

TIMELINE

		3000		2500		2000
Dynasties		Predynastic period	Early Dynastic Period		Old Kingdom	Middle Kingdom
		c.3000 Upper and Lower Egypt are united; Memphis is founded by Narmer		**2575** Snofru founds the 4th Dynasty and establishes the powerful Old Kingdom, based at Memphis		**2134** End of the Old Kingdom, as Egypt divides into two rival kingdoms
			2920 Traditional Egyptian date for the foundation of the 1st Dynasty		**2400** Royal power goes into decline	
Cultural		**6000** Farming begins in the Nile valley		**c.2630** The Step Pyramid is built at Saqqara		**2150** A succession of low floods brings famine and unrest
			c.4000 Copper is in use in Egypt	**c.2550** The Great Pyramid is built for Khufu at Giza		
			c.3300 The Naqada II period sees the growth of towns in the Nile valley			
			c.3300–3000 The hieroglyphic script is developed			
		3000		2500		2000

1 The First Cataract was the traditional southern frontier of Egypt through most of its history.

2 Hierakonpolis and Naqada were the first towns to develop in Egypt, c.3300. Narmer was probably king of Hierakonpolis.

3 Saqqara is the site of the oldest pyramid, the Step Pyramid, c.2630.

4 Giza is the site of the largest pyramids, including the Great Pyramid of Khufu.

5 The mountains of the Eastern Desert were the chief source of minerals.

6 Graffiti show that the Egyptians were exploiting Sinai's mineral wealth as early as the 3rd Dynasty (2649–2575).

7 The Egyptians maintained a trading post at Buhen in Nubia during the Old Kingdom.

8 Memphis was capital of Egypt for most of the Early Dynastic and Old Kingdom.

to the Levant

timber
from Lebanon

Tell el-Rub'a

Buto

Nile River Delta

LOWER
EGYPT

natron

Great Bitter
Lake

SINAI

Legend:

- fertile area
- conjectural borders of Kingdom of Upper Egypt, c.3000
- southern border of Old Kingdom
- border of Kingdoms of Upper and Lower Egypt, 2134–2040

Old Kingdom pyramids, 2650–2040
- single
- multiple
- non-royal

- capital of Old Kingdom
- Predynastic and Early Dynastic royal tomb, c.3250–2650
- later Old Kingdom tomb, c.2500-2100
- military expansion of Upper Egypt, c.3000
- campaign in the Early Dynastic and Old Kingdom

lead source of commodity
- desert route
- modern coastline and drainage where altered

natron

Wadi
Natrun

Heliopolis

quartzite
limestone

6

copper
turquoise

Abu Rawash

Giza

Zawyet el-Aryan

Abusir

Memphis

Saqqara

copper

3

Dahshur

8

Gulf of Suez

basalt
dolerite
gypsum

Maidum

Seila

Birket Qarun
(ancient shoreline)

Faiyum

Nile

Abu Rawash

Herakleopolis

Dishasha

0   300 km
0   200 mi

flint

Sawaris

Red Sea

copper

MIDDLE EGYPT

Bahariya
Oasis

Gebel el-Teir

Tihna

porphyry
granite
jasper

Zawyet el-Amwat

copper

Bahr Yusuf

Beni Hasan

limestone

lead

Deir el-Malik

Sheik Sa'id

alabaster

Quseir el-Amarna

5

Sheik Atiya

Deir el-Gabrawi

copper

Meir

Dara

Asyut

Hammamiya

Qaw el-Kebir

Western
Desert

Eastern
Desert

Akhmim

granite

Farafra
Oasis

Nag el-Deir

Dendara

Nag el-Gaziriyah

Hagarsa

Koptos

Nile

Abydos

Naqada

Tukh

2

Thebes

limestone

UPPER EGYPT

Gebelan

El-Mo'alla

gold
feldspar
emeralds

El-Kab

limestone

El-Kula

Hierakonpolis

to the Red Sea

TERRACOTTA figure of a
dancing woman from the
Predynastic Naqada I
culture.

2

Edfu

alum

El-Kharga
Oasis

Kurkur
Oasis

Qubbet el-
Hawa

amethyst

Elephantine
1st Cataract

lead
granite
diorite
steatite
quartzite

El-Dakhla
Oasis

Balat

1

ebony
gold
ivory
from Nubia

7

to Buhen

See also 1.07 (writing), 1.10 (Mesopotamia),
1.18 (Middle and New Kingdoms)

The reunification of Egypt in 2040 BC by Mentuhotpe (r.2061–2010), of the Theban dynasty of Upper Egypt, marks the start of the Middle Kingdom. A few decades later royal authority and political stability had been restored and the power of the provincial governors reduced. To rebuild a loyal administration, the Middle Kingdom rulers promoted propagandist literature, while statuary presented the king as the care-worn "good shepherd" of his people. Pyramid building was revived, though more modestly than in the Old Kingdom.

Egypt's neighbors were now becoming organized in chiefdoms and petty kingdoms, and the Middle Kingdom rulers had to pursue a more aggressive foreign policy than their predecessors. Under Amenemhet I (r.1991–1962), Lower Nubia was conquered; the frontier at the Second Cataract was garrisoned and heavily fortified by his successors. Egyptian influence was extended over the Levant during the reign of Senwosret III (r.1878–1841) and local rulers were forced to become vassals of Egypt. During the 18th century the bureaucracy began to grow out of control and for much of the time the effective rulers of Egypt were the viziers. In the 17th century there was considerable immigration from the Levant into the Delta. Most immigrants were absorbed into the lower classes of Egyptian society but one, Khendjer, became king around 1745.

Around 1640 Egypt was invaded by the Hyksos, a Semitic people from the Levant, who overran Lower Egypt, which they ruled from their capital at Avaris in the Delta. Upper Egypt remained independent under a vassal Theban dynasty but control over Lower Nubia was lost to the nascent kingdom of Kush. Hyksos rule, in what is known as the Second Intermediate period, made Egypt more open to foreign influences. Bronze came into widespread use, war chariots were introduced, as were weapons such as the composite bow and scale armor. New fashions in dress, musical instruments, domestic animals and crops were adopted through Hyksos influence. Otherwise, the Hyksos accepted Egyptian traditions and historical continuity was unbroken.

Under the Theban king Seqenenre II (died c.1555) the Egyptians began a long struggle to expel the Hyksos which was finally completed by Ahmose in 1532. This victory marks the beginning of the New Kingdom, under which the power and influence of ancient Egypt reached its peak. The Hyksos invasion had shown the Egyptians that their borders were no longer secure, and the New Kingdom was overtly militaristic and expansionist, reaching its greatest extent around 1500 under the warrior king Tuthmosis I. Tuthmosis conquered the entire Levant and established a frontier on the Euphrates. Lower Nubia was reconquered and Kush was overrun to beyond the Fourth Cataract. The primary motive of expansion into the Levant was to establish a buffer zone between Egypt and the aggressive powers of the Middle East; in Nubia, which had rich gold deposits, the motive was economic. In the Levant, local rulers were kept under the supervision of Egyptian officials and key cities were garrisoned. Nubia was subjected to full colonial government under a viceroy directly responsible to the king. Nubia was a great source of wealth to the New Kingdom but the Egyptians faced a constant struggle to keep control of the Levant, against local rebellions and expansionist powers such as the Hittite empire.

The power of Egypt declined after the reign of Amenophis IV (r.1353–1335). Amenophis, who changed his name to Akhenaten, was a radical religious reformer who attempted to replace Egypt's traditional polytheism with the monotheistic cult of the Aten or sun disk. Akhenaten founded a new capital and promoted radically new art styles to symbolize the break with the past, but there was little popular enthusiasm for the new religion, which was abandoned after his death. In the ensuing period of political instability, Egypt lost control of the Levant to the Hittites. Campaigns by the kings (or pharaohs as they were now known) Sethos I (r.1305–1290) and Ramesses II "the Great" (r.1290–1224) to restore the Egyptian position were only partially successful and Ramesses eventually made peace with the Hittites. Around 1200 the entire region was disrupted by

Middle Kingdom (12th Dynasty, 1991-1783)

- zone of direct control
- zone of dominance

Second Intermediate period

- Hyksos Kingdom (15th Dynasty, 1640-1532)
- Theban (17th Dynasty, 1646-1550)
- Kingdom of Kush
- maximum extent of New Kingdom under Tuthmosis I, 1504-1492

- royal capital, with dynasty
- city

royal tomb

- Middle Kingdom
- New Kingdom

fort or garrison

- Middle Kingdom
- New Kingdom

- sacked c.1200, probably by Sea Peoples
- Giza temple
- desert route used for communication between the Hyksos and Kushite allies
- gold deposit
- major migration
- modern coastline and drainage where altered

Libyan

| 0 | | 300 km |
| 0 | | 200 mi |

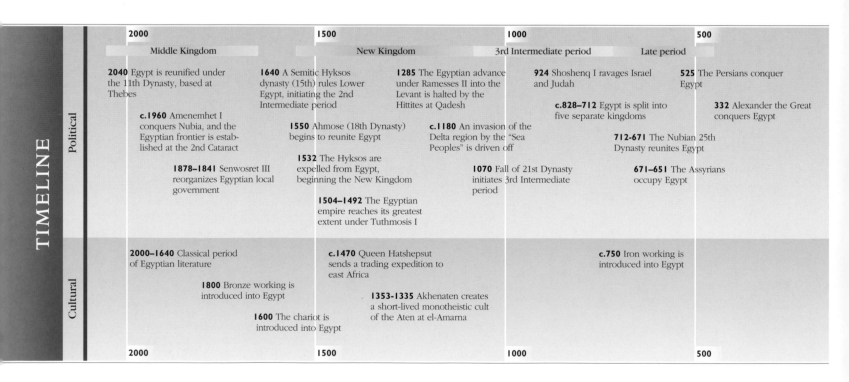

TIMELINE

Political

2040 Egypt is reunified under the 11th Dynasty, based at Thebes

c.1960 Amenemhet I conquers Nubia, and the Egyptian frontier is established at the 2nd Cataract

1878–1841 Senwosret III reorganizes Egyptian local government

1640 A Semitic Hyksos dynasty (15th) rules Lower Egypt, initiating the 2nd Intermediate period

1550 Ahmose (18th Dynasty) begins to reunite Egypt

1532 The Hyksos are expelled from Egypt, beginning the New Kingdom

1504–1492 The Egyptian empire reaches its greatest extent under Tuthmosis I

1285 The Egyptian advance under Ramesses II into the Levant is halted by the Hittites at Qadesh

c.1180 An invasion of the Delta region by the "Sea Peoples" is driven off

1070 Fall of 21st Dynasty initiates 3rd Intermediate period

924 Shoshenq I ravages Israel and Judah

c.828–712 Egypt is split into five separate kingdoms

712-671 The Nubian 25th Dynasty reunites Egypt

671–651 The Assyrians occupy Egypt

525 The Persians conquer Egypt

332 Alexander the Great conquers Egypt

Cultural

2000–1640 Classical period of Egyptian literature

1800 Bronze working is introduced into Egypt

1600 The chariot is introduced into Egypt

c.1470 Queen Hatshepsut sends a trading expedition to east Africa

1353-1335 Akhenaten creates a short-lived monotheistic cult of the Aten at el-Amarna

c.750 Iron working is introduced into Egypt

Periods (top bar): Middle Kingdom | New Kingdom | 3rd Intermediate period | Late period

Scale markers: 2000 | 1500 | 1000 | 500

Sea peoples
c.1180

HITTITE EMPIRE

MITTANI

■ Carchemish

♨ Aleppo
♨ Alalakh

Euphrates

Orontes

♨ Ugarit

♨ Hamath

*Syrian
Desert*

Arvad ■

LEVANT

Qadesh
1285 ✕

Cyprus

Byblos ■

■ Damascus

Mediterranean Sea

Sidon ■

Tyre ■

Hazor ■ **5**

Acco ■

Megiddo ✕
c.1456

■ Beth-shean

Jerusalem ◆

■ Amman

Joppa ◆

6

✕ 1180

◆ Gaza

Hyksos
17th century

Hebrews
late 13th century

Raqote ■

Buto ■
Sakha ■ **14**

Sais ■

Tanis ■

□ Sile

Kom el-Hisn ■

Athribis ■

Bubastis ■

Avaris
15, 19, 20

LOWER
EGYPT

Giza 🔺
Heliopolis

Dahshur ■

Memphis
12, 13, 18, 19

SINAI

Hawara ■
El-Lisht
12, 13

Kom Medinet Ghurab ■
El-Lahun

Herakleopolis

• Serabit

*Bahariya
Oasis*

El-Ashmunein

El-Amarna
18

*Farafra
Oasis*

7

Asyut ■

Nile

*Eastern
Desert*

Akhmim ■

■ Mersa Gawasis

*Western
Desert*

Abydos

El-Dakhla
Oasis • Balat

El-Kharga
Oasis

Red Sea

Valley of the Kings 🔺 **8**
🔺 Karnak

Armant ■ 🔺 Thebes
11, 17, 18

Luxor ■ **2**

Hierakonpolis ■ El-Kab

Edfu ■

UPPER EGYPT

Elephantine ◆

*Kurkur
Oasis*

≈ 1st Cataract

*Dunqul
Oasis*

◆ Beit el-Wali

Ikkur ◆ ◆ Gerf Hussein

3

◆ Quban

Aniba ◆

LOWER
NUBIA

◆ Abu Simbel

Buhen ◆

Kot

◆ Faras

Mirgissa ◆

◆ Meinarti

*Salima
Oasis*

Dorginarti
2nd Cataract

Uronati ◆
Semna ◆ **1**

◆ Kumma

Sai ◆

◆ Amara West

UPPER
NUBIA

◆ Amara East

🔺 Soleb

◆ Sesebi

◆ Tombos
3rd Cataract ≈
◆ Kerma

Kawa ◆

4

KUSH

≈ 4th Cataract

Nile

■ Napata

5th Cataract ≈

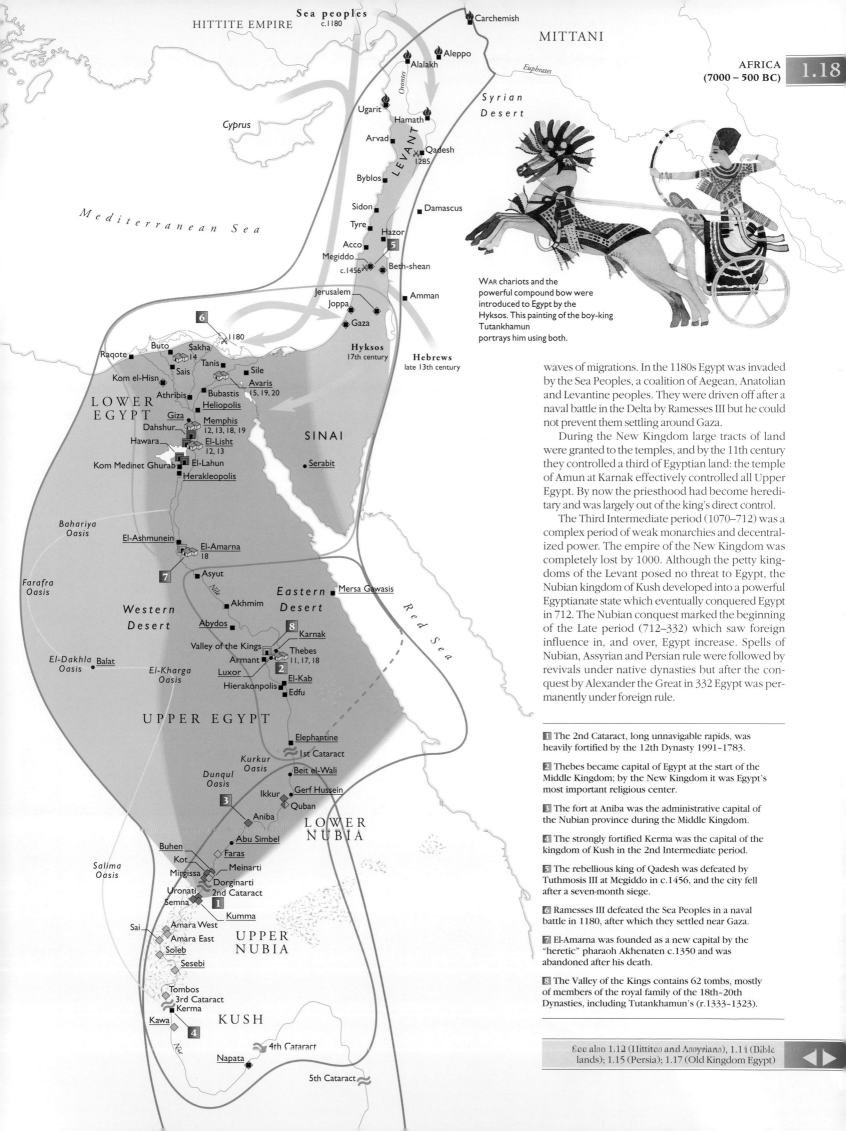

Wᴀʀ chariots and the powerful compound bow were introduced to Egypt by the Hyksos. This painting of the boy-king Tutankhamun portrays him using both.

waves of migrations. In the 1180s Egypt was invaded by the Sea Peoples, a coalition of Aegean, Anatolian and Levantine peoples. They were driven off after a naval battle in the Delta by Ramesses III but he could not prevent them settling around Gaza.

During the New Kingdom large tracts of land were granted to the temples, and by the 11th century they controlled a third of Egyptian land: the temple of Amun at Karnak effectively controlled all Upper Egypt. By now the priesthood had become hereditary and was largely out of the king's direct control.

The Third Intermediate period (1070–712) was a complex period of weak monarchies and decentralized power. The empire of the New Kingdom was completely lost by 1000. Although the petty kingdoms of the Levant posed no threat to Egypt, the Nubian kingdom of Kush developed into a powerful Egyptianate state which eventually conquered Egypt in 712. The Nubian conquest marked the beginning of the Late period (712–332) which saw foreign influence in, and over, Egypt increase. Spells of Nubian, Assyrian and Persian rule were followed by revivals under native dynasties but after the conquest by Alexander the Great in 332 Egypt was permanently under foreign rule.

1 The 2nd Cataract, long unnavigable rapids, was heavily fortified by the 12th Dynasty 1991-1783.

2 Thebes became capital of Egypt at the start of the Middle Kingdom; by the New Kingdom it was Egypt's most important religious center.

3 The fort at Aniba was the administrative capital of the Nubian province during the Middle Kingdom.

4 The strongly fortified Kerma was the capital of the kingdom of Kush in the 2nd Intermediate period.

5 The rebellious king of Qadesh was defeated by Tuthmosis III at Megiddo in c.1456, and the city fell after a seven-month siege.

6 Ramesses III defeated the Sea Peoples in a naval battle in 1180, after which they settled near Gaza.

7 El-Amarna was founded as a new capital by the "heretic" pharaoh Akhenaten c.1350 and was abandoned after his death.

8 The Valley of the Kings contains 62 tombs, mostly of members of the royal family of the 18th-20th Dynasties, including Tutankhamun's (r.1333-1323).

See also 1.12 (Hittites and Assyrians), 1.14 (Bible lands); 1.15 (Persia); 1.17 (Old Kingdom Egypt)

Anatomically modern humans from Africa reached what is now the Middle East some 90,000 years ago, but it was not until the beginning of the Upper Paleolithic period, about 40,000 years ago, that they were able to move into Europe. Unlike the indigenous Neanderthals, who were physically adapted to the harsh Ice Age climate, the early anatomically modern humans were poorly equipped to survive in Europe until, some 50,000–40,000 years ago, they also acquired a fully modern human mental capacity. This enabled them to adapt to the cold climate through technological and social innovation, and compete on more than equal terms with the Neanderthals. The Neanderthals became extinct about 28,000 years ago. Whether it was as a result of a war of extermination or because superior modern human hunting techniques drove them into marginal environments is a subject of debate: current archeological opinion favors the latter.

Two parallel toolmaking traditions, the Châtelperronian and the Aurignacian, are found in Europe during the 10–12,000 years that modern humans and Neanderthals shared the continent. The Châtelperronian is apparently a development of the Mousterian tool culture and is thought to have been used by the Neanderthals. The Aurignacian has similarities with contemporary tool cultures in the Middle East and is therefore thought to have been introduced to Europe by anatomically modern humans. The Aurignacian and the succeeding Gravettian tool cultures both show considerable uniformity over wide areas but there is greater regional variation in later Upper Paleolithic tool cultures. These variations are often stylistic rather than functional and probably served as a way of expressing emerging ethnic identities. Typical Upper Paleolithic stone tools include scrapers, sharpened blades, burins – engraving tools used for antler harpoons – and bone points and needles were also used. The Solutrean culture introduced a sophisticated technique of pressure flaking which produced beautiful leaf shaped spear heads.

The most impressive characteristics of the Upper Paleolithic cultures are their art traditions, both decorated artifacts and cave-wall painting. The earliest Upper Paleolithic art dates from around 31,000 years ago but the traditions reached their peak in the Magdalenian (17,000–11,000 years ago), in the cave paintings of sites such as Lascaux and Altamira. The

greatest concentration of Upper Paleolithic cave art is to be found in southwest France and northern Spain, an area with a particularly dense population at the time. The function of cave art is unknown but it is thought to have played a religious role. The most distinctive decorated artifacts are female "Venus" figurines made around 25,000 years ago. These have been found across Europe – evidence, perhaps, of a widespread religious cult.

Despite the cold, the tundras and steppes of Ice Age Europe were a very favorable environment for hunters, being filled with easily tracked herds of large grazing mammals. Upper Paleolithic hunters used a combination of semi-permanent base-camps – often sited at bottlenecks on animal migration routes, such as river crossings – and seasonal camps where particular game species were intensively exploited. Caves and south-facing rock shelters were favored camp sites, but in more exposed areas tents and huts were built.

The end of the last glaciation, around 10,000 years ago (8000 BC) marks the end of the Upper Paleolithic and the beginning of the Mesolithic

Legend

Upper Paleolithic, 40,000–10,000 years ago
- Levantine Aurignacian culture
- Aurignacian culture
- ◆ cave site
- ✋ cave site with painting
- ● open site
- ▲ open site with structure
- Venus figurine find

Mesolithic, 10,000–6000 ya (8000–4000 BC)
- major site
- 🐚 site with shell midden

- maximum extent of ice sheet during last glaciation, c.18,000 ya
- extent of ice sheet, 7000 BC
- .... northern limit of deciduous woodland, c.18,000 ya
- .... northern limit of deciduous woodland, 7000 BC
- ➤ migration of anatomically modern humans from Middle East, c.40,000 ya
- - - - ancient course of Thames/Rhine, 7000 BC
- —— modern coastline and drainage where altered

```
0                          800 km
0                          600 mi
```

"VENUS" figurines with exaggerated sexual characteristics were a feature of the Gravettian culture and probably symbolized fertility. This example is from Willendorf in Austria.

Oronsay Oban
Mount Sandel
Star Carr
Creswell Cr
Paviland
Pincevent
ATLANTIC OCEAN
Loire
Douro
Tagus
Cabeço da Arruda
PYRENEES

8
1
7

TIMELINE

		40,000 years ago (ya)	30,000	20,000	10,000 ya (8000 BC)
	Mousterian	Châtelperronian			
		Aurignacian	Gravettian	Solutrean Magdalenian	
Cultural		c.41,000 Blade tool technology introduced to Europe	c.30,000 The earliest cave paintings in southwest France and northern Spain	c.20,000 The pressure-flaking technique of tool manufacture is adopted	14,000 Production of cave paintings at Altamira, Spain
			25,000–22,000 "Venus" figurines are found widely from Spain to Russia	17,000 The cave paintings at Lascaux, France, are made	8000 (6000 BC) Beginning of the transition to a farming way of life in southeast Europe
				16,000 Microlithic tools are developed	
Physical		c.40,000 The first anatomically modern humans enter Europe	c.28,000 The last remaining Neanderthals become extinct in Spain	18,000–15,000 The Ice Age is in its coldest phase	10,000 End of the last glaciation
	MID PALEOLITHIC		UPPER PALEOLITHIC		MESOLITHIC

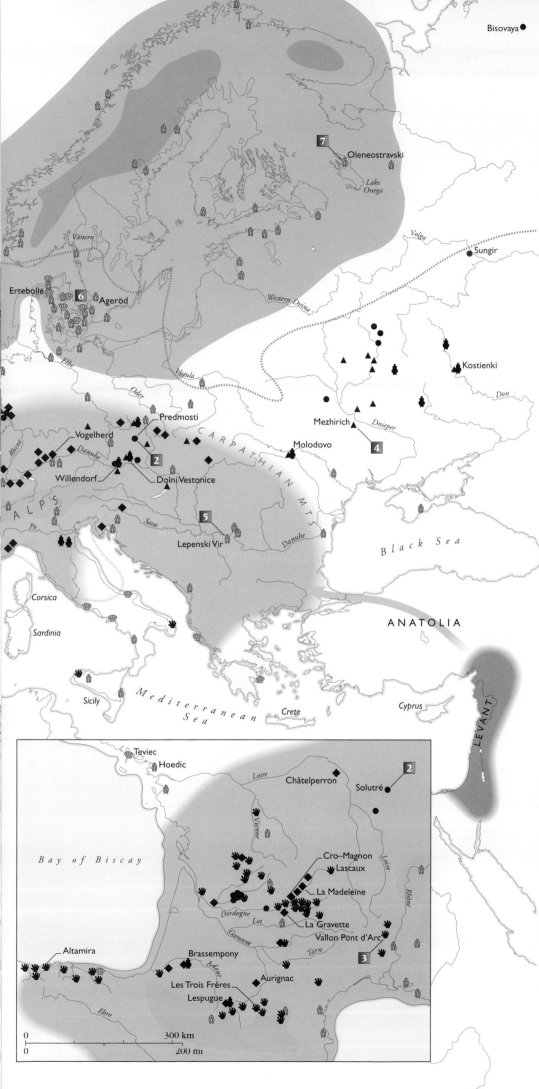

period. As the climate became warmer, sea levels rose and dense forests advanced over most of Europe, bringing the big-game hunting way of life to an end. Large mammals were now fewer and more elusive, but a far greater diversity of plant foods, shellfish, fish, birds and small mammals was available. Mesolithic hunter–gatherers introduced many new devices to exploit these new food sources. The most important technological change was a reliance on microliths – small stone blades or flakes – used in combination to make composite tools such as knives, harpoons, fish spears and lightweight arrow heads. Nets, fish traps, shellfish scoops and dug-out canoes also came into widespread use for the first time in the Mesolithic.

Many areas of northern Europe which had previously been uninhabitable because of extreme cold or ice sheets received their first modern human inhabitants during the Mesolithic, while some which had been relatively densely populated, such as southwest France and the southwest steppes, became comparatively depopulated. The densest population moved to areas such as the Atlantic coast and southern Scandinavia. Hunter–gatherers here were able to adopt an increasingly sedentary way of life, making fewer and shorter migrations between camps. In southern Scandinavia and eastern Europe there were even permanent settlements occupied all year round. Task groups set out from these settlements to spend short periods at temporary seasonal camps to exploit locally abundant food resources.

The Mesolithic period came to an end with the adoption of the Neolithic farming way of life, a process which began about 6000 BC in southeast Europe and about two thousand years later in the British Isles and Scandinavia. In extreme northerly areas, an essentially Mesolithic way of life continued until the domestication of the reindeer early in the Christian era.

1 In the Upper Paleolithic, southwest France had light woodland for fuel, sheltered valleys with many caves, and lay across major animal migration routes; it was therefore Europe's most densely populated area.

2 Upper Paleolithic hunters used temporary camps to exploit particular game species. Solutré was a base for horse hunters, Predmosti for mammoth.

3 Cave paintings of woolly rhinoceros, horses and buffalo found at Vallon Pont d'Arc in 1994 are, at 30,000 years old, the oldest yet found.

4 On the treeless steppes, mammoth bones were used to build huts; a well-known example, c.18,000 years old, was found at Mezhirich.

5 The well-preserved Mesolithic settlement of Lepenski Vir includes many fish-head sculptures, perhaps indicating worship of a fish-deity.

6 Denmark, with marine, freshwater and terrestrial food sources in close proximity, was densely populated in the Mesolithic.

7 The first cemeteries, such as those at Cabeço da Arruda and Oleneostravski (about 170 burials each) date from the late Mesolithic (c.4250 BC).

8 Late Mesolithic hunter-gatherers (c.4000–3400 BC) visited Oronsay island several times a year for fish and shellfish.

See also 1.02 (peopling the earth);
1.08 (Middle East); 1.20 (Neolithic Europe)

The Bronze Age saw chiefdoms and warrior elites established across most of Europe. Beyond the Aegean, states were not formed until the Iron Age was well advanced and in northern and eastern Europe not until the early Middle Ages. The chiefdoms were competitive communities: fortifications were built in great numbers and new weapons such as swords and halberds were invented. Superb crafted display objects – ornaments, weapons, "parade-ground" armor, tableware, cult objects – made of bronze and precious metals, express the competitiveness of the period. Long-distance trade , particularly in tin and amber, arose to satisfy the demand for metals and other precious objects in areas where such resources were lacking. The increase in trade aided the spread of ideas and fashions and led to a high degree of cultural uniformity.

The earliest known use of bronze in Europe, in the Unetice culture in central Europe about 2500 BC, was probably an independent development and not the result of influence from the Middle East. Bronze came into use in southeast Europe, the Aegean and Italy two hundred years later, followed by Spain and, finally, the British Isles in about 1800. Scandinavia, with no workable deposits of copper or tin, continued in the Stone Age until the middle of the 2nd millennium BC. By this time bronze had entered Scandinavia, brought by traders in exchange for amber and, probably, furs.

Bronze technology led to a rapid increase in the use of metals. Bronze weapons and tools kept an edge better than stone or copper, could easily be resharpened and when broken could be melted down and recast. It was expensive, however, and its use was largely confined to the social elites in the early Bronze Age. Stone tools, sometimes copying the style of prestigious bronze tools, continued in everyday use. Large quantities of bronze artifacts, often of the highest quality, were buried or sunk in bogs as offerings to the gods.

The social distinctions of Bronze Age society are apparent in burial practices: a minority of burials being richly furnished with grave goods and the majority with few offerings. In the earlier Bronze

early Bronze Age cultures, c.2300–1800
- late megalithic cultures
- Bell Beaker cultures
- Nordic late Neolithic cultures
- Cord Impressed Pottery cultures
- Catacomb Grave cultures
- Unetice culture
- Danubian–Carpathian Bronze Age cultures
- Balkan Bronze Age cultures
- early Aegean Bronze Age cultures
- North Italian Bronze Age cultures
- South Italian Bronze Age cultures

spread of Urnfield cultures in late Bronze Age
- by 14th century
- by 12th century
- by 9th century

- early Bronze Age barrow burial
- fortified site
- late Bronze Age urnfield
- metal hoard
- shipwreck
- settlement
- other site
- source of tin
- source of copper
- source of gold
- source of amber
- Mycenaean trade route
- main amber trade route

0   600 km
0   400 mi

Age three distinct burial practices are found. In southeast Europe the normal practice was burial of rich and poor alike in flat grave cemeteries. In most of eastern, northern and western Europe the poor were buried in flat graves but the rich were buried under earth mounds known as barrows. Barrows required a communal effort to build and are evidence of the power of the elites. In some parts of western Europe Neolithic-style communal burials in megalithic tombs continued until about 1200.

In southern and central Europe, large villages, often fortified, developed but in northern and western Europe the settlement pattern was one of dispersed homesteads. Population rose across Europe and agricultural settlers moved into many marginal upland areas. These were abandoned late in the Bronze Age, perhaps because of climatic deterioration or because the poor soils had been exhausted. As agricultural land rose in value, clear boundaries were laid out between communities in

TIMELINE

South and east Europe

2000	1500	1000
c.2500–1800 The Unetice culture appears in central Europe	c.1650 The Mycenaean civilization develops and traders are active in south Italy	c.1350 The Urnfield culture appears in central Europe
c.2300 Bronze working begins in southeast Europe		c.1200 Fall of the Mycenaean civilization
c.2000 Hillforts are built in central Europe		c.1000 Iron comes into widespread use in Greece
c.2000 The first European state emerges, in Crete		c.750 Beginning of the Hallstatt ("Celtic") Iron Age
c.2000 Trade routes across Europe appear for amber and metals		

West and north Europe

2000	1500	1000
c.2000 The Wessex culture flourishes in Britain, with rich barrow burials		1100 Hillforts are built in western Europe
c.2000 The main stage of Stonehenge, in southern Britain, is completed		1000 Urnfield cultures spread to western Europe
		c.700 Iron in widespread use throughout Europe

NEOLITHIC | BRONZE AGE | IRON AGE

sub-Neolithic forest hunters and gatherers

Rickeby
Hallunda
Vänern
Vättern
Tromøy
Kvarnby
Bulbjerg
Lake Peipus
Rezne
Western Dvina

VOTIVE offerings, thrown into the bogs, include this bronze and gold "chariot of the sun" from Trundholm (Denmark).

Trundholm
Brudevaelte
Egtved
Voldtofte
Kivik

4
Drenthe
Barger-Oosterveld
Perleberg
Biskupin
Jankowo
Kamieniec
Nieder-Neundorf
3
Schweinert
Miejsce
Toterfout
Leubingen
Grossenheim
Iwanowice
Pustinka
Court St Etienne
Helmsdorf
Bad Nauheim
Ivanja
Gedinne
Flörsheim
Postoloprty
Spissky Stvrtok
Donec group
Havré
Heidesheim
5
Unetice
Velatice
Barca
Moska
Dnieper
Mannheim
Blucina
Veterov
Rostov
Hagenam
Kelheim
Malé Kosihy
Wasserburg
Ettins
Unter-Radl
Mohi
Rixheim
Baldegg
Nitriansky Hrádok
Vál
Füzesabony
Usatove
Volders
Caka
Suciu du Sus
Tudoromo
1
Hölting
Ptuj
Kamenka
Cortaillod
Wittnauer Horn
Kisapostag
Tószeg
Monteoru
Crestaulta
Bled
Czorvas
Periam
Ledro
Angarano
Polada
Dobova
Gomalova
Vattina
Canegrate
Sava
Girla Mare
Danube
Fontanella
Cîrna
Black Sea
Bismantora
Tarnava
Ezerovo
Luni
Ezero
Corsica
Allumiere
Danja Slatina
Filitosa
Narce
ANATOLIA
Nuraghe
Phlegraean
Scoglio del
Albucci
Fields
Tonno
Troy
Barumini
Hittites
Sardinia
6
Lipara
Millazzo
Mycenae
Sicily
Cyprus
Borg in-Nadur
Crete
Malta
Knossos
Minoan civilization
Mediterranean Sea

Alps
Rhine
Danube
Po
Elbe
Oder
Vistula
CARPATHIAN MTS

---

many areas, especially northwest Europe, and farmland was enclosed into small fields that could be managed more intensively. Farmers benefited from the introduction of heavier plows, wheeled vehicles and horses. European wild oats were domesticated at this time, probably as horse fodder.

Around 1350 the Urnfield culture, named for its distinctive burial practices, appeared in Hungary. Bodies were cremated and the ashes buried in funerary urns in flat grave cemeteries of hundreds, even thousands, of graves. As with earlier Bronze Age burial customs, a minority of graves included rich offerings, weapons and armor. Some of these graves were covered with barrows, demonstrating a degree of continuity with the past, but this was by no means universal: the powers enjoyed by chieftains in the early Bronze Age may have been undermined to an extent by the emergence of a warrior class. By the 9th century Urnfield customs had spread over most of continental Europe. Except in the west where it

was probably taken by migrating Celtic peoples, the Urnfield culture spread mainly as a result of the wide-ranging contacts on trade links. The later Bronze Age saw increased militarization, with extensive fortress building in western Europe and the introduction of the bronze slashing sword. Bronze armor was introduced, but probably for display only: it offers less protection than leather.

Small numbers of iron artifacts appeared in many areas about 1200. However, iron tools first became common only around 1000 in Greece and two hundred and fifty years later in northern Europe.

1 Bronze Age settlements along the northern fringes of the Alps were often built on islands in lakes for defense.

2 One of the last megalithic tombs to be used was at Island, in Ireland; it was still in use about 1200 BC about a millennium later than most megalithic tombs.

3 At Leubingen, an early Bronze Age barrow contains the remains of an elderly man accompanied by a girl, pottery, stone and bronze tools and weapons, and gold jewelry.

4 A late Bronze Age dismantled wooden "temple" was deliberately sunk into a peat bog at Barger-Oosterveld.

5 The Urnfield cemetery at Kelheim of 900–800 BC had more than 10,000 burials.

6 Defensive towers called nuraghe were built about 1800 BC in Sardinia; similar structures are found in Corsica and the Balearic islands.

7 A shipwreck from 800 BC off the southwest coast of Spain included more than 200 bronze weapons made in the Loire region.

See also 1.20 (Neolithic Europe);
1.22 (Minoans and Mycenaeans)

The first cities and states in the western Mediterranean developed in the early Iron Age. The first were the Etruscan city-states of northern Italy, which had emerged by 800 BC. Then in the 8th century many cities were founded on the coasts of southern Italy, France, Spain and north Africa by Phoenician and Greek colonists. The Greeks had a strong impact on the Etruscan civilization while the Phoenician colonies in Spain influenced the growth of cities and states among the native Tartessian, Turdetanian and Iberian peoples by 500 BC.

The origin of the Etruscans is uncertain. Their language was unrelated to any other European language, suggesting that the Etruscans may have migrated into Italy from the Middle East. There is no convincing evidence of this, however, and it is more likely that the Etruscans were an indigenous people. The forerunner of the Etruscan civilization was the Villanova culture – the first iron-using culture in Italy – which developed in Tuscany around 900 and later spread north into the Po valley. This culture itself seems to have developed out of local Urnfield cultures. In Tuscany the Villanova culture was replaced by the Etruscan civilization in the 8th century BC but it survived in the Po valley until the 6th century when the area was overrun by the Etruscans.

Etruria was rich in iron and copper ores, had good agricultural land and a coastline with many natural harbors which encouraged the Etruscans to become active seafarers and traders. Most early Etruscan cities were sited a few kilometers from the coast, close enough for convenience but not vulnerable to pirate raids. Each city was an independent state ruled by a king but the twelve most important cities were loosely united in the Etruscan league. From the 8th century the Etruscans faced competition from Greek and Phoenician colonies in the western Mediterranean. The foundation of the Greek colony at Massilia around 600 was a particularly serious development as it shut the Etruscans out of the important trans-Gallic tin routes. To some extent this was offset by Etruscan expansion into the Po valley in the 6th century, which brought them control of the transalpine and Adriatic trade routes

and diverted some trade away from the Greek colonies. With Carthaginian help, the Etruscans succeeded in driving the Greeks out of Corsica in 535 but attacks on the Greeks at Kymai (Cumae) in southern Italy were repulsed in 524, 505 and 474. Despite these hostilities, Etruscan culture had become very Hellenized by the 6th century.

The other major group of peoples in Italy were the Italic speakers who had probably migrated into Italy from central Europe during Urnfield times. Though most of the Italic peoples were still organized into tribes in 500 BC, city-states had developed among the Latins as a result of Etruscan influence. The leading Latin city was Rome. The Romans expelled their Etruscan king in 509 and founded a republic but Rome was still little more than a market town.

Carthage was not the earliest Phoenician colony in north Africa but its fine harbor and strategic position had made it into the most important by the mid 7th century.

Map legend

- Villanova early Iron Age culture, c.900
- Etruria, c.600
- area under Etruscan domination, c.500
- Carthaginian empire, c.500
- area settled and controlled by Greeks, c.500
- Iberian peoples
- Tartessian–Turdetanian peoples
- Italic peoples
- Illyrian peoples
- Celtic and related peoples, c.500
- Hallstatt heartland, c.700
- ■ Etruscan city
- ■ Greek city
- ■ other city
- trans-Gallic tin route
- transalpine trade route
- → major migration

0   400 km
0   300 mi

Map labels

ATLANTIC OCEAN

Elviña · Coaña
Rianxo · Cameixa · El Redal
Cortes de Navarra
Ebro
Douro
Terroso · Soldeana · Azaila
Lusitanians · Celtiberians · Iber[i]
Tagus
Pedra de Oiro · Saguntum
Guadiana · Hemeroskopei[on]
KINGDOM OF TARTESSOS c.600 · Lucentum · Elche
Guadalquivir · Porcuna
Tartessians
Niebla · El Carambolo · Turdetanians
Tartessos (Huelva) · Osuna
[1]
Gades · Mainake · Malaca · Sexi · Abdera
Carteia
Tingis · Rusaddir
Lixus
Berbers

Side notes

[1] By 600 BC, Tartessos was the capital of a wealthy kingdom, and the region saw rapid urban growth under Phoenician and Carthaginian influence in the 6th century.

[2] The Hallstatt Iron Age culture (c.750–450) is named for a rich cemetery at an ancient salt-mining center in the Austrian Alps.

[3] The stone defenses of the 6th-century Celtic fort at Heuneburg show the influence of Greek architecture.

[4] Until the end of the 6th century, the main importance of the small market town of Rome was its control of the main crossing point of the river Tiber.

[5] The Lipari Islands were the base for Greek pirates in the 6th and 5th centuries.

[6] A joint Carthaginian–Etruscan force defeated the Greeks off Corsica in 539, halting Greek colonization in the western Mediterranean.

[7] Populonia was the main iron-working center of Italy from the 6th century; around 10,000 tonnes of iron ore were imported from Elba and smelted there annually.

TIMELINE

Etruscans and Italy

800		600	
c.900 Emergence of the Villanova culture	733 Foundation of the Greek colony of Syracuse on Sicily	550 The Etruscans gain control of the Po valley	
c.800 Emergence of Etruscan civilization	616 An Etruscan monarchy is set up in Rome	499 Rome defeats the Latins	
	753 Traditional date of the foundation of Rome	c.600 Formation of the Etruscan league	

Carthage

814 Traditional date of the foundation of Carthage	c.654 Phoenician colonies are set up on the Balearic Islands	539 An Etruscan-Carthaginian force expels the Greeks from Corsica	
800–600 Main period of Phoenician and Greek colonization in the west	c.620–540 Rule of King Arganthonios at Tartessos, and urban development in southern Spain	500 Beginning of Carthaginian expansion in southern Spain	
c.800 A Phoenician trading post is set up at Gades in southern Spain	580 The Carthaginians defeat Greek settlers at Lilybaeum		

Celts

Hallstatt Iron Age culture (central Europe)

c.600 The Celts settle in Iberia

800   600

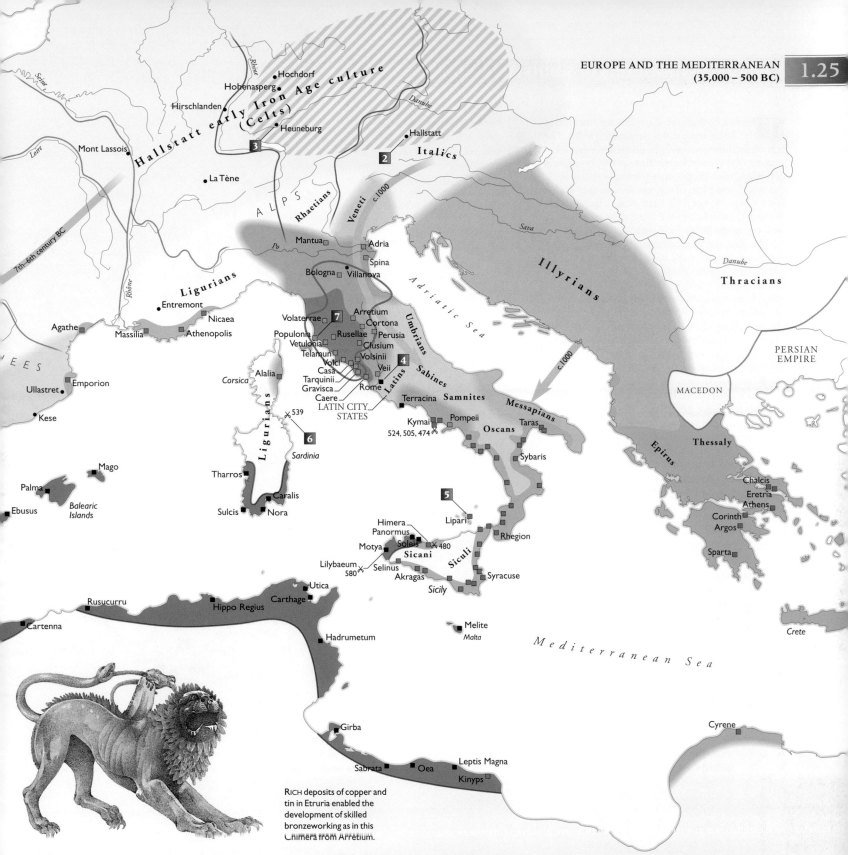

Hallstatt early Iron Age culture (Celts)

Hochdorf
Hohenasperg
Hirschlanden
Heuneburg
3
Mont Lassois
La Tène

Rhine
Seine
Loire

Danube

Hallstatt
2
Italics

ALPS

7th–6th century BC

Rhône
Po

Rhaetians
Veneti c.1000

Ligurians
Entremont
Nicaea
Agathe
Massilia
Athenopolis

Mantua
Adria
Spina
Bologna
Villanova

Volaterrae
7
Arretium
Cortona
Populonia
Rusellae
Perusia
Vetulonia
Clusium
Telamun
Volsinii
Volci
Veii
Casa
4
Tarquinii
Rome
Gravisca
Caere
LATIN CITY STATES
Latins

Umbrians

Sabines

Adriatic Sea

Illyrians

Sava

Danube

Thracians

PERSIAN EMPIRE

MACEDON

c.1000

Epirus
Thessaly

Emporion
Ullastret
Kese

Corsica
Alalia
×539
6
Sardinia

Ligurians

Terracina
Samnites
Messapians
Kymai
524, 505, 474 ×
Pompeii
Oscans
Taras
Sybaris

Chalcis
Eretria
Athens
Corinth
Argos

Mago
Palma
Ebusus
Balearic Islands

Tharros
Caralis
Sulcis
Nora

5
Lipari

Himera
Panormus
Motya
Soleis
× 480
Sicani
Siculi
Lilybaeum
580 ×
Selinus
Akragas
Sicily
Rhegion
Syracuse

Sparta

Rusucurru
Cartenna

Utica
Carthage
Hippo Regius

Hadrumetum

Melite
Malta

Mediterranean Sea

Crete

Girba

Sabrata
Oea
Leptis Magna
Kinyps

Cyrene

RICH deposits of copper and tin in Etruria enabled the development of skilled bronzeworking as in this Chimera from Arretium.

Although technically still subject to its parent city Tyre, Carthage had by this time begun its own independent colonization of the Balearic Islands. In 580 Carthage intervened in Sicily to protect Motya against the Greek city of Selinus and shortly after to support the Phoenician colonies in Sardinia against the natives. These actions established Carthage as the protector of the Phoenician colonies in the west and by 500 it had become the capital of a loose-knit maritime empire which dominated the western Mediterranean trade routes. The Greeks, however, succeeded in gaining control of most of Sicily in 480.

The area most influenced by the Phoenicians and Carthaginians was southern Spain. Gades (Cadiz) was an important Phoenician trading post from at least the 8th century, if not earlier, and Huelva –

almost certainly the ancient city of Tartessos – was a port with trading links with the Greeks, Phoenicians and Atlantic Europe by around 800. Excavations at Huelva have yielded huge quantities of imported pottery. Huelva's prosperity was based on exports of silver and other metals from southern Spain and of tin from Galicia, Brittany and Cornwall. By the 6th century a Tartessian kingdom had developed and fortified towns were being founded in the Guadalquivir valley. Phoenician techniques were incorporated into local metalworking and sculpture and a script based on the Phoenician alphabet was adopted. Urban development was also beginning in the Iberian area on the east coast of Spain by 500. Here too a Phoenician-based script was adopted.

The dominant influence in west and central

Europe in the 7th and 6th centuries was the Hallstatt culture, which is generally identified with the Celts. The Hallstatt culture began to develop in the 12th century BC from the Urnfield cultures of the upper Danube region. Bronze-using in its earlier stages, the Hallstatt culture adopted iron working in about 750. In the early 7th century the Celts spread west across Germany and France and by the early 6th century they had crossed the Pyrenees and occupied over half of the Iberian peninsula. The Celts there were quickly assimilated with the native peoples to produce a distinctive Celtiberian culture.

See also 1.21 (Bronze Age Europe), 1.23 (Greek and Phoenician colonization)

The first civilization of east Asia developed in the Yellow river valley in the 18th century BC from indigenous Neolithic cultures. Farming began as early as 5800 BC on the broad band of loess soils that stretches across the Yellow river basin. By 5000 millet farming villages of the Yangshao culture were spread across much of the region. At the same time rice farming communities were spreading among the wetlands of the Yangtze valley. Rice farming spread to the Yellow river valley in the late 4th millennium and the Longshan cultures emerged. In favorable areas, the Longshan cultures practiced intensive rice cultivation using irrigation. The population rose, copper came into use, regional trading networks developed and a warrior class emerged. There is evidence of warfare, such as rammed earth fortifications and massacres of prisoners. A system of divination based on the use of "oracle bones" was developed.

According to Chinese traditions, civilization was founded by the emperor Huang Di around 2698 BC while the first dynasty, the Xia, was founded by Yu the Great in about 2205. However, there is no evidence for states in China in the 3rd millennium.

The first historically and archeologically attested Chinese dynasty is the Shang. This was founded about 1766 BC by King Tang, around the time of the appearance of the Erlitou culture. Cities with monumental buildings began to develop craft specialization and advanced bronze-casting techniques were adopted. The appearance of rich burials points to the emergence of a powerful ruling elite. A pictographic script came into use: the modern Chinese script is its direct descendant. Shang cultural influence extended across most of northern China and as far south as the Yangtze river. Like many early states, the Shang kingdom combined directly run provinces and vassal states.

Around 1122 the Shang king Di-xin was defeated and overthrown by his vassal king Wu of Zhou. The dynasty established by Wu became the longest lived of Chinese history and the early centuries of its rule were looked back on as a golden age. To legitimize their rule after their usurpation of the Shang, the Zhou rulers introduced the theory of the "Mandate

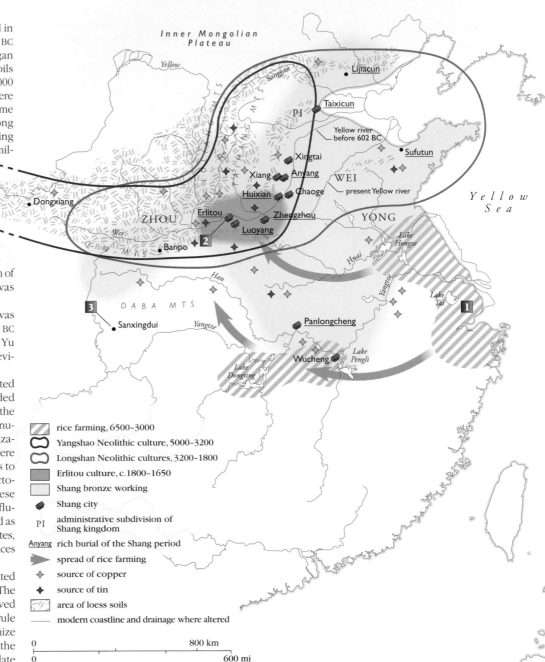

rice farming, 6500–3000

Yangshao Neolithic culture, 5000–3200

Longshan Neolithic cultures, 3200–1800

Erlitou culture, c.1800–1650

Shang bronze working

Shang city

PI administrative subdivision of Shang kingdom

Anyang rich burial of the Shang period

spread of rice farming

source of copper

source of tin

area of loess soils

modern coastline and drainage where altered

0   800 km
0   600 mi

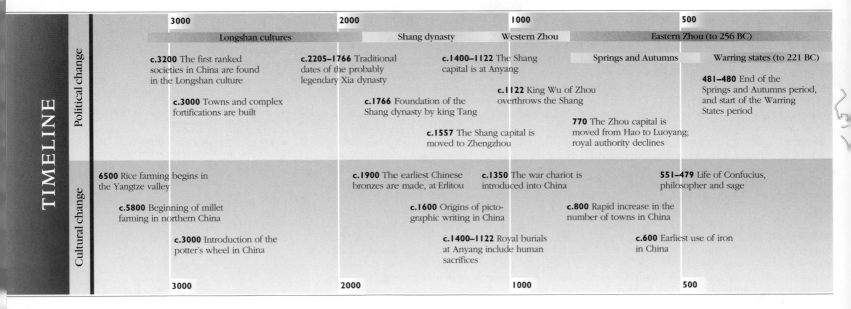

TIMELINE

	3000	**2000**	**1000**	**500**
	Longshan cultures	Shang dynasty	Western Zhou	Eastern Zhou (to 256 BC)
Political change	**c.3200** The first ranked societies in China are found in the Longshan culture	**c.2205–1766** Traditional dates of the probably legendary Xia dynasty	**c.1400–1122** The Shang capital is at Anyang	Springs and Autumns / Warring states (to 221 BC)
				481–480 End of the Springs and Autumns period, and start of the Warring States period
	c.3000 Towns and complex fortifications are built	**c.1766** Foundation of the Shang dynasty by king Tang	**c.1122** King Wu of Zhou overthrows the Shang	
			770 The Zhou capital is moved from Hao to Luoyang; royal authority declines	
		c.1557 The Shang capital is moved to Zhengzhou		
Cultural change	**6500** Rice farming begins in the Yangtze valley	**c.1900** The earliest Chinese bronzes are made, at Erlitou	**c.1350** The war chariot is introduced into China	**551–479** Life of Confucius, philosopher and sage
	c.5800 Beginning of millet farming in northern China	**c.1600** Origins of pictographic writing in China	**c.800** Rapid increase in the number of towns in China	
	c.3000 Introduction of the potter's wheel in China		**c.1400–1122** Royal burials at Anyang include human sacrifices	**c.600** Earliest use of iron in China
	3000	**2000**	**1000**	**500**

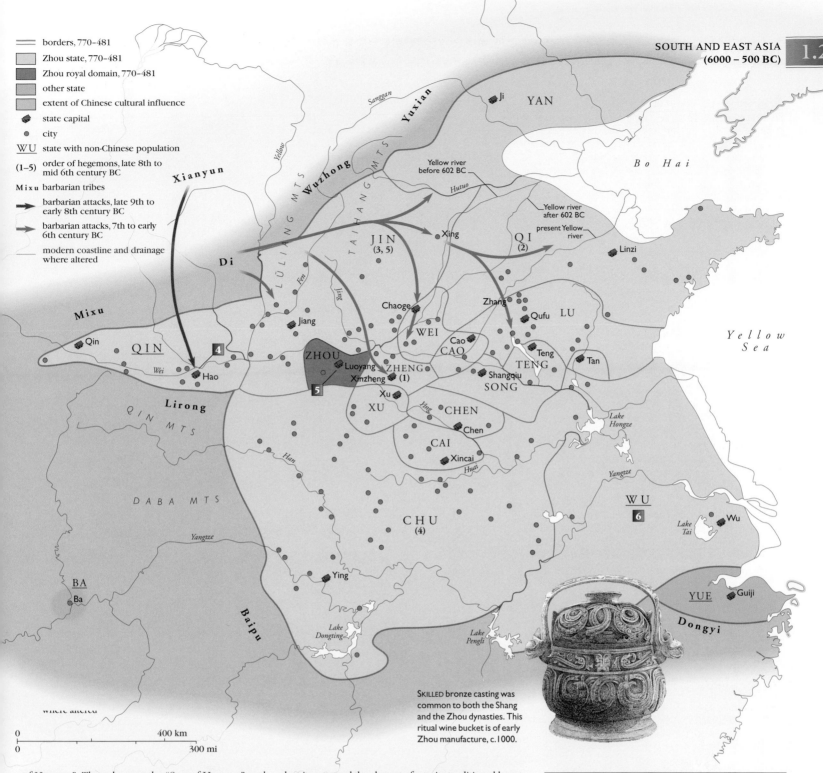

Legend:

- borders, 770–481
- Zhou state, 770–481
- Zhou royal domain, 770–481
- other state
- extent of Chinese cultural influence
- state capital
- city
- **WU** state with non-Chinese population
- (1–5) order of hegemons, late 8th to mid 6th century BC
- **Mixu** barbarian tribes
- barbarian attacks, late 9th to early 8th century BC
- barbarian attacks, 7th to early 6th century BC
- modern coastline and drainage where altered

SKILLED bronze casting was common to both the Shang and the Zhou dynasties. This ritual wine bucket is of early Zhou manufacture, c.1000.

0 | 400 km
0 | 300 mi

---

of Heaven". The ruler was the "Son of Heaven" and "All under Heaven" was his lawful domain so long as he was just and moral. Should a ruler become unjust, Heaven would send him a warning and if he failed to reform, the Mandate would be given to another. Di-xin had been a sadist so Heaven had transferred the right to rule to the Zhou. This theory, which could be used both to condemn disobedience to the ruler and to justify successful usurpation, remained central to Chinese imperial ideology.

The Zhou kingdom was a decentralized feudal state, divided into fiefs governed by dukes chosen from among the king's relatives and trusted supporters. Only the royal domain was directly ruled by the king. In 770 barbarian attacks on Hao forced the Zhou to move their capital to Luoyang. This event was a turning-point in the history of the dynasty and marks the beginning of the period of disorder and fragmentation known as the Springs and Autumns period (after the title of the annals of the state of Lu).

Luoyang was more centrally situated than Hao

but it removed the dynasty from its traditional heartland in the west; its authority began to decline. By this time the king controlled less land than most of his dukes who now became, in effect, the rulers of independent states, making almost constant war on one another. However, the dukes continued to recognize the sovereignty of the king and also recognized the duke of the leading state of the time as hegemon (with general primacy over all other states). The Springs and Autumns period turned into the Warring States period (480–221), which saw the decline of feudal relationships and the rise of a professional bureaucracy.

The Springs and Autumns period was a brutal age but it saw great creativity in literature and religious and philosophical thought. The end of the period saw Confucius found the ethical system which remains fundamental to Chinese thought. Iron working was adopted around 600, probably in Wu, though iron tools and weapons did not replace bronze in everyday use until the 2nd century BC.

1 More than a hundred wet-rice farming villages (using flooded fields) were established in this region 6500–4000 BC.

2 Erlitou was the site of the first Chinese bronzes c.1900 BC; it was probably also the first Shang capital.

3 The city and ritual offering pits at Sanxingdui, discovered in the 1990s, are evidence of a bronze-using civilization contemporary with the Shang.

4 Hao, in the original Zhou heartland, was abandoned as the capital in 770 after barbarian attacks. The move initiated a decline in Zhou authority.

5 The Zhou royal domain was limited to a small area around Luoyang by the 7th century.

6 Wu, the dominant state in southern China in the late 6th century, was destroyed by Yue in 473 BC.

See also 1.03 (agriculture)

The domestication of maize around 2700 made possible the development of permanent farming villages in Mesoamerica by 2300. Most early farmers practiced slash-and-burn agriculture, which cannot support dense populations. However, on fertile river flood-plains in the tropical forests of southeastern Mexico, reliable rainfall and year-round warmth made it possible to raise four crops of maize a year, which provided the economic base for the Olmec civilization.

By 1250 BC the Olmec lived in chiefdoms or small states ruled by a powerful hereditary elite. The most important sites were ceremonial centers with earth pyramid mounds and monumental stone sculptures of gods and chiefs. Associated with the ceremonial centers were settlements of two to three thousand people. The ritual centers were periodically destroyed and sculptures defaced or buried. Though possibly due to warfare between chiefdoms or states, it is more likely that this served a ritual purpose, marking the end of calendrical cycles, the death of a ruler or the accession of a new dynasty. Trade and gift exchange played an important part in the Olmec way of life. The Olmec lands have few natural resources and the raw materials for everyday tools, stone sculpture and status enhancing display objects had to be imported over long distances. Gift exchange played an important part in the diffusion of Olmec culture as the emerging elites of neighboring communities took up Olmec beliefs and artifacts to enhance their prestige. Late in their history, the Olmec developed a rudimentary hieroglyphic script which was used mainly for astronomical inscriptions. They used – and may have originated – both the Mesoamerican 260-day sacred year and the 52-year "long-count" calendar.

The Maya originated about 1200 BC in the Guatemalan highlands, developing from earlier Archaic cultures, and began to spread out into the lowlands of the Yucatán peninsula around 1000. By draining and canalizing swamps the Maya were able to

CARVED in rare blue jade, this tiny bust of a woman has the distinctive monumental quality which characterizes all Olmec sculpture.

Olmec, c.1250–400
Maya, c.1000
Maya, c.800
Zapotec, c.1400–400
Olmec ceremonial center
site with Olmec or Olmec influenced art
Olmec trade route
source of basalt
source of hematite
source of jade
source of obsidian
source of serpentine
northern limit of farming cultures, c.500 BC

0   600 km
0   400 mi

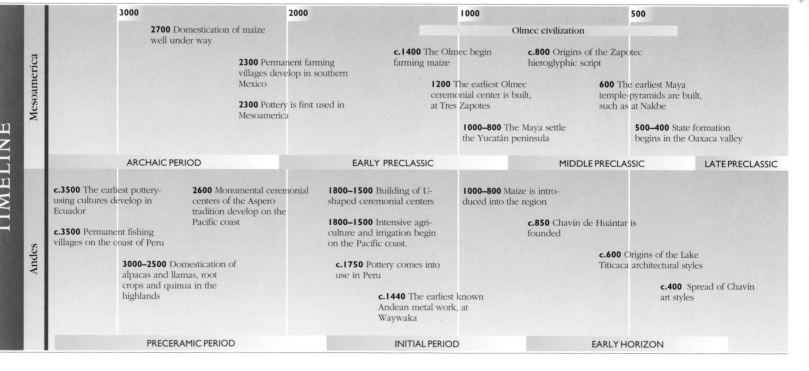

		3000		2000		1000		500	

Mesoamerica

2700 Domestication of maize well under way

Olmec civilization

c.1400 The Olmec begin farming maize

c.800 Origins of the Zapotec hieroglyphic script

2300 Permanent farming villages develop in southern Mexico

1200 The earliest Olmec ceremonial center is built, at Tres Zapotes

600 The earliest Maya temple-pyramids are built, such as at Nakbe

2300 Pottery is first used in Mesoamerica

1000–800 The Maya settle the Yucatán peninsula

500–400 State formation begins in the Oaxaca valley

ARCHAIC PERIOD   EARLY PRECLASSIC   MIDDLE PRECLASSIC   LATE PRECLASSIC

Andes

c.3500 The earliest pottery-using cultures develop in Ecuador

2600 Monumental ceremonial centers of the Aspero tradition develop on the Pacific coast

1800–1500 Building of U-shaped ceremonial centers

1000–800 Maize is introduced into the region

c.3500 Permanent fishing villages on the coast of Peru

1800–1500 Intensive agriculture and irrigation begin on the Pacific coast.

c.850 Chavín de Huántar is founded

3000–2500 Domestication of alpacas and llamas, root crops and quinua in the highlands

c.1750 Pottery comes into use in Peru

c.600 Origins of the Lake Titicaca architectural styles

c.400 Spread of Chavín art styles

c.1440 The earliest known Andean metal work, at Waywaka

PRECERAMIC PERIOD   INITIAL PERIOD   EARLY HORIZON

TIMELINE

produce sufficient food to support a complex society and by 600 towns, such as Nakbe and Komchen, with monumental temple pyramids, were developing. Complex societies also developed among the Zapotec people of the Oaxaca valley by the 1st millennium BC. Here food production was increased by simple irrigation techniques and terracing. By 400 BC there were at least seven small states in the valley, the most important of which was centered on Monte Albán, and a system of hieroglyphic writing had been developed. In the Valley of Mexico highly productive agriculture using *chinampas* – raised fields built on reclaimed swamps – led to the development of trading networks, a market economy, craft specialization and large villages by around 200 BC.

The earliest complex societies in South America developed on the desert coast of Peru in settled fishing communities during the Preceramic period (3750–1800 BC). The marine resources of this area are unusually rich and these communities were able to free labor for the construction of temples and ceremonial centers under the direction of village leaders. One of the earliest such centers was built at Aspero around 2600: it consisted of six mounds nine meters high, topped with masonry ceremonial structures. Cotton, squash and gourds (used as floats for fishing nets) were cultivated but farming did not make a significant contribution to the diet. In the highlands, herding alpacas or llamas and cultivation of root crops such as potatoes, ullucu and oca or quinua, a cereal, gradually replaced hunting and gathering during the Preceramic; permanent villages with small ceremonial buildings also developed.

During the Initial Period (1800–800 BC) the area of cultivable land in the coastal lowlands was greatly extended through irrigation works, diverting water from the rivers which flowed from the Andes through the desert to the coast. Pottery was adopted. Huge U-shaped ceremonial centers, requiring the control of considerable resources of labor, food supplies and raw materials, were constructed: one at Garagay is estimated to have required 3.2 million work-days to complete. These sites were probably focal points for local chiefdoms but burial practices show few distinctions of wealth or rank. Interaction between the fishing communities on the coast and the farming communities in the desert river valleys and the mountains was considerable, with salt, seaweed and dried fish from the coast being exchanged for carbohydrate foods such as root crops and grain from the highlands and river valleys.

The Early Horizon (about 800–200 BC) saw the development of sophisticated architecture and complex sculptural styles at the highland ceremonial center of Chavín de Huántar. The Chavín style was the culmination of styles which had originated as early as 1200 in other Andean and coastal sites and by 400 its influence had spread over a wide area of coastal and highland Peru. Chavín had a population of two to three thousand at its peak in the 4th century but thereafter it declined, without developing into a full urban civilization. Complex societies, united by common beliefs, also developed in the Lake Titicaca basin during the Early Horizon. Particularly important is the ceremonial center at Chiripa, built 600–400 BC, in which can be seen the origins of the architectural styles of the 5th-century AD Tiahuanaco state. Maize became an important crop in the Andes during this period.

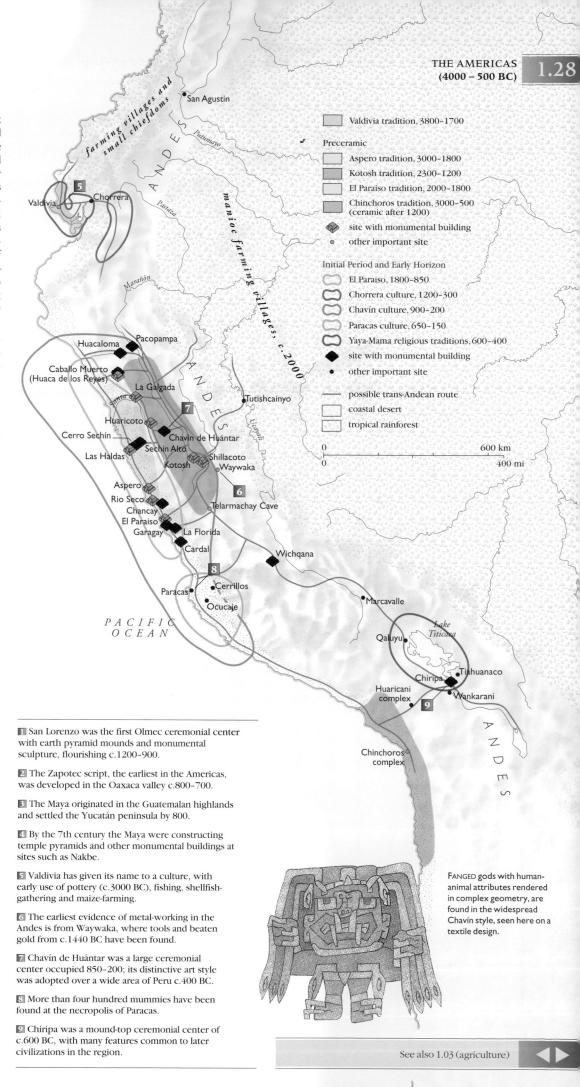

1 San Lorenzo was the first Olmec ceremonial center with earth pyramid mounds and monumental sculpture, flourishing c.1200-900.

2 The Zapotec script, the earliest in the Americas, was developed in the Oaxaca valley c.800-700.

3 The Maya originated in the Guatemalan highlands and settled the Yucatán peninsula by 800.

4 By the 7th century the Maya were constructing temple pyramids and other monumental buildings at sites such as Nakbe.

5 Valdivia has given its name to a culture, with early use of pottery (c.3000 BC), fishing, shellfish-gathering and maize-farming.

6 The earliest evidence of metal-working in the Andes is from Waywaka, where tools and beaten gold from c.1440 BC have been found.

7 Chavín de Huántar was a large ceremonial center occupied 850-200; its distinctive art style was adopted over a wide area of Peru c.400 BC.

8 More than four hundred mummies have been found at the necropolis of Paracas.

9 Chiripa was a mound-top ceremonial center of c.600 BC, with many features common to later civilizations in the region.

Valdivia tradition, 3800-1700

Preceramic

Aspero tradition, 3000-1800

Kotosh tradition, 2300-1200

El Paraiso tradition, 2000-1800

Chinchoros tradition, 3000-500 (ceramic after 1200)

site with monumental building

other important site

Initial Period and Early Horizon

El Paraiso, 1800-850

Chorrera culture, 1200-300

Chavín culture, 900-200

Paracas culture, 650-150

Yaya-Mama religious traditions, 600-400

site with monumental building

other important site

possible trans-Andean route

coastal desert

tropical rainforest

0   600 km
0   400 mi

FANGED gods with human-animal attributes rendered in complex geometry, are found in the widespread Chavín style, seen here on a textile design.

See also 1.03 (agriculture)

Cross-referencing
References to other dictionary entries are identified in small capitals (e.g. ACROPOLIS*); references to map spreads are denoted by the use of an arrow (eg.* ▷ 1.21*).*

Dating
For the purposes of this dictionary, the end of the Paleolithic period of early human prehistory, about 10,000 BC/12,000 years ago (i.e. the end of the Pleistocene Ice Age), is taken as the boundary between geological and historical time. Earlier dates are therefore given in years ago (ya), while dates after the end of the Paleolithic are given using the conventional BC/AD system.

Chinese spellings
Since 1979 the standard international system for the transliteration of Chinese names into Roman characters has been Pinyin, and this is the system used throughout this dictionary.

ABU SIMBEL
The site of two massive rock temples built by the Egyptian PHARAOH RAMESSES II (r.c.1290–1224 BC) on the Nile, 250 kilometers (155 miles) south of Aswan. The largest temple is fronted by four colossal statues of Ramesses. The smaller temple is dedicated to Ramesses' queen, Nefertari. In the 1960s, the temples were lifted and reconstructed above the waters of Lake Nasser. ▷ 1.18

ACHEA, ACHEANS
A region in the northwestern Peloponnese. The Achaeans were one of the peoples of Greece mentioned by HOMER as fighting at TROY. They were divided among a number of settlements, which shared common citizenship and COINAGE. Achaea formed a confederacy with other Peloponnesian cities in the Hellenistic period, but was overwhelmed by ROME in 146 BC. ▷ 1.23, 1.24

ACHEMENES
Founding ancestor of the ACHEMENID royal dynasty of Persia. He probably ruled the kingdom of Parsumash in western Iran in the early 7th century BC as a vassal of the MEDIAN EMPIRE. Achemenes may have led an army against King SENNACHERIB of ASSYRIA in 681 BC. ▷ 1.15

ACHEMENID EMPIRE
Persian empire ruled by the Achemenid dynasty (550–331 BC), named after its founding ancestor, ACHEMENES. The empire was established by CYRUS 11(559–530 BC), who took over the MEDIAN throne (550 BC) and conquered LYDIA, BABYLONIA, Bactria and GANDHARA. By the reign of DARIUS I (522–530 BC), the empire extended from Greece to the Indus, and from the Persian Gulf to the Aral Sea, with an administrative capital at SUSA and royal center at PERSEPOLIS. This period is often regarded as a golden age

of Persian artistic and architectural achievement, and was important for the cultural contacts made possible between the Mediterranean civilizations and those of the Middle East and south Asia.

The empire was administered by 20 provincial governors (satraps), with a regular system of tribute and a large army of regular soldiers and levies controlled by the king. Imperial expansion came to an end after defeats by the Greeks in 490 and 480 BC. The empire gradually declined until it was conquered by Alexander the Great, who deposed the last of the Achemenids, Darius III, in 330 BC. ▷ 1.15, 1.26

ACHEULIAN
Cultural tradition of the LOWER PALEOLITHIC period that originated in Africa and spread to Europe with HOMO ERECTUS populations, about 1.5–0.2 million ya. The Acheulian is distinguished by the use of hand-axes, multi-purpose animal butchery and processing tools with a continuous, sharp working edge and a tapered or pointed end, that were designed for piercing, chopping, cutting and scraping. ▷ 1.01

ACROPOLIS
Literally the "high part" of any Greek city, often used as a center for defense. The most famous acropolis is in Athens; it became the ceremonial and religious center of the city and home of the Parthenon.

ADAD-NIRARI II
King of ASSYRIA (r.911–891 BC), who initiated renewed Assyrian expansion and the establishment of the Neo-Assyrian empire. He undertook campaigns against ARAMEANS and Babylonians, securing Assyrian dominance in central MESOPOTAMIA. ▷ 1.13

ADENA
Complex HUNTER-GATHERER and farming culture of the middle Ohio river valley, in the eastern woodlands of North America (c.1000 BC–AD 100). Adena communities lived in permanent villages and had a rich material culture including pottery, smoking pipes, and COPPER, mica and seashell ornaments. Their mixed hunting, fishing, food-gathering and farming economy supported a large population, and their impressive burial and ceremonial monuments (such as Great Serpent Mound) suggest the development of social ranking and chiefly authority. This cultural tradition was elaborated by the succeeding Hopewell culture. ▷ 1.06

AEOLIA, AEOLIAN GREEKS
According to legend, the Aeolian Greeks fled from the Greek mainland after the collapse of the MYCENAEN world in the 11th century BC. They came to settle on the west coast of Asia Minor, including the island of Lesbos, where they retained a distinctive dialect and developed their own style of architecture. Like

other Greeks, they developed city-states (POLIS) from the 8th century BC. ▷ 1.23, 1.24

AFANASEVO CULTURE
NEOLITHIC culture of southern Siberia from about 2300 to 1500 BC, in the steppe/taiga region to the north of the Altai mountains, along the upper reaches of the Yenisey and Ob rivers. It had a mixed hunting, farming and herding economy (domestic SHEEP, CATTLE and HORSES), a ROUND BARROW funerary tradition, and decorated pottery and COPPER metallurgy. Similar cultures occupied the steppes further to the west, from the Altai to southern Russia. ▷ 1.04

AGADE
See AKKAD

AGAMEMNON
Legendary king of MYCENAE and leader of the Greek forces to TROY. His quarrel with the hero Achilles is the main theme of HOMER's epic, the ILIAD. On his return to Mycenae he was murdered by his wife, Clytemnestra, and her lover, Aegisthus. ▷ 1.22

AHAB
King of ISRAEL (r.c.874–853 BC) and son of Omri. Often at war with JUDAH and ARAM-DAMASCUS, in 854 BC he led the alliance of Levantine states that were opposed to Assyrian expansion. ▷ 1.14

AHMOSE
Egyptian PHARAOH (r.1550–1525 BC) who successfully drove the HYKSOS from Egypt and led campaigns into Syria and southwards into NUBIA. Ahmose firmly established the foundations of the NEW KINGDOM (1532–1070 BC). ▷ 1.18

AKHENATEN
Egyptian PHARAOH (r.1353–1335 BC), also known as Amenophis IV, who reacted against the power of the priests at the sacred city of THEBES by establishing a monotheistic religion based on Aten, the sun disk, whose rays were shown in paintings as shining on Akhenaten ("glory of the sun disk") and his family. He set up his own capital at Akhetaten (now known as EL-ARMANA) in Middle Egypt. After his death Akhenaten was treated as a heretic, and the old gods were restored. ▷ 1.18

AKKAD
A region of south MESOPOTAMIA lying between the Euphrates and Tigris rivers to the northwest of SUMERIA. It was named after the unlocated city of Agade and was founded by SARGON OF AGADE in about 2300 BC, probably near BABYLON on the Euphrates. Akkad was the power base of Sargon's short-lived Akkadian dynasty, which established the first imperial STATE in world history (c.2330–2193 BC). At the height of its power, under Sargon's grandson, NARAM-SIN

(c.2254–2218 BC), the Akkadian empire dominated all of MESOPOTAMIA, the northern LEVANT and possibly southeast Anatolia and western Iran, before collapsing as a result of internal weakness and AMORITE and GUTIAN invasions. The Akkadians established their Semitic dialect as the official language and adopted Sumerian CUNEIFORM as a writing system. Akkadian formed the basis for later Babylonian and Assyrian writing. ▷ 1.04, 1.07, 1.10, 1.11

ALEUTS
Culture inhabiting the Aleutian Islands in the north Pacific, which extend from southwest Alaska towards the east coast of Siberia. The Aleuts had colonized the islands from the Alaskan mainland by about 2000 BC, living primarily by hunting marine and land mammals, and fishing. They had complex fishing technologies, sea-going boats and notable art traditions, particularly ceremonial masks, and bone and ivory carvings. ▷ 1.04, 1.05, 1.06

ALIGNMENT (MEGALITHIC)
Ceremonial monuments of the European NEOLITHIC that were probably used for processions and consist of large stones erected in lines. They are found mainly in Brittany (notably at CARNAC) and in western Britain (c.4000–2000 BC). Timber versions may also have existed. ▷ 1.20

ALTAMIRA
Cave site in northern Spain famous for its UPPER PALEOLITHIC paintings of bison and other animal and anthropomorphic figures. The cave was used by hunting communities over a long period, though the paintings are probably associated with SOLUTREAN and MAGDALENIAN occupation levels, (c.22,000-17,000 ya). ▷ 1.19

AMAKELITES
A group of nomadic tribes in southern JUDAH and Sinai in the early 1st millennium BC. The Amalekites were enemies of the HEBREWS, often raiding ISRAEL, but by the 8th century BC they were no longer a major threat. ▷ 1.14

AMENEMHET I
Egyptian PHARAOH of the MIDDLE KINGDOM (r.1991–1962 BC), who founded the 12th Dynasty and enforced strong Egyptian control over NUBIA. He initiated the practice of installing his son as co-ruler, so as to ensure a smoother succession from one pharaoh to the next. ▷ 1.18

AMENOPHIS IV
See AKHENATEN

AMORITES
Semitic people of Arabia, originally nomadic, who are mentioned in MESOPOTAMIAN records from about 2400 to 2000 BC, when their invasions contributed to the collapse of the

Akkadian empire (c.2193 BC) and later the Third Dynasty of UR (c.2000 BC). In the early 2nd millennium BC, Amorite kings established ruling dynasties in many Babylonian and Assyrian cities, assimilating Sumero-Akkadian culture. Amorites also settled in parts of Palestine in this period, and were sometimes associated with the CANAANITES. ▷ 1.11, 1.13

AMPHICTONIES
Leagues of cities associated with a particular Greek shrine (e.g. DELPHI). Amphictonies would oversee the arrangements for visitors and punish those who offended the dignity of the shrine. ▷ 1.24

ANDEAN CIVILIZATIONS
The cultures of the Andean region and adjacent coastal areas of western South America that developed CHIEFDOMS and later STATE systems, ceremonial centers, cities, and complex iconography and material culture. The history of Andean civilizations is divided into the following periods: PRECERAMIC (c.3750–2000 BC), INITIAL (2000–900 BC), EARLY HORIZON (900–200 BC), Early Intermediate (200 BC–AD 500), Middle Horizon (AD 500–1000), Late Intermediate (AD 1000–1475) and Late Horizon (AD 1475–1530). ▷ 1.04, 1.05, 1.06, 1.28

ANYANG
The last and most enduring of the SHANG capital cities ("Yin", c.1400–1100 BC), situated on a tributary of the Yellow river in Honan province, China. The urban settlement surrounded a palace and temple complex built on a massive, rammed earth platform. All the buildings were constructed of timber and clay, with thatch roofs, some elaborately painted. Stone and jade carvings, ORACLE BONES and evidence of bronze working and pottery manufacture have been found at the site. The royal cemetery nearby had at least 14 richly furnished tombs with grave goods that included magnificently decorated bronze vessels and other objects, and human and animal sacrifices. ▷ 1.27

ARAM, ARAMAEANS
Nomadic people who originally lived in Aram, a desert region in modern Syria, Jordan and western Iraq. The Arameans are first mentioned in Assyrian inscriptions in about 1100 BC, when they raided and settled in MESOPOTAMIA and the LEVANT. By 1000 BC Aramaean kingdoms were established from the Levant to BABYLONIA (where they were known as CHALDEANS). Western Aramaean kingdoms were eventually destroyed by the Assyrian king TIGLATH-PILESER III in 740–720 BC, while Aramaean dynasties in the east merged with the Babylonians. ▷ 1.12, 1.13, 1.14

ARAM-DAMASCUS
ARAMAEAN kingdom founded in about 1100 BC, with a capital at Damascus. It was a

major enemy of ISRAEL from the 10th to 8th centuries BC, until it was annexed by the Assyrians in 732 BC. ▷ 1.14

ARAMAIC LANGUAGE
Semitic language widely adopted in the Middle East following the ARAMAEAN migrations and the development of written Aramaic, using a phonetic script derived from the CANAANITE alphabet (by c.1100 BC). This became the main script used in the Middle East when it was adopted by the Assyrians from about 800 BC, replacing CUNEIFORM. ▷ 1.07, 1.12, 1.13, 1.15

ARCADIA
The central region of the Peloponnese. Although it is relatively unfertile, the Roman poet Virgil portrayed it as a haven of rural bliss, an image that has remained in the European imagination. ▷ 1.24

ARCHAIC PERIOD
A period of MESOAMERICAN CIVILIZATION from about 7000 to 2000 BC, in which HUNTER-GATHERER societies intensified food collection practices and modified plant habitats, domesticating several plant species, notably MAIZE (by c.2700 BC). Population growth, the development of permanent village settlements, intensive farming systems, the use of CERAMICS and long-distance OBSIDIAN exchange are all evident in Mexico by the late 3rd millennium BC.

ARCHAIC PERIOD (GREECE)
The period in Greek history before the Classical period, usually dated from about 750 to 480 BC. It saw the major expansion of the Greeks throughout the Mediterranean, the consolidation of the city-state (POLIS) and the appearance of important PAN-HELLENIC sites, such as OLYMPIA (the four-yearly OLYMPIC GAMES) and DELPHI (the ORACLE). The period also witnessed the birth of the Greek orders of architecture, the first marble sculptures and early lyric poetry. ▷ 1.24

ARDIPITHECUS RAMIDUS
The divergence of the evolutionary lineages of hominids and apes occurred about 6 million ya. Fossil remains of the earliest known hominid, *Ardipithecus ramidus* (found in Ethiopia), dating from about 4.4 million ya, show that it was a small animal about the size of a chimpanzee. It is not yet known whether it had developed the upright, bipedal gait characteristic of modern humans. This species probably evolved into the early australopithecines. ▷ 1.01

ARGOS
Greek city-state in the eastern Peloponnese and according to legend, the first to develop the HOPLITE phalanx as a means of defense. Argos was also a long-term rival of SPARTA, with whom it fought many wars between the 7th and 5th centuries BC. ▷ 1.24

ARVAD

City on the Levantine coast (modern Tripoli in Lebanon), probably founded by about 1000 BC. It was later the capital of a PHOENICIAN city-state, at times owing allegiance to a succession of Assyrian, BABYLONIAN and ACHEMINID kings. ▷ 1.12, 1.13, 1.14

ARYANS

Pastoralist people from central Asia with an INDO-EUROPEAN LANGUAGE, who invaded Iran and India in about 1500 BC. They may have been related to the KASSITES, who invaded the Middle East in about 1600 BC. The Aryans are described in Indian epic poems, the Rigvedas, which were first composed orally in archaic Sanskrit (c.1500–800 BC) and only later recorded in writing. They absorbed aspects of local culture and, by 900 BC, ruled most of northern India, establishing small kingdoms, which coalesced into larger states in the following centuries. The relevance of the Aryans to the question of Indo-European language origins is much disputed, and the identification of an Aryan "race" has no foundation in biological anthropology. ▷ 1.05, 1.06, 1.26

ARZAWA

Kingdom in western Anatolia that was conquered on several occasions by the HITTITES, and a vassal of the Hittite empire for a period in the 17th century BC. Arzawa was at its most powerful from the 15th to 14th centuries BC, but was reconquered by the Hittites in about 1300 BC and later became embroiled in power struggles within the Hittite empire. The collapse of the Hittites in about 1200 BC left Arzawa fragmented and it lost its separate political identity. ▷ 1.12

ASHUR

City in north MESOPOTAMIA situated on the river Tigris, at a strategic point on trade routes from SUMERIA to Anatolia and the LEVANT. It was founded in the 3rd millennium BC and had become a major trade center by about 1800 BC, when it was seized by the Amorite king, SHAMSHI-ADAD. An Akkadian dynasty ruled Ashur from about 1600 BC, overthrowing Mittanian domination in about 1330 BC, and renaming their kingdom ASSYRIA (after Ashur). It remained the Assyrian capital until about 878 BC, and, continued to be the religious capital when the political center moved elsewhere. The city was destroyed by the BABYLONIANS in 614 BC. ▷ 1.11, 1.12, 1.13

ASHURBANIPAL

The last great king of ASSYRIA (r.668–627 BC). He completed the conquest of Egypt, installing Necho I as vassal ruler. Assyrian garrisons were later expelled, but Egypt was no longer a threat to Assyrian dominance. He suppressed rebellions in the LEVANT, expelled the CIMMERIANS, reconquered BABYLONIA and

conquered ELAM by 639 BC. Ashurhanipal greatly overstretched the resources of the empire, while his tyrannical rule created wide discontent. After his death the empire rapidly declined, due to MEDIAN invasions and the resurgence of BABYLON. ▷ 1.13, 1.15

ASHURBANIPAL II

King of ASSYRIA (r.883–859 BC). Ashurbanipal III conquered north MESOPOTAMIA and the Levantine coast, using cavalry on a large scale, and enforced Assyrian dominance by means of terror tactics and the resettlement of conquered populations. He moved the royal capital to KALHU. ▷ 1.13

ASPERO TRADITION

Cultural tradition of the Andean PRECERAMIC PERIOD that produced the first ceremonial monument complexes in South America (c.3000–1800 BC), with sedentary settlement and an increasing reliance on agriculture. It is named after the site of Aspero, one of the earliest ceremonial sites in lowland Peru, consisting of six large earthen mounds with masonry temples (c.2600 BC). ▷ 1.04, 1.28

ASSYRIA

Region of north MESOPOTAMIA centered on the Upper Tigris in modern Iraq. The name derives from ASHUR, an early city-state that was seized by SHAMSHI-ADAD (c.1800 BC), who established a short-lived empire (the Old Assyrian period). The Akkadian dynasty, which ruled Assyria from about 1600 BC, were vassals of MITTANI or BABYLON until Ashuruballit I overthrew Mittanian domination in about 1330 BC. This initiated the Middle Assyrian empire (c.1330–1076 BC), which at its greatest extent under Tukulti-Ninurta I (r.1243–1207 BC) controlled MESOPOTAMIA and dominated most of the LEVANT, Anatolia and ELAM. The empire collapsed in the face of ARAMAEAN invasions.

The Neo-Assyrian empire (c.911–612 BC), the period of Assyria's greatest expansion and cultural achievement, was initiated by ADAD-NIRARI II (r.911–891 BC) and maintained by a series of powerful and warlike kings. The empire reached its greatest extent under ASHURBANIPAL (668–627 BC), but disintegrated after his death and was destroyed by the MEDES and Babylonians in 612 BC. Assyrian imperialism is notable for its military innovations (the mass production of iron weaponry, huge professional armies and mass cavalry tactics), and its extreme ruthlessness (the use of terror and resettlement of conquered populations). The Assyrians are also noted for their architectural and sculptural achievements, especially monumental temples, fortifications, narrative friezes depicting campaigns and hunts, and huge gateway statues of winged bulls. ▷ 1.11, 1,12, 1.13

ATTICA

The territory of Athens, extending for 2,500 square kilometers (965 square miles) around

the city. Originally controlled by aristocratic clans, by the 5th century BC its inhabitants were well integrated into the city's democratic system through their membership of demes, local "village" communities. ▷ 1.24

AURIGNACIAN CULTURE

The earliest UPPER PALEOLITHIC stone tool industry in Europe (c.40,000–29,000 ya), associated with the colonization of the region by anatomically modem humans. It was characterized by a diverse new range of specialized stone and bone tools, such as burins, scrapers and projectile points, and by the appearance of complex works of art, including engraved pebbles, bone and ivory carvings, clay figurines and cave paintings (by 30,000 ya). ▷ 1.19

AUSTRALOPITHECUS AFARENSIS

The earliest australopithecine hominid, living about 4 million to 3 million ya. Fossil remains have been found at HADAR in Ethiopia and at LAETOLI in Tanzania. Lightly built and fully bipedal (though not a tool user), this species evolved into two later types of hominid – gracile AUSTRALOPITHECUS AFRICANUS and the larger AUSTRALOPITHECUS ROBUSTUS – and was possibly ancestral to the genus Homo. ▷ 1.01

AUSTRALOPITHECUS AFRICANUS

Hominid that lived in Africa about 3 million to 2 million ya and was contemporary with the related, but more heavily built, AUSTRALOPITHECUS ROBUSTUS. Fossils from Taung and Makapansgat in South Africa and KOOBI FORA in Tanzania suggest that this was a small, gracile hominid with teeth similar to those of humans. It is possibly the ancestor of HOMO HABILIS, though the human genus may have evolved from AUSTRALOPITHECUS AFARENSIS at an earlier date. ▷ 1.01

AUSTRALOPITHECUS ROBUSTUS

A heavily-built hominid that lived in Africa about 3 to 1 million ya, alongside the gracile AUSTRALOPITHECUS AFRICANUS and the earliest humans. It was characterized by massive jaws and teeth that were adapted to the consumption of tough vegetable foods rather than meat. Fossil remains have been found in eastern and southern Africa (notably at KOOBI FORA, OMO, OLDUVAI, SWARTKRANS and Sterkfontein). This species probably became extinct when HOMO ERECTUS, a sophisticated tool user, began to colonize new habitats, becoming more numerous and marginalizing australopithecine populations. ▷ 1.01

AVEBURY HENGE

Late NEOLITHIC enclosure in southern Britain, built in about 2800–2500 BC. It consists of a massive circular embankment, about 425 meters (1,394 feet) in diameter with an interior quarry ditch, enclosing the three largest STONE CIRCLES in Europe. The site was approached by an avenue of standing stones,

1.6 kilometers (1 mile) long, which lead from another stone circle (the Sanctuary). SILBURY HILL is located to the south. ▷ 1.20

BA

Early state with a non-Chinese population near the confluence of the Yangtze and Jialing rivers in Sichuan province, China. Ba became a feudal state, with Chinese overlords, that owed allegiance to the Western ZHOU in the 11th century BC. It was incorporated into the QIN empire from the late 4th century BC. ▷ 1.27

BABYLON

City on the Euphrates and the most important religious and cultural center of ancient MESOPOTAMIA. Probably founded in the mid-3rd millennium BC, it was the capital of an AMORITE dynasty from about 1895 BC, the best-known ruler being HAMMURABI, until it was destroyed by the Hittites in 1595 BC. It was the capital of a KASSITE dynasty from 1570 until 1158 BC, when it was sacked by the Elamites.

Babylon was subsequently ruled by a series of short-lived ARAMAEAN and CHALDEAN dynasties under Assyrian dominance, until the restoration of Babylonian independence in 626 BC. It was reconstructed by NEBUCHADNEZZAR (c.600 BC) to become the largest city in the world, covering 1,000 hectares (2,500 acres) with a population of over 100,000, and was defended by a massive double wall on both sides of the Euphrates. The most famous buildings in Babylon date from this period, including the ZIGGURAT of Marduk (the Tower of Babel) and the Ishtar Gate. The Greek historian Herodotus also mentions the Hanging Gardens, possibly part of one of the two palace complexes. Babylon was captured by the Persians in 539 BC and a revolt in 482 BC led to the widespread destruction of its ancient temples and fortifications. ▷ 1.11, 1.12, 1.13, 1.14, 1.15, 1.23

BABYLONIA

A region of south MESOPOTAMIA named after the city of BABYLON. It became a province of the Third Dynasty of UR in the late 3rd millennium BC and was established as an independent kingdom during the Old Babylonian period (c.1095–1595 BC), under the AMORITE dynasty founded by King Sumuabum (c.1895). Expansion into northern Mesopotamia by King HAMMURABI in about 1790–1755 BC briefly established Babylonia as the leading imperial power in the Middle East. After Hammurabi's death, Babylonia declined and after Babylon was sacked by the HITTITES in 1595 BC, it was so weakened that it was unable to resist a KASSITE invasion (c.1570 BC). Under the Kassites, Babylonia became a powerful state once again, and was frequently at war with its ASSYRIAN, Elamite and ARAMAEAN neighbors. This dynasty was swept away when the Elamites sacked Babylon in 1157 BC, opening the way to a series of ARAMAEAN and CHALDEAN dynasties. Babylonia became a mere vassal of the Assyrian empire from the mid-9th century BC, until its revival in the 7th century BC. During the Neo-Babylonian empire (c.626–539 BC), Babylonian independence was reasserted by King NABOPOLASSAR, who attacked Assyria and destroyed NINEVEH in 612 BC, ending Assyrian power and taking over their domains. His son, NEBUCHADNEZZAR, defeated the Egyptians in 605 BC, ensuring supremacy in the Middle East. The empire lasted until 539 BC, when Babylonia was taken over by CYRUS the Great, becoming the wealthiest satrapy of the ACHEMENID EMPIRE. The rich cultural heritage of SUMER and AKKAD was adopted by later Babylonian rulers, who maintained their religious, artistic, architectural and literary traditions until conquest by the Persians in the 6th century BC. ▷ 1.12, 1.13, 1.15

BANAS CULTURE

Culture of the Banas valley, Rajasthan, influenced by the late INDUS CIVILIZATION, with stone and clay houses, Black-and-Red ware pottery and bronze tools. The principal settlement at Ahar is dated from about 2200 to 1500 BC. The Banas culture survived the collapse of the Indus civilization and Black-and-Red ware pottery became widespread across southern India after 1800 BC. ▷ 1.26

BANDKERAMIK CULTURE

The earliest farming culture of the central European NEOLITHIC, from 5400 to 4500 BC, characterized by distinctive round-based decorated pottery, large timber LONGHOUSES, and slash-and-burn horticulture. It spread through a gradual colonization process from the Balkans across the loess lands of central Europe, as far as Poland, the Netherlands and France, exploiting domestic plant and animal species that were derived from the Near East. ▷ 1.20

BANTU

An African language group that originated in the equatorial region of Cameroon. Bantu-speaking herders and farmers, with their iron-working technology, spread eastwards and southwards from about 500 BC, replacing or influencing indigenous populations. Bantu speakers were dominant throughout central and southern Africa by AD 400. ▷ 1.06

BARLEY

Cereal plant native to the temperate regions of the Old World, from China to southern Europe and Egypt. Two varieties of barley were domesticated in the Middle East by 8000 BC. It was one of the staple crops of NEOLITHIC farming communities. ▷ 1.03, 1.08, 1.09, 1.16

BARROW, LONG

A type of early NEOLITHIC burial monument found in Europe in about 5000–2500 BC, consisting of an elongated rectangular, trapezoidal or oval mound built of earth or rock. The mounds cover one or more burials, often collective deposits of disarticulated skeletons, sometimes housed in timber or MEGALITHIC mortuary houses. ▷ 1.20

BARROW, ROUND

Multi-period burial monument found in many parts of the Old World, especially associated with NEOLITHIC and BRONZE AGE cultures of temperate Europe from about 3000 to 1000 BC, and steppe cultures (such as the SCYTHIANS) from about 3000 to 200 BC. Built of turf, earth and/or rock, sometimes with timber structures and mortuary houses, they usually cover single articulated burials, some with lavish grave goods. ▷ 1.21

BASILEUS

Literally Greek for "king", the word is normally used to describe Greek nobles of the 10th to 8th centuries BC, a class portrayed by HOMER. A CATTLE-owning aristocracy, they idealized feasting and the heroism of war. In the medieval Byzantine empire the word was used to describe the emperor.

BELL BEAKER CULTURES

Late NEOLITHIC and early BRONZE AGE cultures of Europe associated with distinctive decorated drinking vessels (beakers) and other objects, including COPPER and bronze items, often found as grave goods with single burials under ROUND BARROWS in about 2800–1800 BC. This tradition emerged in the Rhineland and the Netherlands and spread to Britain, central Europe, Atlantic France and Spain, probably adopted by local populations as a cult package. ▷ 1.04, 1.20, 1.21

BERINGIA

Continental shelf between Siberia and Alaska that was exposed as dry land several times during the last glaciation (c.45,000–40,000 ya; 33,000–28,000 ya; 22,000–12,000 ya), forming the Bering land-bridge across which humans migrated from Asia to America. The date of this is disputed, but PALEOINDIAN populations were present in North America by about 15,000–12,000 ya. ▷ 1.02

BIBLE LANDS

A region of the Middle East comprising most of modern Israel, Jordan, Lebanon and Syria. It is referred to in detail in the Old Testament, during the period of HEBREW colonization from the 12th century BC until the destruction of the last of the Hebrew kingdoms in about 587 BC. ▷ 1.14

BIMBISARA

King of Magadha (c.520–491 BC), one of the major Indian states of the Gangetic civilization. He expanded his territory by annexing neighboring kingdoms, forming the core area of the later Mauryan Empire. He was a friend and patron of the BUDDHA. ▷ 1.26

BOEOTIA
Region of central Greece, neighboring ATTICA, that was a fertile area of many settlements, the most prominent of which was Thebes. Its central position made it the focus of many wars between surrounding city-states. ▷ 1.24

BOOK OF THE DEAD
A book of spells that was designed to help Egyptians make the transition into the next world safely. Usually written on papyrus, it was placed beside the mummified body of the deceased.

BOW AND ARROW
A hunting and fighting weapon used for precision killing at a distance from the target. The earliest preserved examples are MESOLITHIC in date, but stone and bone arrow points found in Europe and Africa suggest that they were first used by modern humans about 20,000 ya. The bow was introduced into the Americas from Asia in about 2000 BC. ▷ 1.18

BOWL CULTURES
First farming cultures of northwest Europe (c.4500–3300 BC), with regional traditions of round-based CERAMICS, tomb building (PASSAGE GRAVES and LONG BARROWS), and ceremonial enclosures. These cultures developed from MESOLITHIC communities who adopted ceramics and agriculture, at first perhaps more for ritual than subsistence purposes. ▷ 1.20

BOXGROVE
LOWER PALEOLITHIC fossil beach in southern Britain with the earliest human remains yet found in Europe (HOMO ERECTUS), about 500,000 years old. ACHEULIAN hand-axes and animal remains found *in situ* on the ancient beach surface provide important information about tool manufacture and butchery practices, with implications for early human cognition. ▷ 1.01

BRONZE AGE
A subdivision of the THREE AGE SYSTEM. It is now recognized that the idea of a Bronze Age is of limited value, being applicable only to Eurasia and north Africa, beginning at different times in different regions (e.g. c.4000 BC in MESOPOTAMIA and c.2000 BC in China), and being too general to describe the great variety of bronze-using cultures. ▷ 1.04, 1.05, 1.06, 1.09, 1.10, 1.11, 1.12, 1.16, 1.20, 1.21, 1.26, 1.27

BUDDHA (SIDDHARTHA GAUTAMA)
Founder of the Buddhist religion who was born at LUMBINI in north India in about 563 BC, son of the king of the Sakyas. He renounced his royal status and embarked on a period of learning, formulating a doctrine of personal spiritual enlightenment that attracted a growing number of disciples. He

was highly regarded by King BIMBISARA of Magadha. His teachings inspired a religious movement that spread rapidly, though it did not become a major organized religion until the 3rd century BC. The Buddha died at Kusinagara in about 483 BC. ▷ 1.06, 1.26

BYBLOS
NEOLITHIC settlement on the Levantine coast that became a major trading center, especially for the export of cedar wood to Egypt, by 2500 BC. It was the main city of PHOENICIA in the 11th century BC, but later declined as its rivals SIDON and TYRE grew more powerful. ▷ 1.09, 1.10, 1.11, 1.12, 1.13, 1.14

CALENDAR
Once it was realized that there was a regular year of 365 days, calendars came into operation to mark the passing of the year. They could be based on the cycles of the moon (hence the 12 months of the Egyptian, Greek and Roman calendars), or the sun. Any calendar based on full (e.g. 365) days is bound to become inaccurate with time (the true length of a year is approximately 365 ¼ days), so additional days or even months have to be entered to maintain accuracy. The Roman emperor Julius Caesar adapted an Egyptian solar calendar to solve inaccuracies in the Roman calendar, and it is this Julian calender, with some modifications (Pope Gregory, 1582), that is used today. The practice of dividing a day or night into 12 hours is Egyptian, and that of dividing hours into 60 minutes, Babylonian.

CAMBYSES II
ACHEMENID king of Persia (r.529–522 BC) and the son of CYRUS II. He annexed Egypt after the Battle of Pelusium and the capture of MEMPHIS in 525 BC, but failed to conquer the Nubian state of MEROË. He was possibly murdered in Syria in 522 BC by his brother, SMERDIS, who was deposed by DARIUS. ▷ 1.15

CANAANITES
Semitic people who had settled in the LEVANT, from Sinai to the Orontes river, by about 2000 BC, and established small city-states with a shared religion and alphabet. The Canaanites were culturally heterogenous with elements of pre-Semitic, Semitic and Mesopotamian culture, and Egyptian, Anatolian and Aegean influences. In southern Palestine they were conquered by the Israelites and PHILISTINES (c.1200 BC), the last enclaves being annexed by King DAVID in the early 10th century BC. Further north, the PHOENICIANS were partly descended from the Canaanites and maintained some Canaanite cultural traditions. ▷ 1.05, 1.07, 1.11, 1.12, 1.14, 1.23

CANAANITE ALPHABET
The Canaanite language appears to have been an early form of HEBREW. The CANAANITES developed the first known

phonetic alphabet, which was widely adapted in the LEVANT and Middle East from the late 2nd millennium BC. The PHOENICIAN version of this alphabet was the basis for the Old HEBREW, GREEK and LATIN (via Etruscan) alphabets. ▷ 1.07, 1.12, 1.14, 1.23

CARCHEMISH
City situated on the upper Euphrates, that was strategically placed to command the main trade routes from MESOPOTAMIA to the LEVANT and Anatolia. It was important in the 2nd millennium BC as a trading city and the administrative center of Mittani (c.1500–1350 BC), a vassal state dominated by the HITTITES (c.1350–1200 BC), and the most powerful of the Neo-Hittite city-states (c.1200–880 BC). Carchemish later became a vassal of the Neo-Asyrian empire and was annexed by SARGON II in 716 BC. In 605 BC it was the site of a battle between the Egyptians and Babylonians, which ended Egyptian attempts to regain their power in the Near East. ▷ 1.12, 1.13, 1.14

CARNAC
NEOLITHIC ceremonial center to the north of the Gulf of Morbihan in Brittany, with a dense concentration of MEGALITHIC tombs and alignments (c.4500–2000 BC). The alignments consist of parallel lines of menhirs (standing stones) in several segments on a line about 4 kilometers (2.5 miles) in length, some with enclosures at the ends, that were probably used for processions and other rituals. ▷ 1.20

CATACOMB GRAVE CULTURES
Early BRONZE AGE pastoral nomad cultures of the south Russian steppes (c.2300–1800 BC), characterized by ROUND BARROWS covering burial chambers, some of which contain wheeled vehicles. This was one phase of the longer Kurgan tradition (*kurgan* means "mound"), preceded by the Pit Grave culture, (c.3500–2300 BC) and followed by the Timber Grave phase. SCYTHIAN round-barrow burials are a later version of this tradition. ▷ 1.21

CATTLE
Animals derived from the wild aurochs (*Bos primigenius*), that were domesticated in Anatolia and the Balkans by about 6500 BC, giving rise to *Bos taurus* breeds in Europe and the Middle East, and *Bos indicus* (or humped zebu) breeds in India and east Asia. Central to early farming economies for meat and leather, cattle were increasingly exploited for dairy products and traction from about 4500 BC. The water buffalo (*Bubalus bubalis*) is derived from a different ruminant species domesticated in Asia by about 5000 BC. ▷ 1.03, 1.05, 1.08, 1.16, 1.20

CAUSEWAYED CAMP
A type of NEOLITHIC enclosure found in Britain (e.g. WINDMILL HILL) and Denmark, built in about 3800–3000 BC, that consists of one or more ditch and bank circuits

interrupted by causeways. Most had settlement or ceremonial functions (including possible exposure of the dead). ▷ 1.20

CAVE AND ROCK ART

The earliest examples of art, consisting of paintings and engravings on the walls of caves and rock shelters, produced by the UPPER PALEOLITHIC hunters of Europe, Africa and Australia. In Africa and Australia these traditions continued into modern times. In the case of Upper Paleolithic Europe, the cave art is associated with modern humans, dating mostly from about 25,000 to 10,000 ya, and is dominated by representations of animals, some of them extraordinarily naturalistic, human figures, hand prints and abstract symbols. Especially impressive friezes survive at LASCAUX (France) and ALTAMIRA (Spain). These paintings are believed to have had considerable religious and social significance. ▷ 1.02, 1.16, 1.19

CERAMICS

Materials and objects made of fired clay, including pottery (containers and other vessels) and terracotta (fine building materials, clay tablets and statuary). The earliest known fired-clay objects are the "Venus" figurines and animal models of the UPPER PALEOLITHIC GRAVETTIAN CULTURE of Europe. The use of pottery is sometimes equated with early farming cultures, though the first NEOLITHIC societies of the LEVANT (9th millennium BC) were aceramic, while the HUNTER-GATHERER JOMON CULTURE of Japan made pottery from about 12,500 ya. ▷ 1.04, 1.06, 1.08, 1.10, 1.12, 1.17, 1.27

CHALDEANS

ARAMAEAN people of northern Arabia who settled in MESOPOTAMIA in the early 1st millennium BC, establishing ruling dynasties in several cities. The famous Chaldean 11th dynasty of BABYLON destroyed the Assyrians and re-established the Babylonian empire. ▷ 1.12, 1.13

CHAMBERED TOMB

A type of collective burial monument found in many parts of the world, that consists of a stone mortuary chamber covered by an earth or stone mound. The earliest examples are the early NEOLITHIC MEGALITHIC tombs of Europe, such as passage graves and chambered LONG BARROWS, built by the earliest farming societies in France and Britain in about 4500–3400 BC, with later types found throughout western Europe. ▷ 1.20

CHATAL HUYUK

An exceptionally large early agricultural settlement, sometimes described as a town, that is situated on the edge of the Konya plateau in southern Anatolia and dates from about 6500 BC. The densely-clustered clay-built houses were entered through rooftop openings, some with shrine rooms which

contained clay-modeled bull's heads and frescoes. The settlement had a mixed farming economy that supported a population of about 6,000 people, importing materials such as OBSIDIAN for tools. There is evidence in late occupation levels of early COPPER WORKING. ▷ 1.03, 1.09

CHÂTELPERRONIAN CULTURE

Initial stage of the European UPPER PALEOLITHIC, defined by a distinctive set of stone tools, including backed knives. Dating from about 40,000 to 30,000 ya, it was once thought to be the earliest cultural evidence of modern humans in Europe, though it is now believed to be a product of late Neanderthal populations, copying the AURIGNACIAN blade-tool technologies of the modern human communities. ▷ 1.19

CHAVÍN DE HUÁNTAR

Ceremonial center in the Andes, occupied from about 850 to 200 BC, with several large temple platforms and sunken courts linked by pavements and stairs. The stone buildings, especially gates, are decorated with relief carvings of humans and animals. The site gives its name to the Chavín style of art and architecture (c.900–200 BC), and is probably related to a religious cult that had spread throughout the Andes and coastal Peru by 400 BC. ▷ 1.06, 1.28

CHAYONU

A rare transitional HUNTER-GATHERER and early agricultural settlement in north MESOPOTAMIA, occupied from about 8500 to 6500 BC. It is also notable for the very early evidence (c.7300 BC) of COPPER metallurgy (cold hammering of "native" copper in its free metallic state) to make tools and ornaments. ▷ 1.08

CHESOWANJA

LOWER PALEOLITHIC site in ancient lake sediments and tuffs at Lake Baringo, Kenya, dating from about 2.4 to 1.3 million ya, with remains of AUSTRALOPITHECUS ROBUSTUS, layers containing OLDOWAN chopper tools, and a later ACHEULIAN hand-ax industry. There is also possible evidence of the earliest controlled use of FIRE (c.1.6 million ya). ▷ 1.01

CHIEFDOM

A type of social system characterized by centralized chiefly and religious authority, tribute-giving, the exchange and redistribution of prestige goods, the building of ceremonial centers, alliance networks, and competition between polities. Chiefdoms are usually regarded as an evolutionary stage following tribal or simple ranked societies, and preceding the development of STATES and urbanism, and are recognized in many parts of the world at different times. ▷ 1.04, 1.05, 1.06

CHINCHOROS TRADITION

Long-lived HUNTER-GATHERER culture of the coastal region of South America, in modern

north Chile, spanning both the PRECERAMIC and INITIAL periods (3000–500 BC). As well as fishing and hunting equipment, the Chinchorros had knowledge of basketry and textiles, and made pottery from about 1200 BC. ▷ 1.04, 1.06, 1.15

CHINESE LANGUAGE AND SCRIPT

Chinese is a language group of the Sino-Tibetan language family and consists of a number of separate languages, though all use a common writing system. The earliest Chinese scripts were pictographic, of the SHANG period (from c.1600 BC), when they were used for recording divinations. Refinements to this writing system gave rise to a LOGOGRAPHIC SCRIPT from about 900 BC (standardized in the 3rd century BC), in which each sign represented a unit of meaning rather than sound. This script is the world's oldest continually used writing system. ▷ 1.07, 1.27

CHIRIPA CULTURE

Culture of the Andean EARLY HORIZON PERIOD named after the ceremonial center at Chiripa (600–400 BC), at the south end of Lake Titicaca, Bolivia. Little is known about its origins or development, but the communities of the Titicaca Basin probably shared a religious tradition (YAYA-MAMA), and the architectural styles seen at Chiripa are similar to those of the later Tiahuanaco state in the same area in about AD 500. ▷ 1.05, 1.28

CHOGA MAMI

Early agricultural settlement of the 7th to 6th millennia BC, to the east of the Tigris river on the edge of the Mesopotamian plains. It is the site of the earliest recorded canal IRRIGATION system, built by about 5500 BC. ▷ 1.09

CHORRERA CULTURE

Early farming culture in southern Ecuador with a sophisticated CERAMIC tradition spanning the INITIAL and EARLY HORIZON periods (1200–300 BC), which expanded from the long-settled VALDIVIA coastal region into the Andean highlands to grow MAIZE and manioc. ▷ 1.05, 1.06, 1.28

CHU

Major feudal state of the ZHOU kingdom in southern China in about 1100-250 BC, with a capital at Ying. It was constantly at war with its powerful northern enemy, JIN, during the later SPRINGS AND AUTUMNS PERIOD and briefly became the leading state (hegemon) in about 710–690 BC, under King Zhuang. It lost its position as the pre-eminent southern Zhou state as its rivals, WU and Yue, grew more powerful in the late 6th century BC. ▷ 1.27

CIMMERIANS

Nomadic people of the steppes to the north of the Caucasus who migrated southwards in the 8th century BC. They were repulsed by the Assyrians and driven into Anatolia, where they conquered PHRYGIA (705–696 BC) and LYDIA (652 BC). Their power was broken by the Lydians and Babylonians in the late 7th century BC. ▷ 1.13

CLOVIS CULTURE
Earliest distinct PALEOINDIAN culture of North America (c.9500-9000 BC), characterized by stone tools, including projectile points with concave bases (Clovis points) used for big-game hunting of mammoths and bison. The origins of the Clovis culture are unclear but must lie in the preceding little-known Lower Lithic Paleoindian traditions. ▷ 1.02

COINAGE
Stamped pieces of metal were first given to the Greek mercenaries of the king of LYDIA in about 600 BC and spread quickly into the Greek world. (Coinage was invented independently in China at about the same time.) At first they were used for state transactions and for the receipt of taxes. By the end of the 6th century BC, many Greek cities were minting their own smaller coins in silver, and these were used for everyday transactions. The use of coin faces for propaganda and for the glorification of a city, ruler or successful victory was soon widespread. Coinage quickly spread from Greece to Italy, and then the rest of Europe. ▷ 1.24

COLCHIS
An area enclosed by the Caucasus mountains, stretching from the east coast of the Black Sea. The coastline was colonized by the Greek city of MILETOS in the 6th century BC, and the area was later absorbed into the Roman province of Cappadocia. ▷ 1.15, 1.23

CONFUCIUS
Chinese philosopher and teacher born in 551 BC in the state of LU, who was a member of the minor aristocracy, or bureaucratic class. Confucius advocated moral rectitude, education for all, service to the state and responsible government. His writings established an influential ethical code for the exercise of power and citizenship. He died in 479 BC. ▷ 1.06, 1.27

COPPER WORKING
Copper was one of the first metals used for making tools and ornaments. It is easily worked and may exist in a pure form, though it usually requires extraction from ores by smelting. Copper working began independently in different parts of the world: in MESOPOTAMIA by about 7000 BC, China by about 3000 BC and the Americas by about 1000 BC. In the western Old World, a Copper Age is sometimes identified as a separate period. ▷ 1.08, 1.27, 1.28

CORD IMPRESSED WARE CULTURE
Late NEOLITHIC culture of central Europe that influenced the farming societies of northern

Europe from the Meuse to the Volga in 3000-2400 BC. It is distinguished by its pottery beakers with cord-impressed decoration, stone battle-axes, and burials under ROUND BARROWS. The Cord Impressed Ware culture marked a new emphasis on PASTORALISM and social hierarchy, and was a precursor of the BELL BEAKER cultures of western Europe. ▷ 1.04, 1.20

CORINTH
The leading Greek city-state of the 7th century BC, heavily involved in Mediterranean trading and shipbuilding, and the pioneer of Doric architecture. Corinth's central position meant that it was drawn into the wars of the 5th and 4th centuries BC, at first in support of SPARTA (Peloponnesian War) and then against it. The Romans sacked Corinth in 146 BC, but later founded a new colony there, which regained the original city's prosperity. It was the home of an early Christian community made famous by the letters it received from St Paul. ▷ 1.22, 1.23, 1.24

CORTAILLOD
Early farming and fishing village beside Lake Neuchâtel in Switzerland, that gave its name to the early NEOLITHIC of the north Alpine region in about 3800–3000 BC. Cortaillod settlements are famous for the preservation of wooden houses and artifacts in the lake sediments. ▷ 1.20

COTTON
Seed-hair fiber from plants of the genus *Gossypium*, found in sub-tropical regions and cultivated for making textiles and thread. The earliest use of cotton was in the Indian sub-continent, where it was domesticated by 5000 BC, and in South America, where cotton textiles of the 3rd millennium BC have been recorded (ASPERO culture). ▷ 1.03, 1.26, 1.28

CROESUS
King of LYDIA (r.c.560–546 BC) who lives on in legend for his immense wealth. Croesus had many links with the Greek world, but found himself isolated when he attacked CYRUS of Persia, who defeated him and annexed his kingdom to the ACHEMENID EMPIRE (546–545 BC). ▷ 1.15

CUMAE
See KYMAI

CUNEIFORM
Writing system invented in MESOPOTAMIA in the 3rd millennium BC, derived from Sumerian pictographs that were refined to include phonetic and syllabic values. Early inscriptions were written in Sumerian, but cuneiform was widely adopted in the Middle East for writing other languages, notably AKKADIAN. It fell out of use as ARAMAIC LANGUAGES and versions of CANAANITE phonetic alphabets became widespread in the 1st millennium BC. ▷ 1.07, 1.10, 1.15

CYRUS II (THE GREAT)
King of Persia (r.559–30 BC) who founded the ACHEMENID EMPIRE by overthrowing his MEDIAN overlord, King Astyages, and appropriating his extensive empire. He confirmed his position by destroying his main rival to the west, CROESUS of LYDIA, in Asia Minor (547–546 BC) and annexing BABYLONIAN (539 BC). Cyrus was known for his diplomacy as well as his use of force. His eastern campaigns and fortress-building (546–530 BC) consolidated the empire, but Cyrus was killed in battle on the frontier in 530 BC. ▷ 1.13, 1.14, 1.15

DARIUS I (THE GREAT)
Achemenid king of Persia (r.521–486 BC) who ruled the ACHEMENID EMPIRE when it was at the height of its power. He seized the throne after the death of CAMBYSES and secured the northern frontiers by defeating the SCYTHIANS. He conquered the Indus valley by 518 BC and Thrace by 513 BC, but failed to conquer Greece (490 BC). He reorganized the empire by establishing a federal system of satrapies, efficient taxation and postal systems, and a new military organization. He marked his reign by building a new royal capital at PERSEPOLIS. ▷ 1.15

DAVID
King of ISRAEL (r.c. 1006–965 BC), proclaimed ruler of JUDAH and later of Israel after the death of King SAUL. David conquered JERUSALEM and made it the capital of a united kingdom in about 1000 BC. He defeated the PHILISTINES and consolidated the kingdom of Israel by dominating vassal states such as EDOM, MOAB and ARAM-DAMASCUS. ▷ 1.14

DELPHI
Important shrine of Apollo, situated on the slopes of Mount Parnassus, central Greece. Its famous ORACLE attracted visitors from all parts of the Greek world, and the Pythian Games held at the shrine were second only to those held at OLYMPIA. The site was crowded with treasuries, temples and statues donated by cities and supplicants. Delphi played an important role during the period of Greek colonization, advising migrants where they should settle. ▷ 1.24

DI-XIN
Last king of the SHANG dynasty of China, who was overthrown by his vassal, King WU of the ZHOU family, at the Battle of Chaoge in 1122 BC. He was later seen as a sadistic despot who was morally unfit to rule, and was therefore justly removed according to the doctrine known as the "Mandate of Heaven", under which political power was subject to divine judgement. ▷ 1.27

DIASPORA
Greek word meaning "dispersion" that is used to describe the scattering of Jewish populations and their exile from Palestine.

The first Diaspora took place in 587 BC, when NEBUCHADNEZZAR, king of BABYLON, suppressed a revolt in JUDAH and forcibly resettled HEBREW communities in BABYLONIA. When CYRUS the Great of Persia permitted a return to their homeland in 539 BC, many Jews stayed behind. Later Diaspora scattered the Jews still further. ▷ 1.14

DILMUN

Early state and trading center in the Persian Gulf that is mentioned in Sumerian records and was probably on the island of Bahrain, where a large fortified city existed in about 2800–1800 BC. Dilmun was at the center of a thriving trade system, largely based on commerce between MESOPOTAMIA and the Indus valley in the 3rd millennium BC. It may have been conquered by SARGON OF AGADE, becoming part of the Akkadian empire in the 23rd century BC. ▷ 1.11

DJOSER

Founder of the 3rd Dynasty of Egyptian PHARAOHS, Djoser ruled from 2677 until 2648 BC. He is chiefly remembered for his burial place, the STEP PYRAMID at SAQQARA, designed by the architect Imhotep. ▷ 1.17

DOG

The first animal to be tamed by humans, the wolf probably being its main ancestral species. There is evidence of early domestic dogs in several parts of the world, with the earliest in the Middle East (c.3000 ya), though earlier hunters may have initiated the domestication process. Dogs were used for protection, herding and food (in the Americas), and as pets. ▷ 1.08

DOLMEN

Term used by early European archaeologists to describe MEGALITHIC tomb chambers of the NEOLITHIC period, especially those consisting of upright orthostats with a large capstone on top. The term is now rarely used, except to describe the "portal-dolmen", a specific type of tomb. ▷ 1.20

DORIANS

One of the tribes of Greeks whose foundation myths told of their arrival in the Peloponnese after the fall of TROY. Some archaeologists and historians have dated this to about 1100 BC, but others point to a later foundation (c.900 BC) of the main Dorian City, SPARTA. By the 5th century BC the Dorians were deadly rivals of the IONIANS, whose mother city was Athens. ▷ 1.12, 1.22, 1.23, 1.24

DRAVIDIANS

People of southern India, sometimes regarded as the original pre-ARYAN HUNTER-GATHERER population, which adopted farming from the 4th millennium BC. The ethnic and racial distinctiveness of the Dravidians is open to question, and the term is now used mainly to describe speakers of the Dravidian languages, widely spoken in southern India. ▷ 1.04, 1.05, 1.06, 1.26

DUR-KURIGALZU

City in south MESOPOTAMIA near to the confluence of the Tigris and Diyala rivers, founded in the 14th century BC by a KASSITE king of BABYLON, Kurigalzu I or Kurigalzu II. The city contained a ZIGGURAT and temples dedicated to Sumerian gods, as well as a royal palace. ▷ 1.12, 1.13

DYUKHTAI TRADITION

UPPER PALEOLITHIC stone-tool industry (c.20,000–12,000 ya) that represents the first human colonization of far northeast Asia (eastern Siberia). It is characterized by bifacial spear points for big-game hunting. Communities from this region migrated eastwards in this period and eventually crossed BERINGIA to colonize the Americas. ▷ 1.02

EARLY HORIZON PERIOD

Period of ANDEAN CIVILIZATION from about 900 to 200 BC. it is marked by the spread of the Chavín artistic and temple-building tradition across the formerly diverse regional cultures of the central Andes, after which coastal areas adopted highland architectural styles. This process of cultural integration may have been due to the adoption of a single religious cult. The decline of Chavín influence after 200 BC resulted in the renewed regionalization of cultures such as the Mochica, Nazca and Lima. ▷ 1.28

EARLY DYNASTIC PERIOD

Period of MESOPOTAMIAN CIVILIZATION (c.2900–2334 BC) that saw the emergence of the first documented royal dynasties in the region. A definitive chronology for the period has not been established, due to the fragmentary nature of the sources. The end of the period is marked by the accession of SARGON of AGADE in 2334 BC, which is the first reliable established date in the history of the Middle East. ▷ 1.10

EARLY PRECLASSIC PERIOD

Period of MESOAMERICAN CIVILIZATION from about 2000 to 800 BC, marked by the adoption of farming, the growth of village settlements and the use of pottery throughout Mesoamerica. Most significant was the development of complex hierarchical societies with large settlements and ceremonial centers, such as the Maya, OLMECS and ZAPOTECS, and the emergence of the Olmec civilization in the lowland region to the south of the Gulf of Mexico from about 1200 BC. Extensive trade networks, religious architecture and monumental stone sculpture all appeared in this period. ▷ 1.05, 1.28

EDOM

Region of Palestine between the Dead Sea and the Gulf of Aqaba, occupied by the Edomites from the 14th to the 6th centuries BC. Although well-placed to exploit the Red Sea trade route, Edom was often dominated by ISRAEL or JUDAH (c.1000–843 BC). The region lost its political and cultural identity following its conquest by the Babylonians in about 600 BC. ▷ 1.13, 1.14

EGYPTIAN CIVILIZATION

Ancient Egypt was blessed with annual floods of the Nile, which brought fertile silt and water, making the lower Nile valley the most favorable agricultural area in the ancient world. After 2,500 years of settled cultivation, a unified Egyptian kingdom was created by NARMER (r.c.3000 BC). The Egyptian hieroglyphic writing system and styles of art and architecture emerged with unification. Ancient Egypt was a highly centralized state focused on the semi-divine king (or PHARAOH, as he was later called). The kings showed their authority through grand building projects, such as PYRAMID complexes and temples. Egypt enjoyed long periods of stability (under the OLD KINGDOM, MIDDLE KINGDOM and NEW KINGDOM), broken by periods of fragmentation (Intermediate periods).

Egyptian society was highly ritualized; every activity was related to the gods, who were appeased through elaborate rituals in temples or by means of magic and spells in the home. Those who behaved correctly were promised an afterlife, though this depended on their body being preserved through MUMMIFICATION after death. The Egyptians were expert craftsmen in fields such as sculpture, architecture, painting and jewelry-making. They also had a reputation for wisdom in science, astronomy, mathematics and medicine, though there is little evidence of creative thinking in these areas.

By 1070 BC Egypt was in decline and after the 8th century BC it was usually under foreign rule, but its civilization survived until it was undermined by Christianity in the fourth century AD. ▷ 1.05, 1.07, 1.10, 1.13, 1.14, 1.15, 1.16, 1.17, 1.18, 1.23

EL PARAISO TRADITION

Cultural tradition of coastal Peru in about 1800–850 BC, that was contemporary with the Andean KOTOSH TRADITION. The largest PRECERAMIC monument complex in South America is named after El Paraiso; it consists of massive mounds forming U-shaped platforms, with a temple at the end and central sunken courts. This style of architecture was widely adopted along the coast, together with IRRIGATION farming and pottery, from about 1800 BC. ▷ 1.28

ELAM

Plains region to the east of MESOPOTAMIA, between the Zagros mountains and the Persian Gulf. Cultural developments in Mesopotamia were closely paralleled in Elam, where cities, states and writing (proto-Elamite pictographs) existed by about 3500 BC. The

KINGS OF EGYPT

LATE PREDYNASTIC PERIOD
c.3000 BC

Zekhen
Narmer

EARLY DYNASTIC PERIOD
2920–2575

1st Dynasty	2920–2770
Menes	
Djer	
Djet	
Wadj	
Den	
Adjib	
Semerkhet	
Qa'a	

2nd Dynasty	2770–2649
Hotepsekhemwy	
Reneb	
Ninetjer	
Peribsen	
Khasekhemwy	

3rd Dynasty	2649–2575
Zanakht	2649–2630
Djoser	2630–2611
Sekhemkhet	2611–2603
Khaba	2603–2599
Huni	2599–2575

OLD KINGDOM
2575–2134

4th Dynasty	2575–2465
Snefru	2575–2551
Khufu (Cheops)	2551–2528
Radjedef	2528–2520
Khephren	2520–2494
Menkaure (Mycerinus)	2490–2472
Shepseskaf	2472–2467

5th Dynasty	2465–2323
Userkaf	2465–2458
Sahure	2458–2446
Kakai	2446–2426
Ini	2426–2419
Raneferef	2419–2416
Izi	2416–2392
Menkauhor	2396–2388
Izezi	2388–2356
Unas	2356–2323

6th Dynasty	2323–2150
Teti	2323–2291
Pepi I	2289–2255
Nemtyemzaf	2255–2246
Pepi II	2246–2152

7th/8th Dynasty	2150–2134
Numerous kings including Neferkare	

1ST INTERMEDIATE PERIOD
2134–2040

9th/10th Dynasty	2134–2040
Several kings called	
Khety	
Merykare	
Ity	

11th Dynasty	2134–2040
Inyotef I (Sehertawy)	2134–2118
Inyotef II (Wahankh)	2118–2069
Inyotef III	2069–2061
(Nakhtnebtepnufer)	
Mentuhotpe II	2061–2010

MIDDLE KINGDOM
2040–1640

11th Dynasty	2040–1991
Mentuhotpe II	2061–2010
(ruler of all Egypt from 2040)	
Mentuhotpe III	2010–1998
Mentuhotpe IV	1998–1991

12th Dynasty	
Amenemhet I	1991–1962
Senwosret I	1971–1926
Amenemhet II	1929–1982
Senwosret II	1987–1878
Senwosret III	1878–1841?
Amenemhet III	1844–1797
Amenemhet IV	1799–1787
Nefrusobk	1787–1783

13th Dynasty	1783–after 1640
About 70 kings, including	
Wegaf I	1783–1779
Amenemhet V	
Harnedjheriotef	
Amenyqemau	
Sebekhotpe I	c.1750
Hor	
Amenemhet VII	
Sebekhotpe II	
Khendjer	
Sebekhotpe III	c.1745
Neferhotep I	c.1741–1730
Sebekhotpe IV	c.1730–1720
Sebekhotpe V	c.1720–1715
Aya	c.1704–1690
Mentuemzaf	
Dedumose II	
Neferhotep III	

14th Dynasty	
A group of kings probably contemporary with the 13th or 15th Dynasty	

2ND INTERMEDIATE PERIOD
1640–1532

15th Dynasty (Hyksos)	
Salitis	
Sheshi	
Khian	
Apophis	c.1585–1542
Khamudi	c.1542–1532

16th Dynasty	
Minor Hyksos rulers, contemporary with the 15th Dynasty	

17th Dynasty	1640–1550
Numerous kings, including	
Inyotef V	c.1640–1635
Sebekemzaf I	
Nebireyeraw	
Sebekemzaf II	
Ta'o (or Djehutyi'o) I	
Ta'o (or Djehutyi'o) II	
Kamose	c.1555–1550

NEW KINGDOM
1532–1010

18th Dynasty	1550–1307
Ahmose	1550–1525
(ruler of all Egypt from 1532)	
Amenophis I	1525–1504
Tuthmosis I	1504–1492
Tuthmosis II	1492–1479
Tuthmosis III	1479–1425
Hatshepsut	1473–1458
Amenophis II	1427–1401
Tuthmosis IV	1401–1391
Amenophis III	1391–1353
Amenophis IV (Akhenaten)	1353–1335
Smenkhkare	1335–1333
Tutankhamun	1333–1323
Aya	1323–1319
Haremhab	1319–1307

19th Dynasty	1307–1196
Ramesses I	1307–1306
Sethos I	1306–1290
Ramesses II	1290–1224
Merneptah	1224–1214
Sethos II	1214–1204
Siptah	1204–1198
Twosre	1198–1196

20th Dynasty	1196–1070
Sethnakhte	1196–1194
Ramesses III	1194–1163
Ramesses IV	1163–1156
Ramesses V	1156–1151
Ramesses VI	1151–1143
Ramesses VII	1143–1136
Ramesses VIII	1136–1131
Ramesses IX	1131–1112
Ramesses X	1112–1100
Ramesses XI	1100–1070

Elamites briefly conquered SUMERIA and sacked UR in 2004 BC, and were a major threat to Mesopotamian states in the 2nd millennium BC. In the 13th century BC Elam emerged as a powerful unified kingdom, under a series of warrior kings who conquered much of south Mesopotamia, but it declined rapidly from about 1110 BC, when the capital at SUSA was captured by the Babylonians, later becoming a vassal of Assyrian and Babylonian empires, and one of the richest satrapies of the ACHEMENID EMPIRE. Little is known about Elamite society or religion; its artistic and architectural achievements were predominantly BABYLONIAN in style. ▷ 1.10, 1.11, 1.12, 1.13, 1.15

EL-AMARNA
Modern name for the site of Akhenaten, the capital of the "heretic" PHARAOH AKHENATEN, in Middle Egypt from 1350 to 1325 BC. The city was abandoned at Akhenaten's death and the site remained well-preserved. The ceremonial procession way and great royal hall for public audiences have been recognized as well as residential suburbs. The site also contained the famous El-Amarna letters, detailing the relationship between Egypt and the cities and states of the Near East. ▷ 1.18

ELEUSIS
Important sanctuary west of Athens, known throughout the Greek world for its Mysteries into which suppliants could be initiated. The presiding goddesses were Demeter and her daughter Persephone, themselves at the center of complex cults of fertility and rebirth. ▷ 1.24

ELIJAH
Biblical prophet of the 9th century BC who, with the prophet ELISHA, asserted a monotheistic religious doctrine and successfully encouraged the Israelites to reject CANAANITE beliefs and the worship of Baal (c.860–853 BC). ▷ 1.14

ELISHA
Biblical prophet who, with his mentor ELIJAH, persuaded the Israelites to reject the god Baal. He directed the civil war that led to the death of King AHAB (853 BC) and Jehu's seizure of the throne. Elisha succeeded Elijah as the most influential religious figure in ISRAEL. ▷ 1.14

ENLIL
Sumerian deity (Bel in Akkadian) of the air, winds and farming. One of a triad of gods (with An and Enki), Enlil was especially important because of his role in ensuring fertility and agricultural productivity. Control of the cult center at NIPPUR was essential for Sumerian and Akkadian kings. ▷ 1.11

ENSETE
Plant of the banana family that produces an edible root, domesticated in Ethiopia at a very early date (by c.4000 BC). It is one of several indigenous farming innovations based on local plants (including teff and finger MILLET) that were independent of Middle Eastern agriculture. ▷ 1.16

EPIPALEOLITHIC
Period in the post-glacial period prior to the adoption of agriculture, in which HUNTER-GATHERER societies – including cultures in the LEVANT (such as the NATUFIANS) and north Africa – continued to use UPPER PALEOLITHIC stone-tool and hunting technologies. ▷ 1.08, 1.16

EPIRUS
An area of northwestern Greece known from early times for its ORACLE to Apollo at Dodona. Gradually Hellenized by Greek colonies on the coast, the area was united into a single kingdom under a chieftain from the central Molossian tribe in the 4th century BC. Epirus' greatest period of prosperity then followed. Its most famous king was Pyrrhus. The kingdom collapsed in the 3rd century BC and, in 167 BC, Epirus was conquered by the Romans, who reputedly enslaved 150,000 of its inhabitants. ▷ 1.24, 1.25

ERIDU
Sumerian city to the south of UR, referred to in ancient king lists as the first city of SUMER. Founded in the mid-6th millennium BC, Eridu was one of the leading cities of MESOPOTAMIA by the EARLY DYNASTIC PERIOD (c.2500 BC), and was continuously occupied until about 600 BC. Its political importance declined after the rise of the Third Dynasty of Ur. ▷ 1.09, 1.10, 1.11

ERLITOU CULTURE
The first bronze-using culture of China (c.1900–1650 BC), named after the city of Erlitou situated on the Yellow river in the heartland of the later Shang state. The Erlitou culture is probably equivalent to the first phase of the SHANG CIVILIZATION and is notable for its sophisticated cast-bronze work. ▷ 1.27

ERTEBOLLE CULTURE
Late MESOLITHIC HUNTER-GATHERER-fisher culture of Denmark (c.6000–3500 BC). It is characterized by its distinctive stone tools, massive shell middens at coastal sites, cemeteries with grave goods, and the adoption of pottery, polished stone axes and agricultural methods from neighboring farmers. Several canoes and examples of wood-carved art have been found in water-logged sediments. ▷ 1.19

ESARHADDON
King of ASSYRIA (r.680–669 BC), who re-established peaceful dominion over BABYLONIA but lost control of the northern provinces due to SCYTHIAN and CIMMERIAN invasions. Esarhaddon suppressed revolts in the LEVANT and conquered Egypt, but failed to consolidate Assyrian rule. Esarhaddon's successor, ASHURBANIPAL, was forced to reconquer the country. ▷ 1.13

ESHNUNNA
City on the Diyali river in central MESOPOTAMIA and an important city-state of the EARLY DYNASTIC PERIOD. It was conquered by the Akkadians (c.2250 BC) and later ruled by the Third Dynasty of UR, before regaining its independence in about 2000 BC. It was the last major Mesopotamian state to be conquered by HAMMURABI of BABYLON (1755 BC). ▷ 1.10, 1.11

ETRUSCANS
The leading pre-Roman people of Italy, located between the Tiber and Arno rivers, with offshoots in the Po valley and Campania. Recognizable in the early IRON AGE Villanovan cultural group of the 9th and 8th centuries BC, the Etruscans soon developed prosperous city-states supported by agriculture, COPPER and iron deposits, and extensive trading contacts throughout the Mediterranean. The leading cities were loosely organized in the league of Twelve Cities (the Etruscan league), which met periodically at the sanctuary of Voltumna in central Etruria. From 396 BC, with the fall of Veii, the Etruscans gradually came under Roman control and their assimilation was complete by the end of the republic. They were famed for their artistic skills, and many Etruscan wall-paintings, terracottas and bronzes have been discovered in tombs and sanctuaries dating from the 7th to the 1st centuries BC. ▷ 1.06, 1.07, 1.23, 1.25

FERTILE CRESCENT
Region of the ancient Middle East in which the earliest agricultural economies and sedentary village societies developed (c.9000–7000 BC), with domesticated cereals (einkorn and emmer WHEAT, and BARLEY) and animal species (SHEEP and GOAT). These species co-existed in the wild in the crescent-shaped region extending from the southern LEVANT, through northwest Syria to the Zagros mountains in Iran. ▷ 1.08, 1.09

FIRE, EARLIEST USE
The earliest evidence of the controlled use of fire by hominids (probably HOMO ERECTUS) is dated to about 1.6 million ya, at CHESOWANJA, Kenya and at SWARTKRANS, South Africa. Consistent fire making, however, was probably a later development associated with the human colonization of temperate regions after about 600,000 ya. The earliest evidence of the use of fire in Europe comes from near Bury St Edmunds in eastern England and dates from about 400,000 ya. ▷ 1.01

FLOOD, THE
Biblical story with earlier origins in Middle Eastern culture. CUNEIFORM tablets dating

(after death he gained the status of a god). Little is known about Hittite religion or art.

The later history of the Hittites can be divided into three main periods: the Old Kingdom period, New Kingdom (Empire) period and Neo-Hittite period. During the Old Kingdom period (1750–1450 BC), the Hittites established a capital at Kussara, and then at Hattusas (c.1650 BC), extending their rule into north MESOPOTAMIA. Under King MURSILIS they briefly annexed ASSYRIA and sacked BABYLON (1595 BC), but could not sustain their conquests. Hittite power declined in the 16th century BC in the face of Egyptian and Mittanian expansion and internal instability, and reached a low point in the 15th century BC, when little is known about Hittite affairs.

Under the New Kingdom (Empire) period (c.1450–1190 BC) the revival of the Hittite empire took place, as MITTANI power waned and the Egyptians were distracted by internal affairs. The empire reached its greatest extent in about 1325 BC under King SUPPILULIUMAS, who consolidated Hittite rule in Anatolia and conquered the northern parts of Syria and the LEVANT. Confrontations with the Egyptians in the early 13th century BC over control of the Levant ended in stalemate. The collapse of the empire (c.1205–1190 BC) is attributed to PHRYGIAN invasions (which destroyed the capital at Hattusas), attacks by the SEA PEOPLES and political fragmentation.

After the Phrygian conquests, during the Neo-Hittite period (1190–700 BC), Hittite cultural identity was maintained only in small city-states and kingdoms in south Anatolia and north Syria, the most powerful being CARCHEMISH. Their independence, and the last remnants of Hittite culture, were finally destroyed by the Assyrians in the 8th century BC. ▷ 1.11, 1.12, 1.13, 1.14, 1.18, 1.21, 1.22

HOMER

Greek poet who is associated with the final composition of the two great Greek epics, the ILIAD and the ODYSSEY, in the late 8th century BC. The Ionic dialect of the poems suggests that he may have come from Asia Minor, the eastern Aegean or Euboea. Homer probably brought together earlier oral poems and consolidated them into coherent stories. ▷ 1.22, 1.24

HOMINOID APES

Large primates belonging to three main groups (*Sivapithecus*, *Dryopithecus* and *Proconsul*) that evolved in the MIOCENE EPOCH and spread throughout the Old World. The evolutionary lineage of hominids, including humans, probably diverged from other apes only 6 million ya. ▷ 1.01

HOMO ERECTUS

Human species that had evolved in Africa from HOMO HABILIS by about 1.5 million ya. Though probably slightly taller, *Homo erectus* was physically similar to modern humans. Its

brain size ranged from two-thirds that of a modern human in early examples of the species, to three-quarters in later examples. *Homo erectus* developed more effective technology than *Homo habilis*, notably the use of hand axes, wooden spears and FIRE. *Homo erectus* was so successful adaptively that populations grew to colonize a wide range of new habitats, spreading from Africa to Eurasia, reaching Britain (BOXGROVE), China (ZHOUKOUDIEN) and Indonesia (Sangiran). Between 500,000 and 100,000 ya *Homo erectus* evolved into anatomically modern HOMO SAPIENS SAPIENS in Africa. In Europe it evolved into HOMO SAPIENS NEANDERTHALENSIS, while in southeast Asia it may have survived until about 60,000 ya, becoming extinct only with the arrival of anatomically modern humans in the region. ▷ 1.01, 1.02

HOMO HABILIS

The earliest human species, probably evolved from AUSTRALOPITHECUS AFARENSIS or AUSTRALOPITHECUS AFRICANUS, that lived in eastern and southern Africa, about 2.5–1.5 million ya. Fossils from OLDUVAI GORGE, KOOBI FORA and SWARTKRANS show that this gracile hominid had hands that were capable of the precise manipulation of objects, and discoveries of contemporary stone tools suggest that *Homo habilis* was the first tool-using hominid. Its brain size was about half that of a modern human. ▷ 1.01

HOMO SAPIENS

Although the origins of *Homo sapiens* ("Wise Man") are debated, this species probably evolved from HOMO ERECTUS populations in Africa and Eurasia, with some distinct regional traits, such as the cold-adapted groups in Europe (which later developed into the NEANDERTHALS). As a sophisticated tool user, *Homo sapiens* developed effective hunting equipment for the first time (projectiles for close-impact spearing of animals), had a wider range of specialized tool industries, may have built shelters, and were adept at using FIRE. ▷ 1.01, 1.02

HOMO SAPIENS NEANDERTHALENSIS

(NEANDERTHAL man) Specialized cold-adapted human species that evolved in west Eurasia and the Middle East from late HOMO ERECTUS, about 230,000–150,000 ya. The recent recovery of Neanderthal DNA has shown that they were not ancestral to modern humans. The Neanderthals had short, thick skeletal frames to reduce surface body area exposed to the cold, and heavy facial structures to protect the sinuses and lungs from cold air. They used MIDDLE PALEOLITHIC tools, hunted a range of animals, lived in open settlements and cave sites, and were the first humans to express aesthetic qualities and religious beliefs (formal burials). They became extinct about 28,000 ya, as more numerous and versatile HOMO SAPIENS SAPIENS populations colonized their territories. ▷ 1.01, 1.02, 1.19

HOMO SAPIENS SAPIENS

Anatomically modern man, a regional human adaptation that evolved in Africa about 150,000–100,000 ya, with enhanced cognitive and linguistic capabilities, increasingly complex technologies and social institutions, and new forms of cultural expression in art and ritual. The adaptational success of modern humans, with developed UPPER PALEOLITHIC tool-kits, led to population growth and rapid global colonization, spreading from Africa to east Asia by about 75,000 ya, to Europe by about 40,000 ya, and to the Americas by about 15,000 ya, replacing existing human groups (HOMO SAPIENS variants). All humans today are descendents of the *Homo sapiens sapiens* population that evolved in Africa. ▷ 1.01, 1.02

HOPLITE

Greek infantry soldier of the 7th to 4th centuries BC, notable for his large shield (hoplon), which – joined alongside those of others – enabled him to fight in a heavily protected line. Hoplite battles consisted of tightly packed bodies of troops (phalanxes), about 12 ranks deep, pushing and jabbing their opponents until one side gave way.

HORSE, DOMESTICATION

Probably first domesticated as a food source in the steppe region of southeast Europe and central Asia in the 4th millennium BC, the use of horses as draft animals for pulling wagons and chariots developed in this region from about 2500 BC and spread to the Middle East by about 1700 BC. Horse-riding equipment was invented by the pastoralist cultures of the Eurasian steppes (c.1500–1000 BC), enabling them to adopt a fully nomadic way of life. ▷ 1.03, 1.06, 1.11, 1.19, 1.20, 1.21, 1.22, 1.23

HUANG DI

Mythical third emperor of China and founder of Chinese civilization, traditionally dated to 2698 BC, who "invented" wooden houses, wheeled transport, the bow, writing and moral government. His reign was regarded as a golden age of order and prosperity. ▷ 1.27

HUELVA

See TARTESSOS

HUNTER-GATHERERS

People that depend on wild resources for their subsistence by hunting wild animals, fishing, and gathering plant foods and other materials. All humans were hunter-gatherers until the development of farming about 10,000 ya, each group adapting to local ecological conditions, with highly specialized social and economic systems. By 500 BC agriculture was the dominant mode of livelihood in most parts of the world, and hunter-gatherers were restricted to Arctic regions, North America, parts of South America, southern Africa and Australia. ▷ 1.01, 1.02, 1.03, 1.04, 1.05, 1.06, 1.08, 1.16, 1.19, 1.20

HURRIANS

People closely related to the Urartians, from the area to the southwest of the Caspian Sea, who moved into MESOPOTAMIA and Anatolia in the late 3rd millennium BC. They settled in northern Mesopotamia and Syria, overran ASSYRIA in about 1680 BC, and had established the powerful kingdom of MITTANI by about 500 BC. ▷ 1.11, 1.12

HYKSOS

Literally "chiefs of foreign lands", Semitic peoples who migrated from Asia to the Nile Delta in the 17th century BC, and whose influence spread throughout Lower Egypt at a time when central Egyptian government was weak (the 2nd Intermediate period). They were expelled from Egypt by AHMOSE I in about 1550 BC. ▷ 1.18

ICE AGES

The cold phases of the PLEISTOCENE EPOCH, a period of extreme oscillation in global temperatures with extensions and contractions of the polar ice sheets. The long-accepted sequence of four glacial/inter-glacial phases from 750,000 ya, recognized in the northern hemisphere, is now known to be too simplistic. Recent studies of polar ice cores and ocean sediments have identified at least 22 major warm and cold phases in the same period. ▷ 1.01, 1.02, 1.08, 1.16, 1.18, 1.19

ICE MAN

The frozen body of a man, dating from about 3350–3120 BC, discovered in an Alpine glacier on the Italian–Austrian border. Preserved equipment lying nearby included leather clothing, a fur hat, BOWS AND ARROWS, COPPER and stone tools, and a backpack made of wood and animal skins. The man had several small linear tattoos on his arms, legs and back. The discovery revealed that metal tools had come into use in west-central Europe far earlier than previously supposed. ▷ 1.20

ILIAD

One of Europe's great epics, traditionally ascribed to HOMER, which tells the story of the hero Achilles during the Greek siege of TROY. A poem about war and the pity of war, it explores the nature of heroism and leadership. It was probably brought to its final form in about 750 BC, but contains material that may be dated to MYCENAEAN times. ▷ 1.24

IMPRESSED POTTERY CULTURES

The earliest farming societies (c.6000–4000 BC) of the west Mediterranean region, characterized by pottery with impressed decoration, such as the Cardial Wares of southern France, and village settlements. Their farming economy, based on cereals, legumes and domestic animals, probably spread along the coast from the Balkans. ▷ 1.20, 1.21

INDO-EUROPEAN LANGUAGES

Group of related languages spoken in Europe, the Middle East and India, the origins of which are disputed. The prevailing view is that they derive from dialects spoken in the west Eurasian steppe region in the 4th to 3rd millennia BC, which spread as a result of population migrations. An alternative argument sees Indo-European origins in the adoption of Middle Eastern farming and associated economic and social practices, which spread throughout the Indo-European area in the NEOLITHIC period, from about 7000 to 5000 BC. ▷ 1.11, 1.12, 1.26

INDO-IRANIAN PEOPLES

Peoples who spoke Indo-Iranian languages, the easternmost branch of the INDO-EUROPEAN LANGUAGE group, who were probably originally pastoral nomads of the central Eurasian steppes. These included the ARYANS, who migrated into northern India in the mid-2nd. millennium BC, and the CIMMERIANS, SCYTHIANS, MEDES and Persians who migrated into different parts of the Middle East, Anatolia and Ukraine in the 9th–7th centuries BC. ▷ 1.13, 1.26

INDUS CIVILIZATION

A civilization that had emerged in the Indus valley by 2500 BC, with consistent features across a vast area from the Hindu Kush to the Arabian Sea, and from Baluchistan to Gujarat. STATE formation and URBANIZATION in the early 3rd millennium BC may have been partly stimulated by trade with MESOPOTAMIA. Planned towns, built of mud brick, included walled citadels with monumental buildings, civic granaries and housing areas. The two largest centers, at HARAPPA and MOHENJO-DARO, were probably capital cities, though their relative status is unknown.

The Indus economy was based on IRRIGATION farming of cereals, RICE, legumes and COTTON, with CATTLE for dairy products and traction. Domesticated elephants and camels were also exploited. Evidence exists of long-distance trade in silver, COPPER and lapis lazuli, with distant trading colonies such as SHORTHUGAI in the Hindu Kush, and maritime trade with SUMERIA. Little is known about Indus political organization or religion, but features such as the ritual bath at Mohenjo-daro are found in later Hindu contexts. Monumental art works are rare, but terracotta figurines, painted pottery, stone seals and an undeciphered pictographic script give the impression of a complex cultural life.

The decline and collapse of the Indus civilization in about 2000–1700 BC has not been fully explained, though flooding, soil degradation, over-population and political fragmentation have been suggested, with the final collapse of an already impoverished society at the time of the ARYAN invasions. Urban state cultures did not develop again in the Indian subcontinent for several centuries. ▷ 1.07, 1.26

INITIAL PERIOD

Period of ANDEAN CIVILIZATION from about 2000 to 900 BC, marked by full dependence on agriculture, farming villages, impressive ceremonial and temple complexes, IRRIGATION systems in the coastal lowlands, and the widespread introduction of pottery and COTTON-weaving. Marked regional cultures in this period gave way after 900 BC to the spread of the Chavin tradition. ▷ 1.28

IONIA, IONIAN GREEKS

A division of the Greek peoples, traditionally descendants of settlers from the Ionian "mother city" of Athens, found in communities on the central-western coast and islands of Asia Minor. Ionians pioneered the Ionic style of architecture and fostered early Greek philosophy. ▷ 1.23

IRON AGE

A subdivision of the THREE AGE SYSTEM that commences and ends at different times in different regions (it could be argued that it continued until the modern industrial era, c.AD 1750). It is misleading as a means of characterizing very complex and varied iron-using cultures. Iron metallurgy was practiced in Anatolia by about 1500 BC and spread rapidly throughout the Old World, except southern Africa, from 1100 to 500 BC. ▷ 1.05, 1.06, 1.12, 1.16, 1.21, 1.24, 1.26, 1.27

IRRIGATION

A means of controlling plant growth by ensuring and regulating water supply to produce consistent harvests and intensify production. Irrigation agriculture was a key factor in the development of complex civilizations in many parts of the world, particularly in MESOPOTAMIA and the Indus valley from the 6th to 3rd millennia BC, north China by 4000 BC, and in Mesoamerica and South America from the 2nd to 1st millennia BC. ▷ 1.03, 1.09, 1.17, 1.26, 1.27, 1.28

ISIAH

HEBREW prophet of the mid-8th century BC who warned the Israelites about the impending threat of Assyrian conquest (c.735 BC), which he saw in a vision and interpreted as a sign of divine condemnation of Israelite godlessness. ▷ 1.14

ISIN

City in south MESOPOTAMIA, ruled by an AMORITE dynasty by about 2000 BC. It briefly dominated SUMERIA in the 20th century BC, but lost its political independence to Lama and then BABYLON from about 1800 BC. It reasserted its independence in the 12th and 11th centuries BC, when several kings of Isin dominated BABYLONIA. ▷ 1.11, 1.12

ISRAEL, ANCIENT

HEBREW kingdom founded in the late 11th century BC by King SAUL and consolidated by DAVID (c.1006–965 BC). It reached its greatest

MEDITERRANEAN TRIAD

The so-called Mediterranean triad consisted of three staple crops: cereals, olives and vines. They could be farmed together on the same land and even in the most disastrous of years, at least one would crop. They formed the backbone of the Greek agricultural economy from the 8th century BC, with olives and vines spreading overseas with Greek settlements.

MEGALITHIC MONUMENT

Ceremonial or mortuary structure built of 'large stones" (from the Greek words *megas* and *lithikos*). The term is mainly applied to the NEOLITHIC and BRONZE AGE stone architecture of Europe, including CHAMBERED TOMBS, STONE CIRCLES and avenues, but is also applicable to building traditions such as the Iron Age MEGALITHIC TOMB CULTURE of India. ▷ 1.04, 1.20, 1.21, 1.26

MEGALITHIC TOMB CULTURE (INDIA)

Small-scale Iron Age agricultural societies of southern India in the 1st millennium BC that built distinctive MEGALITHIC tombs and other ceremonial monuments. This cultural tradition had indigenous NEOLITHIC origins and developed largely independently of the urban, state-organized societies of northern India. One of the culture's most important sites, Brahmagiri, contains more than 300 tombs and STONE CIRCLES. ▷ 1.26

MEGIDDO

Strategic town in Palestine, founded in the 4th millennium BC. It was often sacked and rebuilt, and owed allegiance to a succession of Egyptian, CANAANITE and Israelite rulers. It was refortified by SOLOMON OF ISRAEL in about 1000 BC, and was a major fortress of the kingdom of JUDAH. ▷ 1.14

MEHRGAHR

NEOLITHIC village in Baluchistan that was occupied from the 7th to 4th millennia BC. The adoption of Middle Eastern domesticates and similarities with aceramic farming settlements in the FERTILE CRESCENT suggest that agriculture spread rapidly across Iran. The long occupation sequence, with numerous layers of mud-brick houses, also provides important evidence of cultural change from the first village to the proto-urban center of the 4th millennium BC. ▷ 1.26

MEMPHIS

Strategically situated where the narrow Nile valley begins to broaden out into the Delta, Memphis was the natural choice for an Egyptian capital after the first unification of the country in about 3100 BC. The city remained an important administrative center throughout Egyptian history, and only fell into decline when Alexandria was built in the late 4th century BC. ▷ 1.13, 1.15, 1.17, 1.18

MENTUHOTPE II

Egyptian PHARAOH (r.2061–2010 BC) who is remembered for restoring order to the borders of Egypt following the breakdown of authority in the 1st Intermediate period. His impressive burial complex near THEBES, his capital, drew heavily on OLD KINGDOM models, doubtless as a means of asserting his legitimacy. ▷ 1.18

MEROË

Town situated on the Nile in NUBIA. It was the capital city of the Kushite kingdom in the 5th century BC, after the Kushites had retreated southwards from Egypt. An important center for IRON WORKING, the town later gave its name to the Meroitic kingdom, which was at its height from 300 BC to AD 350. Meroitic culture was heavily Egyptianized; its rulers were buried in small PYRAMIDS and worshipped Egyptian gods. ▷ 1.06, 1.15

MESILIM OF KISH

See KISH

MESOAMERICAN CIVILIZATIONS

A series of related Mesoamerican cultures that developed complex societies with STATE systems, ceremonial centers, cities and rich iconography and material culture, as well as the only fully literate culture of the ancient Americas (the Maya civilization of the Classic period). The history of Mesoamerican civilizations is divided into the following periods: ARCHAIC (c.7000–2000 BC), EARLY PRECLASSIC (c.2000–800 BC), MIDDLE PRECLASSIC (c.800–300 BC), Late Preclassic (c.300 BC–AD 300), Classic (c.AD 300–800), and Postclassic (c.AD 800–1520). ▷ 1.04, 1.05, 1.06, 1.07, 1.28

MESOLITHIC

The period of cultural transition in Europe (c.8000–4000 BC), following the end of the last glaciation, when UPPER PALEOLITHIC HUNTER-GATHERERS developed specialized cultural systems adapted to changing climatic conditions and new habitats. Mesolithic communities used sophisticated tool-kits with MICROLITHIC technology and a new emphasis on fishing equipment. In resource-rich coastal areas, such as Brittany and Denmark, the appearance in the late Mesolithic of semi-permanent settlements, ritual sites and formal burials suggests population growth and more complex social systems (e.g. ERTEBOLLE culture). These were the last groups in western Europe to adopt agricultural practices, and the first to build MEGALITHIC tombs. ▷ 1.19, 1.20

MESOPOTAMIAN CIVILIZATION

The distinctive STATE-organized urban cultures of the Tigris and Euphrates river system that formed a core area of civilization from the 4th millennium BC. Its key features include the first cities and large-scale IRRIGATION (by 3500 BC), the earliest writing system (Sumerian pictographs and CUNEIFORM), and

first imperial state (SARGON OF AGADE's Akkadian empire, c.2330 BC). Mesopotamian civilization was highly varied because of its diverse origins in independent city-states and its distinct ethnic communities, but it developed a shared religious and literate tradition with a considerable degree of continuity and integration, as each new dominant state tolerated local customs and adopted cultural and political features of their predecessors.

The complex history of the region can be divided into the following periods (with intermediate periods of political and cultural instability): URUK (c.4300–3100 BC), JEMDET NASR (c.3200–2900 BC), EARLY DYNASTIC (c.2900–2334 BC), Akkadian empire (c.2350–2200 BC), Third Dynasty of UR (c.2100–2000 BC), Old Babylonian and Old Assyrian (c.1900–1600 BC), Middle Assyrian empire (c.1360–1075 BC), Neo-Assyrian empire (c.930–612 BC) and Neo-Babylonian empire (612–539 BC). ▷ 1.04, 1.05, 1.10, 1.11, 1.12, 1.13, 1.14, 1.15

MESSENIA

Plain in the southwest Peloponnese annexed by SPARTA in the 8th century BC. Its native Greek peoples, the HELOTS as they became known, were treated as slaves by the Spartans and forced to work the land for their overlords. The area was liberated from Spartan control by the Thebans in the mid-4th century BC. ▷ 1.24

MEZHIRICH

UPPER PALEOLITHIC settlement in the Ukraine with a hut built partly of mammoth bones, dating from about 20,000 ya. The bones were probably used to weigh down tent awnings, but may also have had some social or religious significance. ▷ 1.19

MICHELSBERG

Late NEOLITHIC post-BANDKERAMIK culture of the Rhineland and northern France, between about 4000 and 2800 BC. It is named after a ceremonial enclosure site in the middle Rhine valley, with distinctive material culture and settlement sites. ▷ 1.20

MICROLITHIC TOOLS

Composite tools made of tiny, stone blade fragments, or "microliths", set in hafts singly (such as arrowheads) or edge-to-edge in groups (such as projectile barbs and sickle blades). Microliths are often geometric in shape and were made by snapping long blades into pieces for more versatile use. Microlithic tools are characteristic of the MESOLITHIC period in Europe but were used by many other cultures. ▷ 1.19

MIDAS

See MITAS

MIDDLE KINGDOM

Period in Egyptian history (c.2055–1650 BC) characterized by stability and prosperity. The

PHARAOH MENTUHOTPE II (12th Dynasty) successfully stabilized the kingdom over a long reign and order was maintained until a succession of weaker pharaohs of the 13th Dynasty lost control of the Delta and allowed the infiltration of the HYKSOS people. At its height the Middle Kingdom saw effective Egyptian control over NUBIA. It was also an age that produced the most famous of the so-called "Wisdom Texts', which extolled the virtues of good administration. ▷ 1.18

MIDDLE PRECLASSIC period
Period of MESOAMERICAN CIVILIZATION from about 800 to 300 BC, in which OLMEC CIVILIZATION reached the height of its cultural achievement, particularly in stone sculpture, jade carving and temple building, before it collapsed in the 5th to 4th centuries BC. Mayan civilization, which emerged in highland Guatemala and the Yucatan peninsula, has many features in common with the Olmecs, but also developed large-scale IRRIGATION farming systems that facilitated settlement growth and STATE formation (c.600–300 BC). Another complex society emerged in this period in the OAXACA VALLEY, Mexico, where the earliest writing system in the New World (ZAPOTEC hieroglyphic) was invented in the 8th century BC. ▷ 1.06, 1.07, 1.28

MILETOS
Important Greek city-state on the west coast of Asia Minor whose wealth came from its rich territory and trade. In the 6th century BC Miletos was an effective colonizer of the Black Sea coast, and the same period saw the work of its famous philosophers, Thales, Anaximander and Anaximenes. A leader of the unsuccessful IONIAN revolt against the Persians (499 BC), it never fully recovered its prosperity. ▷ 1.22, 1.23, 1.24

MILLET
Several species of grasses that produce small edible seeds, domesticated in different parts of the world at different times, notably in China, sub-Saharan Africa and Ethiopia by the 6th millennium BC, and in the Middle East by the 4th millennium BC. ▷ 1.03, 1.16, 1.27

MINOAN PALACE CIVILIZATION
Important civilization that flourished on CRETE between 2000 and 1450 BC. It was centered on large palaces (KHANIA, KNOSSOS, MALLIA and PHAISTOS), which were also religious and administrative centers. Originally relying on an agricultural economy, the Minoans also traded extensively in the Aegean and were fine craftsmen and fresco painters. Their civilization collapsed, probably as the result of a MYCENAEAN invasion. ▷ 1.07, 1.20, 1.22

MIOCENE EPOCH
Period of the Tertiary era (c.25–5 million ya), marked by cooling climatic conditions in which mammal species increasingly dominat-

ed terrestrial fauna, with hominid evolution in eastern Africa. ▷ 1.01

MITAS (MIDAS)
King of PHRYGIA, whose dates are traditionally given as 738–695 BC. A figure of fun for the Greeks, his greed is remembered in the story that he wished for everything he touched to be turned to gold, and then found he could not eat or drink anything. ▷ 1.13

MITTANI
A kingdom of north MESOPOTAMIA and Syria founded by HURRIAN invaders by about 1550 BC, after the decline of the Assyrian and Babylonian states which had ruled the region in the 19–17th centuries BC. Mittani controlled the strategic routes linking Hittite Anatolia, Mesopotamia, the Levantine ports, the Aegean states and Egypt, and was a major regional power from about 1500 to 1350 BC. It collapsed in the early 13th century BC after the HITTITES sacked the capital, WASHUKANNI, and conquered the western part of the kingdom (c.1340 BC), leaving the remainder to be conquered by the Assyrians (by c.1270 BC). Little is known about the political organization or culture of the Mittani state, which left few written records. ▷ 1.12, 1.18

MOAB
Highland region of Palestine to the east of the Dead Sea occupied in biblical times by the Moabites, a Semitic people closely related to the Israelites, who may have settled in Palestine in the 14th century BC. The Moabite kingdom was often at war with ISRAEL and JUDAH, and was destroyed by the Babylonians in about 582 BC. ▷ 1.13, 1.14

MOHENJO-DARO
The largest of the two great cities of the INDUS CIVILIZATION (the other being HARAPPA), situated beside the Indus river in Sind (south Pakistan). The city was probably founded in the early 3rd millennium BC, laid out in a series of residential blocks with a grid street plan and drainage system. On one side of the city was a monumental brick-built citadel which may have served as the royal and religious center of the Indus state, with a huge granary, residential buildings, aisled ceremonial halls and a ritual bath. Massive flooding and local environmental deterioration probably led to its decline and eventual abandonment by about 1700 BC. ▷ 1.26

MOUSTERIAN CULTURE
MIDDLE PALEOLITHIC tool industry of west Eurasia and north Africa, about 150,000 to 40,000 ya, that is often associated with HOMO SAPIENS NEANDERTHALENSIS. The Moustierian culture is characterized by its distinctive flaking techniques and range of tools, including small hand axes, flake tools, and the first hafted projectiles (spears for close-impact hunting of large game). Differences in tool assemblages from site to

site may indicate cultural variation or seasonal specializations. ▷ 1.01, 1.19

MUMMIFICATION
The process, used by the ancient Egyptians, of preserving a corpse in preparation for burial, in the belief that only a preserved body ("mummy") could enjoy an afterlife. Carried out in accordance with strict rules over a period of some 70 days, it involved preserving some organs separately, while soaking the rest of the body in natron, a natural drying agent. The body was then bound in cloth and placed in a coffin.

MURSILIS I
King of the HITTITES (r.c.1620–1590 BC). The most successful king of the Old Kingdom period, he extended Hittite rule in Anatolia and northern Syria, and undertook a campaign down the Euphrates, sacking BABYLON in 1595 BC. He was killed in a palace coup. ▷ 1.11

MUSHKI (MYSIANS)
People who were related to the PHRYGIANS and who settled in northeast Anatolia in the 12th century BC, after the collapse of the HITTITE empire. Allied with native HURRIANS and Kaskas, they invaded MESOPOTAMIA but were defeated by TIGLATH-PILESER I of ASSYRIA in 1115 BC. ▷ 1.12

MUWATALLIS II
King of the HITTITES (r.1295–1271 BC). He opposed the Egyptian attempt under PHARAOH RAMESSES II to regain control of Syria and inflicted a strategic defeat on the Egyptian PHARAOH at the Battle of QADESH (c.1285 BC), successfully extending Hittite control as far south as Damascus. ▷ 1.12

MYCENAE
An impressively fortified hilltop city with a palace and lavishly furnished royal tombs in the Peloponnese, occupied from the 16th to 12th centuries BC. Its most famous features are the famous Lion Gate and the so-called "Treasury of Atreus", actually a magnificent THOLOS tomb. Mycenae was excavated in the 19th century by the pioneering German archaeologist, Heinrich Schliemann, and many spectacular artifacts, including gold death masks, were discovered. ▷ 1.21, 1.22, 1.23

MYCENAEAN CIVILIZATION
First GREEK-speaking civilization (c.1600–1200 BC), named after MYCENAE, its most important site. The Mycenaean civilization centered on a number of independent rulers, each with their own stronghold. Mycenaeans traded extensively overseas and conquered CRETE in about 1450 BC, where they adapted the LINEAR A script to write their own language (LINEAR B). Excavations at many Mycenaean sites, including Mycenae, indicate that the civilization came to a violent end, though its attackers are unknown. ▷ 1.21, 1.22, 1.23

NABATEAN ALPHABET

Variant of the CANAANITE phonetic alphabet developed by the Nabataeans in Arabia for writing their ARAMAIC LANGUAGE (c.1000 BC). It was most widely used in the Nabataean kingdom of Petra from about 150 BC to AD 150, and gave rise to the Arabic scripts of the Middle Ages. ▷ 1.07

NABONIDUS

The last king of BABYLON (r.555–539 BC). An imperial official crowned by the ruling aristocracy, Nabonidus was defeated by CYRUS the Great of Persia in 539 BC, after which BABYLONIA submitted peacefully to ACHEMINID rule. ▷ 1.13, 1.15

NABOPOLASSAR

King of BABYLON (r.626–605 BC) and the king of the CHALDEAN 11th dynasty, who reasserted Babylonian independence. Nabopolassar drove the Assyrians out of BABYLONIA before attacking ASSYRIA. He destroyed the Assyrian capital at NINEVEH in 612 BC and took over Assyrian domains. ▷ 1.13

NAPATA

District of Nubia that served as the center of the Kushite kingdom between 1000 BC and 300 BC, before the kingdom moved southwards to MEROË.

NARAM-SIN

King of AKKAD (r.2254–2218 BC), who was the grandson of SARGON of AGADE and ruled the Akkadian empire at the height of its power. He consolidated Akkadian domains, protected key trade routes, founded numerous temples and may have assumed theocratic powers. ▷ 1.11

NARMER

Early Egyptian ruler who was possibly responsible for the first unification of Egypt (c.3000 BC) and the foundation of the capital at MEMPHIS. The famous Narmer palette found at HIERAKONPOLIS shows for the first time a king wearing the Crowns of both Lower and Upper Egypt. ▷ 1.17

NATUFIAN CULTURE

Late glacial and early Holocene EPIPALEOLITHIC culture, dating from about 12,500 to 10,500 ya (8500 BC), of the LEVANT and SYRIAX, with an intensive cereal-collecting and gazelle-hunting economy. They became increasingly settled, living in small villages of permanent houses at sites such as JERICHO, with shrines and formal burials, and selectively modified plant-growing conditions that led to incipient farming. ▷ 1.08

NEANDERTHALS

See HOMO SAPIENS NEANDERTHALENSIS

NEBUCHADNEZZAR

King of BABYLON (r.604–562 BC), the son of NABOPOLASSAR. While he was still crown-prince he defeated the Egyptians at CARCHEMISH in Syria in 605 BC, and undertook campaigns in Syria, ELAM and the LEVANT, ensuring Babylonian supremacy in the Middle East by about 590 BC. He crushed revolts in JUDAH in 597 and 587 BC, and deported the population to BABYLONIA. He rebuilt his capital at Babylon on a vast and magnificent scale. His dynasty was overthrown soon after his death. ▷ 1.13, 1.15

NECHO II

Egyptian PHARAOH (r.610–595 BC), the third of the Saite dynasty, who founded Egypt's first navy and reconquered the LEVANT as the ASSYRIAN EMPIRE disintegrated. He was finally checked by the Babylonians in 605 BC. ▷ 1.13

NEOLITHIC

The final phase of the STONE AGE, in which farming was the main form of subsistence production, leading to population growth, village settlements and ranking, while stone remained the principal material used in tool manufacture. The term is still used to refer to early agricultural societies in the Old World. ▷ 1.03, 1.04, 1.06, 1.08, 1.09, 1.10, 1.16, 1.19, 1.20, 1.27

NEW KINGDOM

The third and final of the three great kingdoms of ancient Egypt (1550–1070 BC). The period saw the extension of Egyptian power into Syria and Palestine and the intense exploitation of NUBIA. Among its great PHARAOHS was the conqueror TUTHMOSIS III, the heretic king AKHENATEN and the great builder RAMESSES II; among its most spectacular legacies are the contents of the tomb of TUTANKHAMUN. In the late New Kingdom the power of the temple priesthoods was greatly increased through excessive grants of land by the pharaohs, leading to the decline of royal authority and the loss of Egypt's empire in Nubia and the Near East. ▷ 1.18

NEWGRANGE

Enormous early NEOLITHIC PASSAGE GRAVE located in the Boyne valley ceremonial center in Ireland, built in about 3000 BC. The passage is oriented on sunrise at the midwinter solstice, when the sun's rays illuminate the central chamber. The stone kerb around the mound is elaborately decorated with carvings. Two similar monuments (Knowth and Dowth) are located nearby, as well as numerous satellite tombs. ▷ 1.20

NINEVEH

Assyrian city situated beside the Tigris in central MESOPOTAMIA. Although an important commercial and religious center by 3000 BC, it did not play a major role in Assyrian history until the 9th to 7th centuries BC, when successive rulers built large temples and palaces. It became the Assyrian capital in 705 BC, provided with magnificent buildings and replanned on a grandiose scale, with wide streets, a water-supply system, monumental gates, arsenal and palaces (including Ashurbanipal's palace and library, from which thousands of clay tablets have been recovered). The city was destroyed in 612 BC when the Babylonians and MEDES overthrew the Assyrian empire. Nineveh was rediscovered by the pioneering Victorian archaeologist, Austen Henry Layard, in 1849. ▷ 1.09, 1.10, 1.11, 1.12, 1.13, 1.15

NIPPUR

Major city and the most important religious center in SUMERIA, founded by 4000 BC. Nippur was the site of the temple of ENLIL, the storm god responsible for sanctifying secular power, making control of the city essential for any ambitious MESOPOTAMIAN king. The final temple sanctuary was built by UR-NAMMU, king of UR, in about 2100 BC. ▷ 1.09, 1.10, 1.12, 1.13

NUBIA

Region along the Nile, south of Egypt, that acted as a corridor between Egypt and the rest of Africa. The more powerful Egyptian kingdoms, especially the NEW KINGDOM, exploited its resources mercilessly, but at times of Egyptian weakness it maintained its own cultures (the KERMA culture) and kingdoms (the Kushite). The Kushite dynasty (747–656 BC) from NAPATA was powerful enough to rule Egypt itself. ▷ 1.14, 1.15, 1.16, 1.17, 1.18

OAXACA VALLEY

Highland area of south Mexico where complex societies developed in the 2nd millennium BC, influenced from about 1200 BC by the OLMECS. It was the core area of ZAPOTEC civilization, which developed in the 1st millennium BC, with an early ceremonial center at Monté Albán and hillside agricultural terraces and settlements. ▷ 1.28

OBSIDIAN

Volcanic glass with flaking properties similar (but superior) to flint, widely used and highly valued for toolmaking in many parts of the world, notably in MESOPOTAMIA, where long-distance trade in obsidian was important by 7500 BC, and in Mesoamerica, where control of obsidian resources was essential for the lowland civilizations of the OLMEC and Maya. ▷ 1.08, 1.09, 1.28

ODYSSEY

Greek epic poem attributed to HOMER (c.700 BC), that tells the story of the hero Odysseus' return from the TROJAN WAR. His adventures include encounters with gods, monsters (the Cyclops) and the hazards of the sea. He eventually arrives at his homeland, Ithaca, to be reunited with his wife, Penelope. The *Odyssey* is the archetypal story of a hero battling against great odds to reach ultimate happiness. ▷ 1.24

OLD KINGDOM
The first of the great kingdoms of ancient Egypt (2686–2181 BC). It was characterized by powerful rulers who diverted enormous resources towards the building of the PYRAMIDS as their burial places. The strain on the economy, possibly intensified by climatic changes, led to the slow disintegration of the kingdom and a period of disorder (the 1st Intermediate period). ▷ 1.17

OLDOWAN CULTURE
The earliest tool industry (c.2.4–1.4 million ya) that is associated with the first humans (HOMO HABILIS) at sites in east Africa, such as OLDUVAI GORGE (after which it is named), KOOBI FORA and OMO. Flaked pebble tools, choppers and flakes were used for crushing, cutting and scraping. The more consistent Developed Oldowan industry (c.1.5–0.7 million ya), contemporary with early ACHEULIAN industries, was probably employed by hand-ax users for specific tasks. ▷ 1.01

OLDUVAI GORGE
A complex of ravines in the African Rift Valley, Tanzania, cutting through volcanic deposits and ancient lake and river sediments. They contain important early hominid remains (HOMO HABILIS, AUSTRALOPITHECUS ROBUSTUS, HOMO ERECTUS and HOMO SAPIENS), and the longest sequence of PALEOLITHIC tool industries (c.2.1 million—15,000 ya), with a succession of OLDOWAN, ACHEULIAN, MIDDLE PALEOLITHIC and UPPER PALEOLITHIC assemblages. ▷ 1.01

OLMEC CIVILIZATION
The earliest MESOAMERICAN CIVILIZATION, which developed in the humid lowland region along the Gulf coast of southern Mexico from 1250 BC. The Olmecs established a set of political, religious and aesthetic traditions which influenced later Mesoamerican cultures, with large ceremonial centers (notably TRES ZAPOTES, LA VENTA and SAN LORENZO), platform mounds and step pyramids, monumental stone carving, expansive and warlike states, and distinctive religious iconography.

Most stone resources used for the building of monuments (basalt and serpentine) and for portable material culture (OBSIDIAN and jade) had to be imported from highland regions, extending the Olmec sphere of influence. Hieroglyphic writing and a complex calendar had been invented for ritual purposes by about 700 BC, though there is no evidence that the Olmecs developed a literary culture. The decline of Olmec civilization and the destruction of its ceremonial centers took place between about 600 and 400 BC, probably as a result of political fragmentation and economic stresses. The Maya, who were deeply influenced by the Olmecs, became the dominant cultural force in Mesoamerica from about 400 BC. ▷ 1.28

OLYMPIA
Site of the OLYMPIC GAMES, Olympia is situated in the fertile Alpheus valley, in the north west Peloponnese. The site was an important PAN-HELLENIC sanctuary to the god Zeus, whose festivals came to be dominated by the famous games. The temple to Zeus, dating from the mid-5th century BC, contains fine classical sculptures. ▷ 1.24

OLYMPIC GAMES
Games held at OLYMPIA every four years between 776 BC and AD 393, at which aristocratic athletes from throughout the Greek world would compete in a range of events, including athletics, wrestling and chariot racing. The prizes were modest, but the honor of winning was great. ▷ 1.24

OMO
Region at the north end of Lake Turkana in Ethiopia, with ancient lake and river sediments dating from about 4 million ya, rich in early hominid fossil remains (australopithecines and HOMO ERECTUS) and tool industries (early pebble tools). Perhaps most significant is the discovery made there of the earliest fossils – about 135,000 years old – of HOMO SAPIENS SAPIENS. ▷ 1.01, 1.02

OPIS, BATTLE OF
Defeat of the last king of BABYLONIA, NABONIDUS, by CYRUS the Great in 539 BC, removing the last serious threat to the early ACHEMENID EMPIRE. ▷ 1.15

ORACLE BONES
Animal bones, especially ox scapulae and turtle shells, with engraved or painted inscriptions (pictographs), that were used for divination in China during the LONGSHAN and SHANG periods (from c.2500 BC). Cracks in the bone caused by applying heat were interpreted according to their patterns and relation to inscriptions (China's first written script). ▷ 1.27

ORACLE, GREEK
Both city-states and individuals used oracles as a means of divining the future or receiving advice on matters as diverse as marriage, overseas settlement or whether to go to war. The most celebrated oracle was at DELPHI, where answers were given by a priestess who entered a trance to consult the god Apollo. ▷ 1.24

ORKNEY, NEOLITHIC
Group of islands off the north coast of Britain with important NEOLITHIC remains dating from about 3500 to 2000 BC. These include the well-preserved SKARA BRAE settlement, the MAES HOWE PASSAGE GRAVE, and many other MEGALITHIC sites (e.g. the Ring of Brodgar and Stenness STONE CIRCLES). This concentration of monuments offers an unusually detailed view of Neolithic settlement, social organization and ritual practices. ▷ 1.20

OSCANS
Proto-historic inhabitants of southern Italy who are difficult to identify with historically documented groups. The language of the same name – Oscan – was spoken by various Italian groups (notably the SAMNITES, Frentani, Lucani, Bruttii and Apuli). Oscan is an INDO-EUROPEAN Italic language that was widely used until the 1st century BC; it then survived in some local dialects into the imperial period. Many Oscan inscriptions survive, most dating from 300 to 90 BC. ▷ 1.25

PAINTED WARE CULTURES
Earliest farming cultures of Anatolia and the Balkans (c.7000–6000 BC), where native populations adopted Near Eastern domesticates, ceramic technologies and similar social institutions, with village communities, mud-brick houses and long-lived TELL settlement sites. These cultures produced distinctive styles of painted pottery. ▷ 1.20

PALEOINDIANS
Earliest human populations in the Americas, the descendants of HUNTER-GATHERER bands who colonized the New World from at least 15,000 ya, crossing the Bering Straits land-bridge from Siberia. The first "Lower Lithic" cultures remain elusive. The best-known Paleoindian cultures are the CLOVIS-FOLSOM big-game hunters of North America. ▷ 1.02

PALEOLITHIC
The first phase of the STONE AGE of the THREE AGE SYSTEM and the earliest period of human toolmaking. The Paleolithic is itself divided into three stages – the LOWER PALEOLITHIC, MIDDLE PALEOLITHIC and UPPER PALEOLITHIC – each with distinctive stone technologies and tool-kits, and each associated with different human species and different forms of human subsistence and social organization. ▷ 1.01, 1.02, 1.19

PALEOLITHIC, LOWER
Tool industries of the early human species HOMO HABILIS and HOMO ERECTUS, dating from about 2.4 million to 230,000 ya. The earliest pebble tool industries, such as the OLDOWAN, were largely replaced by hand-ax industries, such as the ACHEULIAN. These tools were used mainly for scavenging and food processing, rather than hunting. ▷ 1.01

PALEOLITHIC, MIDDLE
Tool industries of the archaic HOMO SAPIENS and regional variants, such as the NEANDERTHALS in west Eurasia (associated with the MOUSTERIAN industry), characterized by an emphasis on the use of flake tools for a more flexible adaptation to local resources and specialized tasks, including the use of spears for hunting. ▷ 1.01, 1.02, 1.19

PALEOLITHIC, UPPER
Tool industries of HOMO SAPIENS SAPIENS that were based on blade technologies and

Rome until 509 BC when the Roman republic was established.

Relatively little is known archaeologically about the city in the regal and earlier republican periods; the extensive remains now visible mainly date to the later republic and empire. The city was embellished by the great patrician families and emperors, with major civic building projects such as forums, temples, theaters and circuses. As Rome's population grew, so did its infrastructure of roads, aqueducts and warehouses. Rome's political importance declined in the 3rd century AD as it was abandoned by the emperors for centers closer to the embattled frontiers. Following the fall of the western Roman empire in the 5th century, Rome's population declined dramatically, but the city retained importance as the leading Christian center in western Europe. ▷ 1.25

SABA
Ancient kingdom of southwest Arabia, known in biblical references as Sheba. Saba was founded by Semitic Sabaeans of the north from about 1200 BC. By the 7th to 5th centuries BC, it was a centralized state with IRRIGATION agriculture, monumental temples, and control over the Red Sea-Indian Ocean trade routes. ▷ 1.05, 1.06

SABEAN SCRIPT AND LANGUAGE
A writing system ultimately based on the proto-CANAANITE phonetic alphabet that was adapted by the Semitic-speaking Sabean people of southwest Arabia from about 1000 BC and used for record-keeping and monument inscriptions. ▷ 1.07

SABINES
A people of ancient Italy occupying the area northeast of ROME, along the west side of the Tiber valley. The Sabines figure largely in the legends of early Rome, though archeological data is scanty. Some recent excavations, however, reveal material culture similarities with LATIUM in the Iron Age. The Sabines were finally defeated by Rome in 290 BC and were granted full citizenship in 268 BC. ▷ 1.25

SAKAS
INDO-IRANIAN pastoral nomad people of the central Asian steppes who raided the northeastern satrapies of the ACHEMENID EMPIRE in the late 6th and 5th centuries BC. CYRUS the Great built a chain of forts to defend the frontier against the Sakas and was killed fighting them in 530 BC. ▷ 1.06, 1.15

SAMARIA
A city in central Palestine that was founded by King Omri in about 880 BC as the new capital of ISRAEL. Some of Samaria's buildings of the 9th century BC have PHOENICIAN features. The city was destroyed by Shalmaneser V of ASSYRIA in 724 BC, after a three-year siege. ▷ 1.14

SAMARRAN CULTURE
Late NEOLITHIC culture of central MESOPOTAMIA, characterized by painted pottery styles with animal and human figures. Dating from about 6000 to 5500 BC, it follows the HASSUNA CULTURE and marks the extension of agricultural societies southwards. Samarran communities lived in large villages and developed large-scale IRRIGATION systems (at CHOGA MAMI), increasing crop yields and allowing for settlement of the Mesopotamian plains. ▷ 1.09

SAMNITES
A warlike OSCAN-speaking people of ancient Italy in the central-south Apennines, divided into a powerful confederation of the Caraceni, Caudini, Hirpini and Pentri tribes. Even after losing the Samnite wars, they supported Pyrrhus and Hannibal against ROME, fought in the Social War and against Sulla in the civil war. Latin colonies were established at Beneventum (268 BC) and Aesernia (263 BC), but Romanization was relatively slow. ▷ 1.25

SAN LORENZO
Earliest OLMEC ceremonial center, situated on a plateau beside the fertile Coatzacoalcos river plain. The main phase of building (c.1200–900 BC) involved construction work to raise the surface of the natural plateau, huge lateral ridges for access, mounds for timber houses (for an elite community of about 1,000 people), temple mounds, altars with stone carvings, and massive sculpted stone heads (portraits of Olmec kings or gods). It was destroyed in about 900 BC, when many sculptures were deliberately broken and buried. ▷ 1.28

SANXINGDUI
City occupied in the 2nd millennium BC, contemporary with the SHANG dynasty, that was recently discovered in central China. Found bronze objects indicate a high degree of technical sophistication and cultural complexity. The relationship between Sanxingdui and Shang China is uncertain. ▷ 1.27

SAQQARA
Important Egyptian site, close to MEMPHIS, and the burial place of many of Egypt's early kings, including NARMER. The most impressive monument is the STEP PYRAMID (c.2630 BC) built for the PHARAOH DJOSER. After THEBES became the focus for royal burials, Saqqara continued to be used for the burials of Memphis officials. ▷ 1.04, 1.17

SARDIS
Capital of the LYDIAN kingdom of western Anatolia from the 7th to 6th centuries BC, with a large citadel and the earliest known coin mint. It was captured, along with King CROESUS, by CYRUS the Great in 546 BC, and became the capital of a satrapy of the ACHEMINID EMPIRE. ▷ 1.15

SARGON OF AGADE (THE GREAT)
Akkadian king of KISH who founded the first imperial state (c.2334–2279 BC), ruling AKKAD and SUMERIA, north MESOPOTAMIA, the north LEVANT and ELAM. He controlled the maritime trade routes to the Persian Gulf, the Indus and the east Mediterranean, and the land routes to central Anatolia and Iran. He founded the city of Agade as a capital for his empire, but its location has not been discovered. His empire lasted for a century and reached its greatest extent under his grandson, NARAM-SIN, before it disintegrated in the early 22nd century BC. Sargon was a model for later Mesopotamian rulers and his life became the subject of many legends. ▷ 1.10, 1.11

SARGON II
King of ASSYRIA (r.721–705 BC), probably the son of TIGLATH-PILESER III, named after SARGON OF AGADE. Sargon II consolidated the conquests of his father, expanded Assyrian rule in URARTU (714 BC) and conquered south MESOPOTAMIA (710–07 BC). The Assyrian empire reached its greatest power and influence under his reign. He was probably killed in battle in Anatolia in 705 BC. ▷ 1.13

SARMATIANS
INDO-IRANIAN pastoral nomad people of the central Eurasian steppes who were closely related to the SCYTHIANS. The Sarmatians migrated into the Ural region in the 5th century BC, before conquering the Scythians and settling in the Ukraine and Balkans in the 4th-2nd centuries BC. ▷ 1.06

SAUL
First king of ISRAEL (r.c.1020–c.1006 BC), proclaimed ruler by the judge Samuel to unify the Israelites against the PHILISTINES and AMALEKITES. He was killed by the Philistines at the Battle of Gilboa. ▷ 1.14

SCYTHIANS
INDO-IRANIAN pastoral nomads of central Asia who migrated westwards and southwards in the 8th–7th centuries BC, displacing the CIMMERIANS and settling in the Ukraine (Royal Scythians) and the Caspian region (Pointed Hat Scythians). They are famous for their warlike character and rich tradition of metalworking, examples of which have been found in ROUND BARROW tombs. They were later absorbed by local populations or dispersed by further nomad invaders, such as the SARMATIANS, in the 4th-2nd centuries BC. ▷ 1.06, 1.15, 1.23

SEA PEOPLES
Groups of migrants of uncertain origin, who may have included elements from Libya, the northern Aegean, Asia Minor and even Sardinia. They raided widely around the eastern Mediterranean, as far south as Egypt, in about 1200 BC. Relatively little is known

about them, though the HITTITE empire and the MYCENAEAN CIVILIZATION may have disintegrated as a result of their attacks. The Egyptians drove them off the Delta in 1180 BC, though one group, the Peleset (PHILISTINES) settled in Palestine, which is named after them. ▷ 1.12, 1.18, 1.22

SEMITES
Speakers of the Semitic languages, which originated in Arabia and western MESOPOTAMIA, and spread as the Semitic peoples migrated and conquered neighboring regions (3rd–1st millennia BC), either replacing existing populations or establishing ruling elites that imposed their own languages. These peoples include the Akkadians, AMORITES, CANAANITES, HEBREWS, ARAMAEANS, CHALDEANS, PHOENICIANS, Sabaeans and Arabs. ▷ 1.04, 1.05, 1.06, 1.07, 1.11, 1.12, 1.13, 1.14, 1.15

SENNACHERIB
King of ASSYRIA (r.704–681 BC) who maintained Assyrian dominance, though threatened by local or CHALDEAN and Elamite-inspired rebellions in BABYLONIA. He suppressed a revolt in Palestine (701 BC), and undertook six campaigns in Babylonia and ELAM, eventually destroying BABYLON in 689 BC. He moved the Assyrian capital to NINEVEH. ▷ 1.13, 1.14

SHALMANESER III
King of ASSYRIA (r.858–824 BC) who attempted, with varying success, to extend Assyrian dominion over the LEVANT and elsewhere. He was resisted at Qarqar in 854 BC by a coalition of Levantine states, including ISRAEL. The Assyrian empire entered a period of instability after his death. ▷ 1.13

SHAMSHI-ADAD
AMORITE king of SHUBAT-ENLIL (r.1813–1781 BC) who seized control of ASHUR in about 1813 BC and established the first major territorial state in north MESOPOTAMIA. The kingdom declined thereafter and was under BABYLONIAN control by 1750 BC. ▷ 1.11

SHANG CIVILIZATION
The first state-organized urban culture of China, known from both historical and archeological sources, that was ruled by the Shang dynasty from their heartland in the Yellow river region. The semi-mythical founder of the dynasty, King Tang, is said to have deposed the last of the morally corrupt XIA kings in 1766 BC, though archeological evidence suggests a more gradual centralization from the 19th to 17th centuries BC.
A notable feature of Shang culture is their magnificent bronze work, using unique piece-mould casting processes to produce highly decorated ceremonial vessels and weaponry. A pictographic script, initially written on ORACLE BONES for divination purposes, was adapted for secular use, such

as inscriptions on bronze vessels. Shang cities such as ANYANG were built of rammed earth and timber, with massive ramparts, monumental buildings and large populations. Evidence from inscriptions, later histories and royal burials (accompanied by bronze and jade artifacts and human sacrifices) suggest that Shang society had a clan structure, with a strict social hierarchy and a warrior aristocracy engaged in constant warfare. Shang China became increasingly centralized, bureaucratic (with standard systems of measurement) and expansive. The last king of the Shang, DI-XIN, was overthrown by the ZHOU DYNASTY in 1122 BC. ▷ 1.05, 1.07, 1.27

SHANIDAR
MIDDLE and UPPER PALEOLITHIC cave site in the Zagros mountains, modern Iraq, with important MOUSTERIAN occupation levels. The site contains Neanderthal burials (including a disabled individual who must have been cared for by his companions). ▷ 1.01

SHEEP
Several species of sheep were domesticated in prehistory, the most important being *Ovis orientalis* in the Zagros mountains (by c.9000 BC) and *Ovis vignei* in central Asia (by c.4000 BC). It is possible that other species, such as the European *Ovis musimon*, were also domesticated. Sheep were important sources of meat in NEOLITHIC economies, and later became important for textile manufacture (WOOL). ▷ 1.03, 1.08, 1.09, 1.20, 1.21, 1.22

SHORTHUGAI
An INDUS CIVILIZATION settlement to the north of the Hindu Kush, near the Oxus (Amu Darya) river in north Afghanistan, 500 kilometers (310 miles) from the nearest Indus towns. It was probably a trading colony, founded by 2000 BC, for importing lapis lazuli and other raw materials. ▷ 1.26

SHOSHENQ I
Egyptian PHARAOH (r.945–924 BC) of Libyan extraction, who temporarily regained control of Palestine after a period of Egyptian weakness and withdrawal. ▷ 1.14, 1.18

SHUBAT-ENLIL
City in north MESOPOTAMIA that was founded as a new capital by King SHAMSHI-ADAD of ASSYRIA in about 1800 BC, on the site of an earlier city that had been abandoned in about 2200 BC. The city declined after his death and was destroyed by the Babylonians in about 1726 BC. ▷ 1.11

SICULI (SICELS)
The name given by the Greeks to the indigenous peoples of east Sicily in the later 8th century BC. It has not been possible to distinguish them archaeologically from the other local groups, such as the Elymi. ▷ 1.25

SIDON
City on the Levantine coast that was founded in the 3rd millennium BC. Sidon was one of the most important PHOENICIAN city-states from about 1000 BC and became the most prosperous of the coastal cities after the annexation of the region by the Persian empire in about 530 BC. ▷ 1.14

SILBURY HILL
The largest prehistoric mound in Europe, situated in the AVEBURY late NEOLITHIC monument complex in the Kennet valley, England. It was built in three phases in the mid-3rd millennium BC for ceremonial purposes, and was sited so that only the top could be seen from contemporary monuments nearby, though its specific function is unknown. ▷ 1.20

SIWA
Remote oasis site in the desert west of Egypt, known for its oracle to Amun. An expedition under the Persian king CAMBYSES failed to reach it, but Alexander the Great succeeded in getting there, believing that the priests had saluted him as the son of Amun and thus the true PHARAOH. ▷ 1.15

SKARA BRAE
NEOLITHIC farming and fishing village on the coast of the largest of the ORKNEY Islands, northern Britain, inhabited in the 3rd millennium BC. The small nucleated group of stone-built houses linked by paved alleys, with central hearths and stone cupboards, were unusually well-preserved under wind-blown sand and occupation debris. ▷ 1.20

SKUDRA
Region of the southern Balkans (Thrace) on the north side of the Aegean, that was established as the only satrapy of the ACHEMINID EMPIRE on the mainland of Europe after the invasion by DARIUS I in 538 BC. It sent horses and weapons as tribute to the Persian emperor. ▷ 1.15

SLAVERY (ANCIENT WORLD)
Slavery, the ownership of one individual by another, was known throughout the ancient world, but Greece and ROME in particular depended heavily on slave labor. In Greece the subjection of the slave served to emphasize the freedom of the citizen. Slaves were used as domestic servants, on farms, in manufacturing and in mines, and their treatment ranged from the benign to the brutal. In Rome slaves were often seized as the fruits of victories, though a flourishing slave trade was also in existence. By contrast with Greece, in Rome slaves could be given their freedom, and many "freedmen" prospered as a result. Slavery was as prevalent in late antiquity as it had been in earlier times, and the coming of Christianity had no impact on the institution. ▷ 1.10, 1.22, 1.24

BC), a design feature of later Mesopotamian temples. ▷ 1.09

TEPE YAHYA
Settlement in southern Iran occupied from the 5th millennium BC, with evidence of the earliest bronze metallurgy to use arsenic to improve the casting properties of smelted ores (c.3800 BC). In the 3rd millennium BC it was a major center for the manufacture of soapstone vessels and seals. ▷ 1.10

TERRA AMATA
LOWER PALEOLITHIC occupation site found in fossil beach deposits in southern France, dating from about 230,000 ya. Evidence of oval brushwood shelters (potentially the earliest known human structures) is disputed by most archaeologists. ▷ 1.01

THEBES (EGYPT)
The Greek name for the southern Egyptian town of Waset. Thebes rose to prominence after its ruling family initiated the MIDDLE KINGDOM and its local god, Amun, became the dominant Egyptian deity. During the NEW KINGDOM period Thebes, the religious capital of Egypt, reached the height of prosperity, with enormous temples to Amun and other gods erected at LUXOR and KARNAK. ▷ 1.18

THERA
Island in the southern Aegean that was the scene of an immense volcanic eruption in about 1626 BC, which some historians believe may have given rise to the Atlantis legend. Its most flourishing town, Akrotiri, has been rediscovered beneath the lava, providing magnificent examples of MINOAN-style frescoes. ▷ 1.22, 1.24

THESSALY
Large region of northeastern Greece, made up of two plains enclosed by mountains, with little access to the sea. For much of its history Thessaly was a federation of states with only the occasional ruler (e.g. Jason, the TYRANT of the 4th century BC) exercising strong central control. The plains were easily subdued by Philip II of Macedon in the 4th century BC. ▷ 1.24, 1.25

THOLOS
A circular building. The term often refers to the vaulted "beehive" tombs of the Mycenaeans that originated in MESSENIA and reached their most sophisticated form at MYCENAE in the 14th century BC (as in the "Treasury of Atreus"). ▷ 1.22

THRACIANS
People of uncertain origin who occupied the southern Balkans between the Aegean and the Danube (Thrace) from the 7th century BC, known from early historical texts (Herodotus) and archeological sources. They were ethnically heterogenous, with a horse-riding elite, possibly drawn from warrior

pastoralists, who migrated into eastern Europe in the early 1st millennium BC. The Thracians developed close trading and cultural links with the Greeks, and had established a STATE system by the 5th century BC. ▷ 1.05, 1.06, 1.12, 1.15, 1.23, 1.24, 1.25

THREE AGE SYSTEM
An evolutionary classification of human culture, based on tool technologies and materials (STONE AGE, BRONZE AGE and IRON AGE), first proposed by the Danish archeologist Christian Thomsen in 1816–19. It is now accepted that the scheme has no analytical value, being applicable in strict terms only to Eurasia and north Africa (with different temporal parameters in different regions). It is considered too crude a means of characterizing the complexity and variety of ancient cultures, and too simplistic as a way of representing cultural change. The terms Bronze Age and Iron Age are sometimes still used for broad descriptive purposes.

TIBETO-BURMESE
HUNTER-GATHERER peoples with closely-related languages who lived in the Himalayan region and who adopted transhumant PASTORALISM from about 1500 BC. They were influenced by contacts with herding communities in India and by the steppe pastoralists of central Asia. ▷ 1.04

TIGLATH-PILESER I
King of ASSYRIA (r.1115–1076 BC). He resisted invasions by HURRIANS and KASKAS of Anatolia, but failed in his attempt to revive Assyrian dominance by controlling ARAMAEAN settlers. The empire declined after his death, and was reduced to control of the region around ASHUR. ▷ 1.12

TIGLATH-PILESER III
King of ASSYRIA (r.744–727 BC) who re-established Assyrian dominance in the Middle East. Once governor of Calah, he deposed Ashur-nirari V and reorganized the empire as a centralized state with a professional army and a provincial administration under direct royal control. He curbed the power of URARTU and imposed Assyrian rule on BABYLONIA and the LEVANT, resettling conquered populations in border areas. ▷ 1.13, 1.14

TIN
Metal used in COPPER-alloy metallurgy, forming about 10 percent of bronze, added to strengthen and harden cast objects. Tin ore sources were of considerable significance in the ancient Old World, and major deposits were exploited in Europe and Asia from the 3rd millennium BC, with large-scale regional trading networks dating from about 2000 BC. ▷ 1.10, 1.21, 1.23, 1.25, 1.26, 1.27

TINGIS
PHOENICIAN trading colony (modern Tangiers) on the Atlantic coast of Africa, to the west of

the Straits of Gibraltar. It was founded in the 7th century BC as a port for west African trade. By about 500 BC, Tingis was the capital of a province of the Carthaginian empire. ▷ 1.23, 1.25

TORRALBA-AMBRONA
Group of LOWER PALEOLITHIC Sites in central Spain where ACHEULIAN hand-ax industries dating from about 600,000–200,000 ya have been discovered, along with evidence of elephant butchery, wooden spears and the use of FIRE. ▷ 1.01

TRES ZAPOTES
An important early OLMEC ceremonial center (c.1200 BC) to the west of the Tuxtla mountains (where basalt for monument construction was obtained), near the Gulf coast in central Mexico. It was the last major Olmec center to be occupied after the destruction of LA VENTA in about 400 BC. ▷ 1.28

TRIPOLYE-CUCUTENI CULTURE
Late NEOLITHIC and early Copper Age culture of the west Ukrainian steppes and Carpathian mountains, dating from about 4200–3800 BC. It is characterized by large fortified villages, painted pottery, and COPPER and gold artifacts such as those deposited in the VARNA cemetery. Tripolye-Cucuteni communities were among the first to domesticate HORSES. ▷ 1.20

TROJAN WAR
Legendary war in which a massed force of Greeks attacked TROY after the abduction of Helen of SPARTA by Paris of Troy. The Greeks eventually sacked the city after a ten-year siege. The war was a major theme in epic poetry and forms the background to HOMER's ILIAD. The legend may rest on actual events of the MYCENAEAN period. ▷ 1.22

TROY
Ancient city on the eastern side of the entrance to the Dardenelles. Its prosperity resulted from the control of sea routes to the Black Sea and east-west land routes. The complex site was occupied, with short interruptions, from 3000 BC until the 9th century AD, and its detailed history has proved difficult to interpret. No clear evidence of a Greek or MYCENAEAN siege has yet been discovered, though the site was destroyed by fire twice in the 13th century, and again in about 1100 BC. ▷ 1.22

TRUNDHOLM
Ancient bog in Zealand, Denmark, where an outstanding example of middle BRONZE AGE metal craftmanship, the "Chariot of the Sun", was deposited in the mid-2nd millennium BC. The composite cast-bronze model, which consists of a horse pulling a vertical disk (gold-plated on one side), mounted on a wheeled carriage, probably had religious significance. ▷ 1.21

TURDETANIANS

People of southern Spain, related to the Tartessians, who traded with PHOENICIAN and Greek colonies, and later with Carthaginian cities on the Mediterranean coast, in about 900–200 BC. They developed an indigenous sculptural tradition influenced by Greek and Phoenician art, and by about 500 BC had established several kingdoms with urban centers, such as Porcuna. ▷ 1.25

TUTANKHAMUN

Egyptian boy-PHARAOH (r.1333–1323 BC). Tutankhamun was of little importance historically, but achieved worldwide prominence when his unplundered tomb was discovered in the VALLEY OF THE KINGS in 1922. ▷ 1.18

TUTHMOSIS I

Probably the greatest PHARAOH of NEW KINGDOM Egypt, Tuthmosis I (r.1504–1492 BC) founded the Egyptian empire in the LEVANT, as well as extending Egyptian power into NUBIA. He was the first pharaoh to be buried in the VALLEY OF THE KINGS. ▷ 1.12. 1.18

TUTHMOSIS III

Egyptian PHARAOH (r.1479–1425 BC) of the NEW KINGDOM period who became sole ruler in 1458 BC after the death of his domineering stepmother, HATSHEPSUT. A fine military commander, Tuthmosis III systematically reduced the cities and kingdoms of Syria and Palestine, thus consolidating the Egyptian empire in the Near East. ▷ 1.18

TUTHMOSIS IV

Egyptian PHARAOH (r.1401–1391 BC) of the NEW KINGDOM period. By marrying his son to the daughter of the king of the rival Near Eastern state of MITTANI, Tuthmosis IV gained a 50-year period of stability for Egypt and an ally against the growing power of the HITTITE empire of Anatolia. ▷ 1.12

TYRANT

In the turbulent period (650–500 BC) when the Greek city-states were evolving their political systems, it was common for single rulers to seize power – often with popular support – from the aristocratic elite. The term tyrant, possibly PHOENICIAN in origin, was used to describe a ruler who had gained power by his own efforts rather than by inheritance. Tyrants were not initially associated with oppressive government. Many, such as PEISISTRATOS of Athens, were able rulers who enjoyed widespread popular support because they challenged aristocratic privileges. As citizen bodies became more confident, however, one-man rule became an anathema, and most tyrants were overthrown or expelled from their cities. ▷ 1.24

TYRE

A port on the Levantine coast that had become the leading PHOENICIAN city by the 10th century BC, establishing trading colonies throughout the Mediterranean, including Carthage. It was sacked by the Babylonian king, NEBUCHADNEZZAR, in 574 BC but remained an important port into Roman times. ▷ 1.13, 1.14, 1.15, 1.23, 1.25

UBAID PERIOD

Late NEOLITHIC period in which farming communities similar to those of the SAMARRAN and HALAFIAN cultures settled in south MESOPOTAMIA in about 5900–4300 BC. They built large-scale IRRIGATION systems and their distinctive CERAMICS are found throughout Mesopotamia from about 5200 BC. Farming villages in this period grew into small towns, such as ERIDU (by c.5000 BC), some with temple buildings, establishing a pattern of urban development and religious architecture that was central to Mesopotamian civilization. ▷ 1.09

UGARIT

Levantine port that became a major state in the 2nd millennium BC, when it handled Cypriot, MYCENAEAN, HITTITE and Egyptian trade. The cosmopolitan character of Ugaritic culture is evident from trade goods, artifacts and records written in four languages and seven scripts. The city was destroyed, probably by SEA PEOPLES, in about 1200 BC. ▷ 1.08, 1.09, 1.10, 1.11, 1.12, 1.13, 1.14

UJJAIN

One of seven sacred Hindu cities, located in the upland area of central India, founded in the 6th century BC as the capital of the powerful Avanti kingdom. Ujjain was defended by massive earth ramparts enclosing an area about 1.5 kilometers (0.9 miles) in diameter. ▷ 1.26

ULU BURUN SHIPWRECK

Shipwreck on the south Anatolian coast dating from the 14th century BC. Its varied cargo, which included COPPER ingots; bronze weapons; pottery from Greece, Canaan and Cyprus; Anatolian TIN; gold jewelry; Egyptian scarabs, and a range of faience, ivory and glass objects, provides a unique insight into the late BRONZE AGE Aegean system of trade. ▷ 1.22

UMBRIANS

Term applied to various geographical, linguistic and cultural entities. Umbria formed part of the 6th region of Italy under Augustus. Umbrian was an INDO-EUROPEAN Italic dialect of central Italy, attested in a number of inscriptions, notably the Iguvine bronze tables. ▷ 1.25

UMMA

Sumerian city that competed with LAGASH, URUK, UR and AKKAD in the 3rd millennium BC. It briefly achieved regional hegemony under King LUGALZAGESI (c.2350 BC), who defeated Lagash and united SUMER and Akkad under one ruler for the first time. Conquered by SARGON OF AGADE in about 2330 BC, it never regained its former power. ▷ 1.10

UNETICE CULTURE

Culture of north-central Europe dating from about 2500 to 1500 BC, whose features widely typify the Early BRONZE AGE cultures of temperate Europe, including rich single burials under ROUND BARROWS, the widespread use of bronze (from c.2000 BC), the development of CHIEFDOMS, and long-distance trade in bronze, amber, faience and gold prestige goods. ▷ 1.04, 1.21

UR

City in SUMERIA that became a major city-state in the EARLY DYNASTIC period (c.2900–2334 BC), and at times the most powerful city in MESOPOTAMIA. The famous "Royal Cemetery" of the 26th century BC, with spectacular grave goods and human sacrifices (slaves, attendants and guards), suggests a powerful and brutal ruling elite. It competed with rival cities such as KISH, LAGASH and UMMA, and was briefly pre-eminent in the 25th century BC under the First Dynasty of Ur (the first dynasty known from written records).

After a period of domination by Akkadian and Gutian rulers in the 24th–22nd centuries BC, the city revived under the Third Dynasty of Ur (2112–2004 BC), which established an extensive empire in southern Mesopotamia. The great ZIGGURAT built by UR-NAMMU was one of the most impressive structures in ancient Mesopotamia. After the sack of Ur by the Elamites in 2004 BC, the city gradually declined in religious and commercial importance until the massive rebuilding works of the Neo-Babylonian kings, NEBUCHADNEZZAR and NABONIDUS, in the 6th century BC. It was abandoned in the 3rd century BC, when the local IRRIGATION system failed. ▷ 1.09, 1.10, 1.11, 1.12, 1.13

UR-NAMMU

First king of the Third Dynasty of UR (r.2112–2095 BC), who established a new imperial state in MESOPOTAMIA, 80 years after the collapse of the Akkadian empire. His success stemmed largely from control of the trade routes into the Persian Gulf. ▷ 1.11

URARTU

Mountain region between Anatolia and the Caspian Sea, inhabited in the 2nd and 1st millennia BC by Hurrian-speaking peoples. By 850 BC Urartu had become a major state, conquering and developing neighboring areas as far as the Caucasus and upper Euphrates. Its power waned in the 8th century BC, as the Neo-Assyrian empire expanded, culminating in 714 BC in SARGON II's defeat of Rusas (the last Urartian king with imperial aspirations) at Lake Urmia. Urartu was conquered by Armenian invaders in the 7th century BC. ▷ 1.05, 1.07, 1.12, 1.13

Acknowledgments & Index

Text, timelines and maps

The authors and publishers readily acknowledge the work of a large number of scholars and published works, on which they have drawn in the preparation of this atlas. Many of these works remain in print, and can be used as reliable secondary reading on the many topics covered in this atlas. Among them are the following:

al Faruqi, Ismail Ragi (ed) *Historical Atlas of the Religions of the World* (New York and London 1974)

Allchin, B and R *The Birth of Indian Civilization: India and Pakistan before 500 BC* (London, 2nd ed 1994)

Balm, Paul G (ed) *Cambridge Illustrated History of Archaeology* (Cambridge and New York 1996)

Baines, John and Malek, Jaromir *Atlas of Ancient Egypt* (Oxford and New York, 1980)

Barraclough, G (ed) *The Times Atlas of World History* (4th ed, London 1993 and New York 1994)

Beek, MA *Atlas of Mesopotamia* (London 1962)

Blunden, Caroline and Elvin, Mark *Cultural Atlas of China* (London and New York, 1986)

Boardman, J *The Greeks Overseas* (London 1964)

Bolton, Geoffrey (ed) *The Oxford History of Australia* (Oxford and Melbourne 1994)

Bonsall, C *The Mesolithic in Europe* (Edinburgh 1989)

Chadwick, Henry and Evans, Gillian R (eds) *Atlas of the Christian Church* (London and New York, 1987)

Champion, T, Gamble, C, Shennan, S, and Whittle, *A Prehistoric Europe* (London 1984)

Chang, KC *The Archaeology of Ancient China* (Yale 1977)

Chard, CS *Northeast Asia in Prehistory* (Madison, USA 1974)

Coe, Michael, Snow, Dean and Benson, Elizabeth *Atlas of Ancient America* (London and New York, 1986)

Coe, Michael *Mexico: from the Olmecs to the Aztecs* (London and New York 4th ed 1994)

Cohn-Sherbok, D *Atlas of Jewish History* (London and New York 1994)

Coles, JM and Harding, AF *The Bronze Age in Europe* (London 1979)

Connah, G *African Civilizations: Precolonial cities and states in tropical Africa* (Cambridge and New York 1987)

Cook, JM *The Persian Empire* (London 1983)

Cornell, Tim and Matthews, John *Atlas of the Roman World* (London and New York, 1982)

Cotterell, A *East Asia* (London 1993, New York 1995)

Crawford, M *The Roman Republic* (London 1978, Cambridge, Mass 1993)

Cunliffe, Barry (ed) *The Oxford Illustrated Prehistory of Europe* (Oxford and New York 1994)

Davies, JK *Democracy and Classical Greece* (London 2nd ed 1993)

Davis, Norman *Europe: a History* (Oxford and New York 1996)

de Lange, Nicholas *Atlas of the Jewish World* (London and New York, 1984)

Elliott, JH (ed) *The Hispanic World* (London and New York 1991)

Fagan, Brian M *The Journey from Eden: the Peopling of our World* (London and New York 1990)

Fagan, Brian M *Ancient North America* (London and New York 1995)

Fagan, Brian M *People of the Earth* (New York and London, 7th ed 1992)

Fage, JD and Oliver, R (eds) *The Cambridge History of Africa* (Cambridge and New York 1975)

Fage, JD *An Atlas of African History* (London 1978)

Falkus, M and Gillingham J *Historical Atlas of Britain* (London and New York revised ed 1987)

Fiedel, SJ *Prehistory of the Americas* (Cambridge and New York, 2nd ed 1992)

Freeman-Grenville, GSP *Historical Atlas of the Middle East* (New York 1993)

Frye, RN *The Heritage of Persia* (London 2nd ed 1976)

Gamble, C *The Palaeolithic Settlement of Europe* (Cambridge 1986)

Gamble, C *Timewalkers: the Prehistory of Global Colonization* (Stroud 1993, Cambridge, Mass. 1994)

Gaur, A *A History of Writing* (London 1984, New York 1994)

Gilbert, Martin *The Atlas of Jewish History* (London and New York 5th ed 1996)

Green, MJ *The Celtic World* (London and New York 1995)

Grosser Historischer Welt atlas (3 vols (Munich 1981)

Hall, DGE *A History of South-east Asia* (London 4th ed 1981)

Hood, S *The Minoans* (London and New York 1973)

Johnson, Gordon, Bayly, C and Richards, JF *The New Cambridge History of India* (Cambridge 1987-)

Johnson, Gordon *Cultural Atlas of India* (London 1995, New York, 1996)

Kemp, BJ *Ancient Egypt* (London 1989, New York 1992)

Kinder, H and Hilgemann, W *Atlas of World History* (2 vols, Munich, London and New York 1974)

Kuhrt, A *The Ancient Near East* (2 vols, London and New York 1995)

Kulke, H and Rothermund, D *A History of India* (London 1990)

Langer, William L *An Encyclopedia of World History* (5th ed, London and New York 1973)

Levi, Peter *Cultural Atlas of the Greek World* (London and New York, 1984)

Ling, TA *History of Religion East and West* (London 1968)

Mallory, JP *In Search of the Indo-Europeans* (London 1989, New York 1991)

Moore, RI (ed) *The Hamlyn Historical Atlas* (London 1981)

Moseley, ME *The Incas and their Ancestors* (London and New York 1993)

Murray, Oswyn *Early Greece* (London 2nd ed 1993)

Phillipson, DW *African Archaeology* (Cambridge, 2nd ed 1993)

Roaf, Michael and Postgate, Nicholas *Cultural Atlas of Mesopotamia and the Ancient Near East* (London and New York, 1990)

Roberts, JM *The Hutchinson History of the World* (London 1976)

Rogerson, John *Atlas of the Bible* (London and New York 1985)

Scarre, Dr Chris *Past Worlds: The Times Atlas of Archaeology* (London and New York, 1988)

Schmidt, KJ *An Atlas and Survey of South Asian History* (New York and London 1995)

Schwartzberg, Joseph E (ed) *A Historical Atlas of South Asia* (Chicago and London, 2nd ed 1992)

Sharer, RJ *The Ancient Maya* (Stanford Ca 5th ed 1994)

Shepherd, William R. *Shepherd's Historical Atlas* (New York and London, 9th ed 1974)

Sinor, D (ed) *The Cambridge History of Early Inner Asia* (Cambridge 1990)

Smith, BD *The Emergence of Agriculture* (New York 1995)

Taylour, W *The Mycenaeans* (London and New York 2nd ed 1990)

The Times Atlas of the World (London and New York, 8th ed 1990)

Todd, M *The Early Germans* (Oxford and Cambridge, Mass. 1992)

Twitchett, D and Fairbank, J (eds) *The Cambridge History of China* (15 vols, Cambridge and New York 1978-91)

Vincent, Mary and Stradling, RA *Cultural Atlas of Spain and Portugal* (London 1994, New York 1995)

Walbank, FW *The Hellenistic World* (London 3rd ed 1992, Cambridge, Mass. 1993)

Watson, F *India, a Concise History* (London and New York 1993)

Whittle, A *Neolithic Europe: a Survey* (Cambridge and New York 1985)

Artwork

Artwork references have been assembled from a wide variety of sources. Any individual or institution who can demonstrate that copyright may have been infringed is invited to contact Andromeda Oxford Ltd.

Photographs

Introduction Telendos: Images Colour Library.

Figures refer to map numbers; **bold** type indicates major references.

Abu Hureyra 1.08
Abu Simbel 1.29
Acarnania 1.24
Achaea, Achaeans 1.23–24, 1.29
see also Mycenae, Mycenaean civilization
Achemenes 1.15, 1.29
Achemenid empire 1.06, **1.15**, 1.26, 1.29
Acheulian culture 1.01, 1.29
Acropolis 1.29
Adab 1.10
Adad-nirari I 11.12
Adad-nirari II 1.13, 1.29
Adena 1.06, 1.29
Aeolia, Aeolian Greeks 1.23–24, 1.29
Afanasevo culture 1.04, 1.29
Africa
  hominid remains 1.01
  Iron Age **1.16**
  Neolithic **1.16**
  single-origins theory 1.01–02
African Rift Valley 1.01
Agade 1.11
Agamemnon 1.22, 1.29

agriculture 1.02, **1.03**, 1.04, 1.06, 1.08
Africa **1.16**
Agricultural Revolution (Neolithic) *see* Neolithic
Americas 1.03, 1.28
animal domestication 1.03, 1.05–06, 1.08–09, 1.11, 1.16, 1.19–20, 1.26, 1.28
Bronze Age Europe 1.21
cereals 1.03, 1.05, 1.08–09, 1.16, 1.20, 1.28
chinampas 1.28
and desertification 1.04
east Asia 1.27
Egypt 1.03, 1.17
Fertile Crescent **1.08–09**
food plant cultivation 1.03, 1.08–09, 1.16, 1.20–21, 1.27–28
irrigation 1.03, 1.08–09, 1.17, 1.28 legumes 1.20
Mediterranean 1.22
Neolithic and proto-Neolithic **1.08, 1.19–20**
pastoralism 1. 05–06, 1.16
plow 1.09
slash-and-burn 1.28
south Asia 1.26
Ahab 1.14, 1.29
Ahar 1.26

Ahhiyawa 1.12
Ahmose 1.18, 1.29
Akhenaten 1.12, 1.18, 1.29
Akkad 1.04, 1.07, 1.10–11, 1.29
  Sargon the Great 1.04, 1.10–11
  Third Dynasty 1.11
  see also Babylon, Babyloni
Akrotiri 1.22
Akshak 1.10
Akshak 1.10
alcohol 1.10, 1.20
Aleppo 1.12
Aleuts 1.04-06, 1.29
Alexander the Great 1.18
Mi Kosh 1.08
Al Mina 1.23
alpaca 1.28
alphabets *see* writing
Altamira 1.19, 1.29
Amalekites 1.14, 1.29
Amazonia 1.05–06
Amekni 1.16
Amenemhet I 1. 18, 1.29
Amenophis IV 1.18
Americas 1.06
  agriculture 1.03
  Amerindians 1.04
  Andean civilizations *see* Andean civilizations
  Archaic period 1.05
  first civilizations **1.28**

Mesoamerica *see* Mesoamerica
  Paleoindians 1.02
Ammon 1.14
Amorites 1.04, 1.11, 1.13, 1.29
amphictonies 1.24, 1.29
Anatolia 1.04–09, 1.11–13
Andean civilizations 1.03, 1.06, **1.28**, 1.29
  Archaic period 1.05
  Early Horizon period 1.28
  Initial period 1.28
  Preceramic period 1.28
Anga 1.26
Aniba 1.18
animal domestication
  see agriculture
Anyang 1.27, 1.29
Arabia, Arabs 1.06, 1.09, 1.15
Arabic language and script 1.07
Arachosia 1.15
Aram, Aramaeans 1.05, 1.12–14, 1.29
Aramaic language and alphabet 1.05, 1.07, 1.15, 1.29
Aram-Damascus 1.14, 1.29
Aram-Zobah 1.14
Arcadia 1.24, 1.29
Archaic period, 1.29
Ardipithecus ramidus 1.01, 1.29
Arganthonios 1.25

Argos 1.24, 1.29
Aria 1.15
Armenia, Armenians 1.11, 1.15
Arpachiyeh 1.09
Arrapna 1.13
Arretium 1.25
Arvad 1.12, 1.14, 1.30
Aryans 1.05–06, 1.26, 1.30
Arzawa 1.12, 1.30
Ashkelon 1.14
Ashur 1.05, 1.11–13, 1.30
Ashurbanipal 1.13, 1.15, 1.30
Ashur-Dan II 1.13
Ashurnasirpal II 1.13, 1.30
Ashuruballit I 1.12
Aspero tradition 1.04, 1.28, 1.30
Assaka 1.26
Assyrian empire 1.05–07, **1.13**, 1.14–15, 1.18, 1.23, 1.30
  Middle Empire **1.12**
  Old Assyrian period **1.11**
Astyages 1.15
Aten (Egyptian deity) 1.18
Athens 1.06, 1.15, 1.22, 1.24
  Acropolis 1.24
  Attica 1.24, 1.30
Aurignacian culture 1.19, 1.30
Australian Aboriginals 1.02, 1.04–06
Australopithecus afarensis 1.01, 1.30

Australopithecus africanus 1.01, 1.30
Australopithecus robustus 1.01, 1.30
Austronesians 1.04–06
Avanti 1.26
Avaris 1.18, 1.22
Aveburyhenge, 1.30

Ba 1.27, 1.30
Babylon, Babylonia 1.05–07, 1.11–13, **1.13**, 1.14–15, 1.23, 1.30 Akkad *see* Akkad
  dark ages 1.11–12
  Neo-Babylonian empire **1.13**
  Old Babylonian period 1.11
  Persian conquest 1.15
  sack of Babylon 1.11–12
Bactria 1.15
Bahrain 1.11
Baipu 1.27
Balearic Islands 1.21, 1.23, 1.25
Balkans 1.07
Balts 1.06
Baluchistan 1.26
Banas culture **1.26**, 1.30
Bandkeramik culture 1.03, 1.20, 1.30
Bantu languages 1.06, 1.30
Barger-Oosterveld 1.21
barley 1.03, 1.08–09, 1.16, 1.30
barrow, long, 1.30

barrow, round, 1.30
basileus, 1.30
basketry 1.09
Bell Beaker cultures 1.04, 1.20–21, 1.30
Berbers 1.04–06, 1.23, 1.25
Beringia, 1.30
Bering Straits 1.02
Beth-horon 1.14
Bethlehem 1.14
Beth-shean 1.14
Bible
  Book of Judges 1.14
  Old Testament 1.10, 1.14
Bible lands **1.14**, 1.30
Bimbisara 1.26, 1.30
Bismarck Archipelago 1.05
bison *see* buffalo
Bluefish Cave (Alaska) 1.02
boat-building 1.02, 1.17
  dug-out canoe 1.19
  Greek civilization 1.23
  outrigger canoe 1.05
  sail 1.09, 1.16
Boeotia 1.24, 1.31
Book of the Dead, 1.31
Bosporus 1.15
bow and arrow 1.18, 1.31
Bowl cultures 1.20, 1.31
Boxgrove, 1.31
Brahmagiri 1.26
bread 1.08
Britain 1.05, 1.23, 1.25
Brittany 1.25
Bronze Age 1.04–06, 1.09–10, 1.20, 1.31
  Africa **1.16**
  Europe **1.21**, 1.25
  Middle East **1.11–12**
  south Asia **1.26**
bronze working 1.03–06, 1.10, 1.16, 1.18, 1.20—23, 1.27
bronze working 1.03–06, 1.10, 1.16,
1.18, 1.20–23, 1.27
Buddha (Siddhartha Gautama) 1.06, 1.26, 1.31
Buddhism 1.06, 1.26
buffalo 1.06
Buhen 1.17
buildings
  glazed bricks 1.12
  mud brick 1.08–09
  pyramids 1.16
  ziggurats 1.09, 1.11
  burial sites, prehistoric 1.04–06, 1.08–09, 1.19–21, 1.26
Burmese 1.05–06
Byblos, 1.31

Cabeco da Arrunda 1.19
Cai 1.27
calendar, 1.31
  "long count" 1.28
Cambyses 1.15, 1.31
camel 1.03
Campa 1.26
Canaan, Canaanites 1.05, 1.07, 1.12, **1.14**, 1.23, 1.31
canal systems
  Egypt 1.17
  Mesoamerica 1.28
  Mesopotamia 1.09
  Nile to Red Sea 1.15
Cao 1.27
Cappadocia 1.15
Carchemish 1.12–13, 1.31
  Battle of 1.13–14
Caria 1.15
Carnac 1.20, 1.31
Carthage 1.06, 1.16, 1.23, **1.25**
Catacomb Grave cultures 1.04, 1.21, 1.31
cattle 1.03, 1.05, 1.08–09, 1.16, 1.20, 1.31
Caucasus 1.06
causewayed camp, 1.31
cave- and rock-art 1.02, 1.16, 1.19, 1.31
Celtiberians 1.05–06, 1.23, 1.25
Celts 1.06, 1.23, 1.25
ceramics 1.04, 1.06, 1.08–10, 1.31
  Americas 1.28
  Chinese 1.27
  earliest 1.03
  Egyptian 1.17
  glazed 1.12
  Japanese 1.03
  kiln 1.03, 1.09
  Neolithic 1.03–04, 1.20
  painted 1.09
  potter's wheel 1.03, 1.09, 1.26–27
  south Asia 1.26
  wavy-line 1.16
Chad, Lake 1.16
Chaldeans 1.12–13, 1.31
chambered tomb, 1.31
chariot 1.11, 1.18, 1.22, 1.27
Chatal Huyuk 1.03, 1.09, 1.31
Châtelperronian culture 1.19, 1.31
Chavin de Huántar 1.06, 1.28, 1.31
Chayonu 1.08, 1.31
Chedi 1.26
Chen 1.27
Chesowanja 1.01, 1.31
chicken 1.03
chiefdom, 1.31
China 1.03–05, 1.27, **1.27**
  Eastern Zhou 1.27
  Longshan culture 1.04-05, 1.27
  Shang dynasty 1.07, 1.27
  Springs and Autumns Period 1.06, 1.27
  Warring States period 1.27
  Western Zhou 1.27 Xia dynasty 1.27
  Zhou dynasty *see* Zhou dynasty
Chinchoros tradition 1.04–06, 1.15, 1.31
Chinese language and script 1.04, 1.07, 1.31
Chiripa culture 1.05, 1.28, 1.31
Choga Mami 1.09, 1.31
Chorasmia 1.15
Chorrera culture 1.05–06, 1.28, 1.31
Chu 1.27, 1.31
Cilicia 1.13, 1.15
Cimmerians 1.05, 1.13, 1.31
climatic change 1.01–03, 1.08, 1.16, 1.19
Clovis culture 1.02, 1.32
coinage 1.24, 1.32
Colchis 1.15, 1.23, 1.32
Confucianism 1.27
Confucius 1.06, 1.27, 1.32
copper working 1.03, 1.06, 1.08–10, 1.16–17, 1.20, 1.26, 1.32
Cord Impressed Ware culture, 1.32
Corinth 1.22–24, 1.32
Cornwall 1.25
Corsica 1.21, 1.25
Cortaillod, 1.32
cotton 1.03, 1.26, 1.28, 1.32
cowpea 1.16
Crete 1.05, 1.20, 1.24
  Minoan civilization 1.04–05, 1.20, 1.22
  Mycenaean civilization 1.05, 1.22–23
Crimea 1.23
Croesus 1.15, 1.32
Cumae *see* Kymai cuneiform writing 1.07, 1.10, 1.15, 1.32
Cyprus 1.05, 1.15, 1.22–23
Cyrenaica 1.23
Cyrillic alphabet 1.07
Cyrus II (the Great) 1.06, **1.13–15,** 1.32

Damascus 1.12–14
Dan 1.14
Darius 1.15, 1.32
David 1.14, 1.32
Delos 1.24
Delphi 1.24, 1.32
Denmark 1.19
Der 1.13
desertification 1.02–04, 1.16
Diaspora 1.14
diet and animal domestication 1.08–09, 1.16
  bread 1.08
  fishing 1.16
  food plant cultivation 1.08–09, 1.16
  salt 1.08
Dilmun 1.11
Dionysus (Greek deity) 1.23
divination 1.24, 1.27
Di-xin 1.27, 1.32
Diaspora, 1.32
Dilmun, 1.32
Djoser 1.17, 1.32
Do-Dimmi 1.16
dog 1.03, 1.08, 1.32
dolmen, 1.32
Dongyi 1.27
Dorians 1.12, 1.22–24, 1.32
Drangiana 1.15
Dravidians 1.04–06, 1.26, 1.32
Dur-Kurigalzu 1.13, 1.32
Dur-Sharrukin 1.13
Dyukhtai tradition 1.02, 1.32

Eannatum of Kish 1.10
Early Dynastic period, 1.32
Early Horizon period, 1.32
Early Preclassic period, 1.32
Easter Island 1.07
eastern woodlands (North America) 1.05–06
Eastern Zhou 1,27
Ecbatana *see* Hamadan
Edom, Edomites 1.13–14, 1.32
Egyptian civilization 1.05, 1.07, 1.10, 1.13–16, 1.23, 1.32
  1st Dynasty 1.17
  4th Dynasty 1.17
  11th Dynasty 1.18
  17th Dynasty 1.18
  18th Dynasty 1.18
  21st Dynasty 1.18
  25th Dynasty 1.18
  1st intermediate period 1.17
  2nd Intermediate period 1.18
  3rd Intermediate period 1.18
  agriculture 1.03, 1.16–17
  Assyrian conquest 1.13, 1.18
  Babylonian campaign against 1.13
  Bronze Ages 1.11
  Early Dynastic period 1.17
  foundation 1.04, 1.16, 1.17
  Greek colonies 1.23
  invasion of Judah and Israel 1.14
  kings of, 1.33
  Kushite rulers 1.06
  Late period 1.18
  Middle Kingdom 1.04–05, **1.18**, 1.38
  Naqada period 1.17
  New Kingdom 1.05, 1.12, **1.18**, 1.39
  Old Kingdom 1.04, 1.17, 1.39
  Persian conquest 1.06, 1.15, 1.18
  pyramids 1.04, 1.16–18
  Sea Peoples 1.05, 1.12, 1.18
  urbanization 1.16
Elam, Elamites 1.04–05, 1.07, 1.10—13, 1.15, 1.32
el-Amarna 1.18, 1.33
Elba 1.25
eleusine 1.16
Eleusis, 1.33
Elijah 1.14, 1.33
Eleusis, 1.33
Elijah 1.14, 1.33
Elis 1.24
Elisha 1. 14, 1.33
El Paraiso tradition 1.05, 1.28, 1.32
Elteken, Battle of 1.14
Emutbal 1.11
Enlil (Sumerian god) 1.11, 1.33
ensete 1.16
Epipaleolithic period 1.16, 1.33
Epirotes 1.23
Epirus 1.24–25, 1.33
Eridu 1.09–11, 1.33
Erlitou culture 1.27, 1.33
Ertebolle culture, 1.33
Esarhaddon 1.13, 1.33
Eshnunna 1.11, 1.33
Ethiopia 1.06, 1.16
Ethiopic script 1.07
Etruscan league 1.25
Etruscans 1.06–07, 1.23, **1.25**, 1.33
Euphrates river 1.09–12
Europe
  Bronze Age 1.21
  first Mediterranean civilizations **1.22**
  Neolithic 1.20
  Paleolithic 1.19
Ezion-geber 1.14

Faiyum 1.17
farming *see* agriculture
Fertile Crescent 1.03, **1.08–09**, 1.12, 1.33
Finno-Ugrians 1.04–06
Finns 1.06
fire, earliest use 1.01, 1.33
fishing 1.04, 1.16, 1.19, 1.28
Flood, the 1.10, 1.33
Folsom culture 1.02, 1.34
food plant cultivation 1.16
Funnel-necked Beaker culture, 1.34

Gades 1.23, 1.25, 1.34
Galicia 1.25
Gandhara 1.15, 1.26, 1.34
Ganges plain 1.03, 1.05–06
Gaul 1.23
Gauls *see* Celts;
Gaul Gavrinis, 1.34
Gaza 1.14, 1.18
Germans, proto- 1.06, 1.34
Gezer 1.14, 1.34
Gilboa, Battle of 1.14
Girsu 1.10
Giza 1.16–17
glass 1.12
goat 1.03, 1.08–09, 1.16, 1.20, 1.34
Godavari river 1.26
gold 1.03, 1.18, 1.20–22
Gordion 1.13, 1.34
Gravettian culture 1.19, 1.34
Greek alphabet 1.07, 1.34
Greek civilization 1.04–06, 1.15, 1.20, **1.23**
  aristocracy 1.24
  city-states 1.06, 1.15, **1.24**
  colonies 1.23–25
  dark ages 1.05, 1.22–24
  democracy 1.15, 1.24
  monarchy, 1.24
  Mycenae *see* Mycenae, Mycenaean civilization
  oligarchy 1.24
  pan-Hellenic festivals 1.24
  Persian invasion defeated 1.23
  trade 1.23–24
  Trojan War 1.22
  tyrants 1.24 *s*
  ee also Athens; Bactria; Sparta
Guadaiquivir valley 1.25
Gutians 1.10–12, 1.34
Guyana 1.04

Habuba Kabira 1.10
Hadar 1.01, 1.34
Halafian culture 1.09, 1.34
halberd 1.21
Hallstatt culture 1.06, **1.25**, 1.34
Hamadan 1.13, 1.15
Hamath 1.14
Hamazi 1.10
Hammurabi 1.11, 1.34
Hao 1.27, 1.34
Harappa 1.26, 1.34. *See also* Indus Valley civilization
Harran 1.13
Hassuna culture 1.09, 1.34
Hastinapura 1.26
Hatshepsut 1.18, 1.34
Hatti 1.12, 1.34
Hattusas 1.12, 1.34
Hazor 1.14
Hebrew language and alphabet 1.07, 1.34
Hebrews 1.05, 1.12–14, 1.183 1.23, 1.34
  exile 1.14
  see also Jews
Hebron 1.14
Hellenes 1.24, 1.34
Hellespont 1.15
helot, 1.34
henges 1.04, 1.20, 1.34
Heuneburg 1.25, 1.34
Hezekiah 1.14
Hierakonpolis 1.17
hieroglyths, 1.34
hillforts 1.05, 1.34
Hinduism 1.06, 1.26, 1.34
Hindu Kush 1.26
Hippias 1.24, 1.34
Hiram 1.23, 1.34
Hit 1.10, 1.34
Hittites 1.04–05, 1.07, 1.11, **1.12**, 1.13–14, 1.18, 1.21–22, 1.34
  Neo-Hittites 1.13–14
Homer 1.22, 1.24, 1.35
hominoid apes 1.01, 1.35
Homo erectus 1.01–02, 1.35
Homo habilis l.01, 1.35
Homo Neanderthalensis 1.02, 1.35
Homo sapiens 1.01–02, 1.35
Homo sapiens neanderthalensis 1.01, 1.35
Homo sapiens sapiens 1.01–02
horse 1.03, 1.06, 1.11, 1.16, 1.19–22, 1.35
Hoshea 1.14
Huang Di 1.27, 1.35
Huelva 1.25
hunter-gatherers 1.01–06, 1.08, 1.16, 1.19–20, 1.35
Hurrians 1.04, 1.07, 1.11 12, 1.35
Hyksos 1.18, 1.35
Iberia, Iberians 1.23, 1.25
Iberian Celts 1.25
Ice Age 1.01–033.08, 1.16, 1.18–19, 1.35
"iceman" 1.20, 1.35
Iliad, 1.35
Illyrians 1.05–06, 1.23–25
Impressed Pottery cultures 1.04, 1.20–21, 1.35
Inca civilization 1.07
India 1.03, 1.06, **1.25**
  Magadha 1.06, 1.26
  Mauryan empire 1.26
  see also Indus Valley civilization
Indian script 1.07
Indo-European languages, 1.35
Indo-Iranian peoples 1.13, 1.35
Indus Valley civilization 1.04–05, 1.07, **1.26**, 1.35
Intial period, 1.35
Ionia, Ionian Greeks 1.15, 1.23–24, 1.35
Iran 1.05–06, 1.10–11, 1.13, 1.15
  see also Persia, Persians
Ireland 1.21
Iron Age 1.06, 1.21, 1.24, 1.35
  Africa **1.16**
  Europe 1.06, 1.25
  Middle East **1.12**
  south Asia **1.26**
iron working 1.03, 1.05–06, 1.12, 1.16, 1.18, 1.21, 1.27
irrigation 1.03, 1.08–09, 1.17, 1.26, 1.28, 1.35
Isaiah 1.14, 1.35
Isin 1.11, 1.35
Israel 1.02, 1.05–06, 1.08, 1.13–14, 1.35
  Assyrian conquest 1.13
  Egyptian invasion 1.14, 1.18
  Jewish settlement 1.14
  split with Judah 1.14
Italics 1.23, 1.25, 1.36
Italy 1.07, 1.23
  Romans *see* Roman republic; Rome

Jainism 1.26
janapadas 1.26, 1.36
Japan 1.03, 1.07
Java 1.07
Jebusites 1.14, 1.36
Jehu 1.14
Jemdet Nasr 1.10, 1.36
Jericho 1.08, 1.36
Jerusalem 1.12, 1.14, 1.237 1.36
  Hebrew capture 1.14
  religious importance 1.14
  sack 1.14
  temple 1.14
Jews 1.14
  Bible lands 1.14
  Diaspora 1.14
  exile 1.14
  Jewish resettlement by Nebuchadnezzar 1.13
  Old Testament 1.10, 1.14
  see also Hebrews
Jin 1.27, 1.36
Jomon 1.03, 1.05, 1.36
Joppa 1.14
Jordan river 1.05
Joshua 1.14, 1.36
Josiah 1.14, 1.36
Judah 1.13–14, 1.18, 1.36
Judaism *see* jews

Kalhu 1.13, 1.36
Kalibangan 1.26
Kanesh 1.12, 1.36
Karasuk culture 1.05, 1.36
Karkheh 1.13
Karnak 1.18, 1.36
Kar-Tukulti-Ninurta 1.12
Kaskas 1.12, 1.36
Kassites 1.04, 1.10–12, 1.36
Kastri 1.22
Kausambi 1.26, 1.36
Kelheim 1.21
Kerma 1.18, 1.36
Khania 1.22
Kharga Oasis 1.15
Khendjer 1.18
Khephren 1.17, 1.36
Khilakku 1.13
Khoisan 1.04–06, 1.36
Khufu 1.17, 1.36
Kish 1.10–11, 1.36
Kition 1.23
Kizzuwatna 1.12, 1.36
[illegible] 1.15, 1.21, 1.36
Kleomenes, 1.36
Knossos 1.22, 1.36
Komchen 1.28
Koobi Fora, 1.36
Korea 1.03–07
Kosala 1.26, 1.36
Kotosh tradition 1.28, 1.36
Kow Swamp, 1.36
Kufic Arabic 1.07
Kulli 1.26, 1.36
Kultepe 1.11
Kummukhu (Commagene) 1.13
Kuru 1.26
Kush 1.05–06, 1.16, 1.18, 1.36
Kusinagara 1.26
Kymal (Cumae) 1.23, 1.25, 1.36
Kynouria 1.24
Kyreskhata 1.15
Kythera 1.22, 1.24

Lachish 1.14, 1.37
Laconia 1.24, 1.37
Lagashl.10, 1.37
Laitoli (Laetoli) 1.01, 1.37
Lapita culture 1.05–06
Lapps 1.05–06
Lascaux 1.19, 1.37
Latin language and alphabet 1.07
Latins, Latium 1.25, 1.37
La Venta, 1.36
lead working 1.09
Lebanon 1.08
Lepenski Vir 1.19, 1.37
Leubingen 1.21
Levant 1.05, 1.07–09, 1.11–14, 1.18, 1.23, 1.37
  Aurignacian culture 1.18–19
Libya, Libyans 1.12
Ligurians 1.23, 1.25, 1.37
Lilybaeum, Battle of 1.25
Linear A script 1.22, 1.37
Linear B script 1.22, 1.37
Linear Pottery culture *see* Bandkeramik culture linen (flax) 1.03, 1.08–09, 1.16, 1.37
Lipari Islands 1.25
Lirong 1.27 literacy 1.07
llama 1.28, 1.37
logographic scripts, 1.37
longhouses 1.20, 1.37
Longshan culture 1.04–05, 1.27, 1.37
Los Millares, 1.37
lost-wax process 1.10
Lothal 1.26, 1.37
Lu 1.27, 1.37
"Lucy" (*Australopithecus afarensis*) 1.01, 1.37
Lugalzagesi 1.10–11, 1.37
Lukka 1.12
Lullubians 1.11, 1.37
Lumbini 1.26, 1.37
Luoyang 1.27, 1.37
Lusitania, Lusitanians 1.25
Luvians 1.05, 1.12, 1.37
Luxor, 1.37
Lycia, Lycians 1.23–24
Lydia, Lydians 1.15, 1.23–24, 1.37

Macedon, Macedonia 1.15, 1.23–25
  Alexander the Great 1.18
Maes Howe, 1.37
Magadha 1.06, 1.26
Magdalenian 1.19, 1.37
Magna Graecia, 1.37
mahajanapadas 1.26
Mahavira 1.26
Mahismat 1.26
maize 1.03–04, 1.28, 1.37
Malatya 1.12
Malla 1.26
Mallia 1.22
Mannea 1.13, 1.37
Marathon, Battle of 1.15
Marduk (Babylonian god) 1.15
Marhashi 1.11
Mari 1.10–11, 1.37
Massilia 1.23, 1.25, 1.37
Massillia 1.23
mastabas 1.17, 1.37
Matsva 1.26
Mauryan empire 1.26
Mayan civilization 1.06–07, 1.28
Medes 1.06, 1.13, 1.15, 1.37
Median empire 1.15
Mediterranean, first civilizations **1.22**
Mediteranean triad, 1.38
megalithic monuments 1.04, 1.20–21, 1.26, 1.38
Megalithic Tomb culture, 1.38
Megiddo, Battle of 1.14, 1.18, 1.38
Mehrgarh 1.26, 1.38

Melanesia 1.04–05
Meluhha 1.26
Memphis 1.13, 1.15, 1.17, 1.38
Mentuhotpe II 1. 18, 1.38
Meroë 1.06, 1.15, 1.38
Mesilim of Kish 1.10
Mesoamerica 1.07, 1.38
  Archaic and Preclassic periods 1.03, 1.05–06, **1.28**
  see also individual cultures
Mesolithic 1.03, 1.19–20, 1.38
Mesopotamia 1.03, 1.06, 1.08–09, 1.12, 1.26, 1.38
  Amorites 1.11
  Aramaeans 1.05
  Bronze Age **1.11–12**
  earliest cities 1.09, **1.10**
  Early Dynastic period 1.10
  Iron Age **1.12**
  Uruk period 1.04, 1.09–10
  see also Akkad; Assyrian empire; Babylon, Babylonia; Chaldeans; Hittites; Kassites; Sumeria
Messapians 1.25
Messenia 1.24, 1.38
metal working casting 1.27
  lost-wax process 1.10
  smelting 1.03
  see also bronze working; copper working; gold; iron working; tin
Mezhirich 1.19, 1.38
Michelsberg, 1.38
microlith tools 1.19, 1.38
Midas 1.13
Middle Kingdom, 1.38
Middle Preclassic period, 1.38
migration, single-origins theory 1.01, **1.02**
Miletos 1.22, 1.38
millet 1.03, 1.16, 1.27, 1.38
Minoan palace civilization 1.04–05, 1.07, 1.20, **1.22**, 1.38
Miocene epoch 1.01, 1.38
Mitas (Midas) 1.13, 1.38
Mittani 1.12, 1.18, 1.38
Mixtec civilization 1.07
Mixu 1.27
Moab, Moabites 1.13–14, 1.38
Mogador 1.23
Mohenjo-Daro 1.26, 1.38
Mongolia, Mongols 1.05, 1.07
Monte Albán 1.28
Motya 1.25
Mousterian culture 1.01, 1.19, 1.38
mummification, 1.38
Mursilis 1.11, 1.38
Mushki (Mysians) 1.12, 1.38
Mu-ti defensive wall 1.11
Muwatallis 111.12, 1.38
Mycenae, Mycenaean civilization 1.05, 1.07, 1.12, **1.21–23**, 1.38
Mysians *see* Mushki

Nabatean alphabet 1.07, 1.39
Nabonidus 1.13, 1.15, 1.39
Nabopolassar 1.13, 1.39
Nahal Hemar 1.08
Nakbe 1.28
Napata, 1.39
Naqada 1.17
Naram-Sin 1.11, 1.39
Narmer 1.17, 1.39
Natufian culture 1.03,
navigation 1.23
Neanderthals 1.01–02, 1.19
Nebuchadnezzar 1.13–15, 1.39
Necho II 1.13, 1.39
Neo-Babylonian empire 1.13
Neo-Hittites 1.13–14
Neolithic 1.03–04, 1.06, 1.09–10, 1.19, 1.39
  Africa **1.16**
  east Asia 1.27
  Europe **1.20**
  Middle East **1.08**
New Guinea *see* Papua New Guinea
Newgrange, 1.39
New Kingdom, 1.39
Nigeria 1.16
Nile river 1.16–17
  canal to Red Sea 1.15
  Cataracts 1.17
  Delta 1.17
  Nina 1.10

Nindowari 1.26
Nineveh 1.09, 1.12–13, 1.39
  sack 1.13, 1.15
Nippur 1.11–12, 1.39
Nok culture 1.16
nomadism 1.03–06
Nubia 1.04–06, 1.14–18, 1.39
nuraghe 1.21

oats 1.03, 1.21
Oaxaca valley 1.28, 1.39
obsidian 1.08–09, 1.39
oca 1.28
Odyssey, 1.39
oil palm 1.16
Old Kingdom, 1.39
Oldowan culture 1.01, 1.39
Olduvai Gorge 1.01, 1.39
Oleneostravski 1.19
olive 1.22
Olmec civilization 1.05–06, **1.28**, 1.39
Olympia 1.24, 1.39
Olympic Games 1.24, 1.39
Omo 1.01, 1.39
Omri 1.14
Opis, Battle of 1.15, 1.39
oracle bones, 1.39
oracle, Greek, 1.39
Orkney 1.20, 1.39
Oronsay 1.19
Orontes river 1.12
Oscaris 1.25, 1.39
Otztaler Alps 1.20

Painted Ware cultures 1.20, 1.39
Paleoindians 1.02, 1.39
Paleolithic
  Europe **1.19**, 1.39
  Lower 1.01, 1.39
  Mid 1.01–02, 1.19, 1.39
  Upper 1.19, 1.39
Palestine 1.15, 1.22
Panchala 1.26
pan-Hellenic festivals, 1.40
Papua New Guinea 1.05
Paracas culture 1.06, 1.28
Parse 1.15
Parthia, Parthians 1.15, 1.40
Pasargadae 1.15, 1.40
  Battle of 1.15
passage grave, 1.40
pastoralism 1.03–06, 1.16, 1.40
Patagonia 1.02
Peisistratus 1.24, 1.40
Peloponnese 1.04, 1.22, 1.24
Pelusium, Battle of 1.15
Persepolis 1.15, 1.40
Persia, Persians 1.06, 1.13, 1.15, 1.18, 1.24–25
  Achemenid empire *see* Achemenid empire
  Parthians 1.15
  Phoenicians conquered by 1.23
Peru 1.03–05, 1.07
Phaistos 1.22, 1.40
pharaohs 1.18, 1.40
Philistia 1.13–14
Philistines 1.12, 1.14, 1.40
Phocs 1.24
Phoenicia, Phoenicians 1.05–07, 1.13–14, 1.16, 1.23, 1.24, 1.40
  alphabet, 1.40
  Babylonian conquest 1.23
  Greek conquest 1.23
  trade and colonies 1.05, 1.13, 1.23, 1.23, 1.25
Phrygia, Phrygians 1.05, 1.12–13, 1.22–23, 1.40
pig 1.03, 1.08–09.1.40
Pithekoussai 1.23
Plataea, Battle of 1.15
Pleistocene epoch 1.01–02, 1.40
Pliocene epoch 1.01, 1.40
plow 1.03, 1.09, 1.20–21, 1.40
Polar ice caps 1.01
polis 1.24, 1.40
Polynesia, Polynesians 1.05–07
population growth 1.03, 1.09–10, 1.20
Populonia 1.25
potato 1.28, 1.40
pottery *see* ceramics
Poverty Point culture 1.05, 1.40
Preceramic period, 1.40
Prednosti 1.19

Predynastic period, 1.40
priesthood 1.10, 1.17
printing 1.09
Psammeticus III 1.15
Pteria 1.15, 1.40
Pylos 1.22, 1.40
pyramids 1.16, 1.40
  Egyptian 1.04, **1.17–18**
  Mesoamerican 1.28

Qadesh 1.18, 1.40
  Battle of 1.12, 1.18
Qafzeh 1.02, 1.40
Qarqar, Battle of 1.13–14
Qi 1.27, 1.40
Qin 1.27, 1.40
Quaternary period 1.01, 1.40
quinua 1.28

rainforests 1.01
Ramesses II (the Great) 1.12, 1.18, 1.40
Ramesses IIII 1. 18
Rehoboam 1.14, 1.40
reindeer 1.19
religion 1.10
  Paleolithic 1.19
  shrines 1.09
  temples 1.09, 1.11
  see also individual religions
Rhaetians 1.25
Rhine river 1.19
Rhodes 1.22, 1.40
Riben *see* Japan
Riblah 1.13
rice 1.03, 1.16, 1.26–27, 1.40
Roman republic 1.06, 1.25
Rome 1.25
  Etruscans 1.25
  foundation 1.25, 1.40
  kings of, 1.40
Rongorongo 1.07
Rudna Glava 1.20
runic 1.07

Saba 1.05–06, 1.41
Sabean script and language 1.07, 1.41
Sabines 1.25, 1.41
Sagartia 1.15
Sahara 1.02–04, 1.16
Sahel 1.16
Sakas 1.06, 1.15, 1.41
Salamis, Battle of 1.15, 1.23, 1.24
salt 1.08
Samaria 1.14, 1.41
Samarran culture 1.09, 1.41
Samnites 1.25, 1.41
Samoa 1.05
San Lorenzo 1.28, 1.41
Sanxingdui 1.27, 1.41
Saqqara 1.04, 1.17, 1.41
Sardinia 1.21, 1.23
Sardis 1.15, 1.41
Sargon of Agade (the Great) 1.04, **1.10–11**, 1.41
Sargon II 1.13, 1.41
Sarmatians 1.06, 1.41
Saul 1.14, 1.41
savanna 1.03
sculpture 1.09
Scythians 1.06, 1.15, 1.23, 1.41
  Black Sea 1.15
  Caspian 1.15
  pointed-hat 1.15
Sea Peoples 1.05, 1.12, 1.18, 1.22, 1.41
Selinus 1.25
Semites 1.04, 1.41
Sennacherib 1.13–14, 1.41
Senwosret III 1.18
Seqenenre II 1.18
Sethos 1.18
Shalmaneser I 1.12, 1.41
Shalmaneser III 1.13
Shalmaneser V 1.13–14
Shamshi-Adad 1.11, 1.41
Shang dynasty 1.05, 1.07, 1.27, 1.41
Shanidar, 1.41
Shechem 1.14
sheep 1.03, 1.08–09, 1.16, 1.20, 1.22, 1.41
Shorthugai 1.26, 1.41
Shoshenq I 1.14, 1.18, 1.41
Shubat-Enlil 1.11, 1.41

Shu-Sin 1.11
Sicani 1.25
Sicily 1.06, 1.23–25
Siculi 1.25, 1.41
Siddhartha Gautama *see* Buddha
Sidon 1.14, 1.41
Silbury Hill, 1.41
Silk Route 1.06
Sinai 1.17
Sind 1.15
single-origins theory 1.02
Sinhalese 1.26
Siwa 1.15, 1.41
Skara Brae, 1.41
Skudra 1.15, 1.41
slavery 1.10, 1.41
  early Mediterranean civilizations 1.22
  Greek civilization 1.24
Slavs 1.06
smelting 1.09, 1.12
Smerdis 1.15, 1.42
Snofru 1.17, 1.42
Sogdiana, Soghd 1.15, 1.42
Solomon **1.14**, 1.23, 1.42
Solomon Islands 1.02
Solon 1.24, 1.42
Solutrean culture 1.19, 1.42
Song dynasty 1.27
sorghum 1.16, 1.42
Spain 1.23, 1.25
Sparta 1.24, 1.42
Sphinx, Great, 1.42
Springs arid Autumns period 1.06, 1.27, 1.42
squash 1.28, 1.42
Starcevo 1.20, 1.42
state, 1.42
steppe pastoralist cultures 1.04
steppes 1.02–06, 1.19
Step Pyramid 1.17, 1.42
Stone Age, 1.42. See also Mesolithic; Neolithic; Paleolithic
  stone circle, 1.42
Stonehenge 1.04, 1.20, 1.42
Subartu 1.12, 1.42
Sudan 1.16
Sumeria 1.04–05, 1.07, 1.09–11, 1.42
  Early Dynastic period 1.10
  King List 1.10
  trade 1.10
Suppiluliumas 1.12, 1.42
Surasena 1.26
Susa 1.10, 1.13, 1.15, 1.42
Swanscombe, 1.42
Swartkrans 1.01, 1.42
Syracuse 1.23, 1.25, 1.42
Syria 1.03

Tadmor 1.12, 1.14, 1.42
taiga 1.03
Tamar 1.14
Tartaria 1.20, 1.42
Tartessos, Tartessians 1.23, 1.25, 1.42
Taruga 1.16
Tarxien 1.20, 1.42
Tasmania 1.04–06
Tassili 1.16, 1.42
Taxila 1.26
teff 1.16
Tehuacán, 1.42
Tell, 1.42
Tell al-Fakhariyeh 1.12
Tell Awayli 1.09, 1.42
Tell Mureybat 1.08, 1.42
Tell Umm Dabaghiyeh 1.09
Teng 1.27
Tepecik 1.09
Tepe Gawra 1.09, 1.43
Tepe Yahya 1.10, 1.43
Tertiary period 1.01
textiles 1.03, 1.08–10
  cotton 1.03, 1.26, 1.28
  linen 1.03, 1.08–09, 1.16
  printed 1.09
  silk 1.03, 1.06
  spinning 1.03
  weaving 1.03, 1.09–10
  wool 1.03, 1.09, 1.22
Thailand, Thais 1.04–06
Thames river 1.19
Thebes 1.13, 1.15, 1.17–18, 1.43
Thera 1.22, 1.24, 1.43

Thessaly 1.24–25, 1.43
tholos 1.22, 1.43
Thrace, Thracians 1.05–06, 1.12, 1.15, 1.23–25, 1.43
Three Age system, 1.43
Tiahuanaco empire 1.28
Tiber river 1.25
Tibeto-Burmese 1.04, 1.43
Tibet, Tibetans 1.05–07
Tiglath-pileser I 1.12, 1.43
Tiglath-pileser III 1. 13–14, 1.43
Tigris river 1.09–12
tin 1.10, 1.21, 1.23, 1.25, 1.27, 1.43
Tingis 1.23, 1.43
Titicaca, Lake 1.28
Tonga 1.05
toolmaking cultures 1.01, 1.03, 1.19–20
Torralba-Ambrona, 1.43
trade
  Assyria 1.11
  Britain 1.23, 1.25
  Bronze Age 1.09, 1.21
  early Mediterranean civilizations 1.22
  Egyptian civilization 1.17–18
  Greek civilization **1.23–24**
  Indus valley civilization 1.26
  Mycenaean 1.21
  Neolithic 1.08–09
  Olmecs 1.28
  Phoenicians 1.05, 1.13, 1.23
  Silk Route 1.06
  Sumerians 1.10
  trading colonies 1.05–06, 1.23
transhumance 1.05–06
transport
  wheeled vehicles 1.033.20–21
  see also boat-building; canal systems
Tres Zapotes 1.28, 1.43
Tripolye-Cucuteni culture 1.20, 1.43
Troy 1.22, 1.43
Trojan War 1.22, 1.43
Trundholm 1.21, 1.43
Tukulti-Ninurta 11.12
Tunis, Tunisia 1.16, 1.23
Turdetanians 1.25, 1.43
Turkey 1.03. *See also* Anatolia
Turko-Mongols 1.05
Tutankhamun 1.18, 1.43
Tuthmosis I 1.12, 1.18, 1.43
Tuthmosis III 1.18, 1.43
Tuthmosis IV 1.12, 1.43
tyrant, 1.43
Tyre 1.13–14, 1.23, 1.25, 1.43

Ubaid culture 1.09, 1.43
Ugarit, 1.43
Ujjain 1.26, 1.43
Ukraine 1.23
ullucu 1.28
Ulu Burun shipwreck 1.22, 1.43
Umbrians 1.25, 1.43
Umma 1.10, 1.43
Unetice culture 1.04, 1.21, 1.43
Ur 1.04, 1.09–13, 1.43
  Chaldean occupation 1.12
  sack 1.11
  Third Dynasty 1.11
Urartu, Urartians 1.05, 1.07, 1.12–13, 1.43
Urmia, Lake, Battle of 1.13
Ur-Nammu 1.11, 1.44
Urnfield cultures 1.05–06, 1.21, 1.25, 1.44
Uruk 1.04, 1.07, 1.09–12, 1.44
Urukagina 1.10, 1.44
urbanization 1.04, 1.09, **1.10**, 1.44
  and agriculture 1.03–04, 1.08–10
  China 1.27
  early Mediterranean civilizations 1.22
  Egypt 1.16
  Indus valley civilization 1.26

Valdivia tradition 1.04, 1.28, 1.44
Valley of the Kings 1.18, 1.44
Vallon Pont d'Arc 1.19
Van Lang 1.04, 1.44
Vanuatu 1.05
Varna, 1.44
Vatsa 1.26

Vedas, *Vedic Hymns* 1.26
Veddas 1.26
Vedic Aryans 1.05–06, 1.26
Villanova culture 1.25
Vinca, 1.44
visual arts 1.09
Vix 1.23, 1.44
Vrijji 1.26

Wadi Kubbaniya 1.16
Warring States period 1.27, 1.44
warrior class 1.04
Washukanni 1.12, 1.44
water buffalo 1.03
wavy line ceramics, 1.44
Waywaka 1.28, 1.44
weaving 1.03, 1.09–10
Wei 1.27, 1.44
Wessex culture 1.05, 1.44
Western Zhou 1.27
wheat 1.03, 1.08–09, 1.16, 1.20, 1.22, 1.44
wheel 1.03, 1.10, 1.20–21, 1.27, 1.44
Willendorf, Venus of 1.19
Windmill Hill, 1.44
wool 1.03, 1.09, 1.22, 1.44
writing **1.04**, 1.07, 1.09–10, 1.20
  Arabic 1.07
  Aramaic alphabet 1.05, 1.07, 1.15
  Canaanite alphabet 1.07, 1.12
  Chinese script 1.07
  cuneiform 1.07, 1.10, 1.15
  Cyrillic alphabet 1.07
  Greek alphabet 1.07, 1.24
  Hebrew alphabet 1.07
  hieroglyphs 1.06–07, 1.17, 1.22, 1.28
  Kufic Arabic 1.07
  Latin alphabet 1.07
  Linear A script 1.22
  Linear B script 1.22
  logographic 1.07
  Nabatean alphabet 1.07
  parchment 1.15
  Phoenician alphabet 1.05, 1.07, 1.23–25
  phonetic alphabet 1.05, 1.07
  pictographs 1.07, 1.10, 1.26–27
  Rongorongo 1.07
  runic 1.07
  Sabean script 1.07
Wu 1.27, 1.44
Wuzhong 1.27

Xerxes 11.13, 1.15
Xia dynasty 1.27, 1.44
Xianyun 1.27, 1.44
Xu 1.27

yak 1.03
yam 1.16, 1.44
Yan 1.27, 1.44
Yangshao culture 1.27, 1.44
Yangtze valley 1.03, 1.27
Yaya-Mama religious traditions 1.06, 1.28, 1.44
Yellow river 1.27
Yong 1.27, 1.44
Yucatan 1.28
Yue 1.27
Yue Qi 1.06
Yu the Great 1.27, 1.44
Yue Qi, 1.44

Yuxian 1.27

Zagros mountains 1.03, 1.08–09, 1.11
Zapotec civilization 1.06–07, 1.28, 1.44
Zawi Chemi Shanidar 1.08, 1.44
Zedekiah 1.14, 1.44
Zheng 1.27
Zhou dynasty 1.05–06, 1.27, 1.44
Zhoukoudien, 1.44
ziggurats 1.09, 1.11, 1.44
Zobah 1.14
Zoroaster 1.15